PRECIOUS NONSENSE

PRECIOUS
NONSENSE

THE GETTYSBURG ADDRESS,
BEN JONSON'S EPITAPHS
ON HIS CHILDREN, AND
TWELFTH NIGHT

STEPHEN BOOTH

University of California Press

Berkeley · Los Angeles · London

University of California Press
Berkeley and Los Angeles, California

University of California Press, Ltd.
London, England

© 1998 by
The Regents of the University of California

Library of Congress Cataloging-in-Publication Data

Booth, Stephen.
    Precious nonsense : the Gettysburg address, Ben
Jonson's epitaphs on his children, and Twelfth night
/ Stephen Booth.
        p.   cm.
    Includes bibliographical references and index.
    ISBN 0-520-21288-6 (cloth)
    1. English literature—Early modern, 1500–1700—
History and criticism.   2. Nonsense literature, English—
History and criticism.   3. Shakespeare, William, 1564–
1616.   Twelfth night.   4. Lincoln, Abraham, 1809–1865.
Gettysburg address.   5. Jonson, Ben, 1573?–1637.   On
my first daughter.   6. Jonson, Ben, 1573?–1637.   On my
first son.   I. Title.
PR428.N65B66   1998
820.9—dc21   97-27979
                                                              CIP

Printed in the United States of America
9 8 7 6 5 4 3 2 1

For William Alfred

Contents

Preface

I should explain why I group together topics so obviously ill-sorted as the Gettysburg Address, Ben Jonson's epitaph for his baby daughter, and *Twelfth Night*. Not only are they three works from three different literary genres, but two are very short, and one is a full-length play; two are from the English Renaissance, and the third is nineteenth-century American; two of the three are death-centered, and the third is anything but; two are long-established cultural darlings, and one—Jonson's "On My First Daughter"—is relatively unknown; and so on. There are, however, good reasons why the three are together. The trouble is that the reasons are not scholarly ones—or, anyway, not scholarly sounding ones. The roots of this book are personal, and I don't see reason to pretend otherwise. When I first began thinking about the three works I focus on here, what they had in common was that they were three of the things I liked best in the world and I could not see what it was about any of them that pleased me. I wanted to know what was good about them.

I didn't start out thinking about the three together. Their conjunction here results from thinking that began when I first began teaching. In the fall term of 1963 I was racking my brain once a week for an essay topic to give to my composition students in English 1A at Berkeley. In the fall of 1963, the United States was making a heavily publicized fuss about the centennial of the dedication ceremony at Gettysburg. My need for an assignment and my need to know what was so good about the Gettysburg Address had come together. I therefore set my students to "WRITE AN ESSAY IN WHICH YOU ACCOUNT FOR THE HIGH VALUE GENERALLY GIVEN THE GETTYSBURG ADDRESS." Among other cautionary materials prefatory to that rubric, I said this: "For most of the hundred years that it has existed, people have been saying that the Gettysburg Address is a great piece of prose. They say what it is *not:* it isn't long; it isn't pretentious; it isn't limited by the transient particulars of the time and situation in which it was delivered. They do not say what it *is*. What is it about the Gettysburg Address that is so positively good?" I figured that by the time I had read and thought through thirty student essays I would probably have some notion of what the speech had that made it thrilling to me and, apparently, to so many other people, American or not. Instead of thirty essays, it has taken me more than thirty years to feel ready to publish some guesses about the sources of the speech's value.

A process similar to the one I went through with the Gettysburg Address got started one morning ten years later, when I was cleaning up my study at the close of the academic year. As I was filing things and throwing others away, I came upon a Norton anthology several layers down on my desk and open to Jonson's "On My First Daughter." I looked at the poem and realized to my surprise that "On My First Daughter" was not only my favorite poem but had been so for a long time. I was further surprised to realize that I could not see what so bland and conventional a verse tidbit was doing for me that made me like it so much. As I had with the Gettysburg Address, I started asking students to talk and write about "On My First Daughter," asking them to wrestle with a poem that presents nothing obviously interesting to an analyst. Once again, it has taken years of classroom discussions and student essays to develop the accounts I give here of the poem and its companion piece, "On My First Son."

As to *Twelfth Night,* I did not know that I had any problem with it until sometime in the 1970s, when I stood up to talk about it in a big Shakespeare course and realized a few sentences into the lecture that, although what I had to say about the play was not untrue, what I had to say and was used to hearing myself and other people say went nowhere near its essence and did nothing to account for its greatness—the greatness of a farce so powerful and so highly valued by so many people that academic commentators regularly insist that it is not a farce at all. I stuttered and stopped and started for a few minutes and then gave up, apologized, and sent everybody home. From there I went into a process like the ones already under way for the Gettysburg Address and "On My First Daughter."

I did not think about the Gettysburg Address, "On My First Daughter," and *Twelfth Night* together—much less imagine considering them together in a book—until a common denominator showed up in the results of my individual studies: each is at least once and in at least one way *nonsense*—but nonsense such that we read it as sense and do not notice the casual superiority to the apparent limits of human mental capability that the work has empowered in us. The pages that follow attempt both to demonstrate the existence of such nonsense in the works I discuss and to explain why I believe such nonsense is so valuable in works strongly woven enough to support it.

The first essay in the *Twelfth Night* section of this book—"*Twelfth Night* 1.1: The Audience as Malvolio"—was published previously in *Shakespeare's "Rough Magic": Renaissance Essays in Honor of C. L. Barber,* ed. Peter Erikson and Coppélia Kahn (Newark, Del., 1985); it is reprinted here by kind permission of Associated University Presses, Inc.

The dedication page belatedly acknowledges the oldest, most general, and greatest of my hitherto unacknowledged debts, but a lot of newer debts particular to this book are going to remain unacknowledged.

As I explained, this book derives largely from classroom experience over my whole career as a teacher at Berkeley. I know that I learned most of what I know about the Gettysburg Address, the Jonson epitaphs, and *Twelfth Night* from questions put to me or observations made to me by students. I am grateful to all of them and I would like to thank them all. Old notes—notes that survive only accidentally from class sessions long ago—attach this name or that to this or that question or observation, but that evidence is so casually selective, so sparse, and so obviously incomplete that it would be unfair and misleading to acknowledge only the few specific debts and debtors I remember and imply a smaller debt than I owe.

It can, however, do no injustice to anyone else if I thank several colleagues who helped me in the late stages of the project; I am grateful to Judith Radner, Bradley Berens, Young Jean Lee, Michael J. Collins of Georgetown University, Bethany Sinnott of Catawba College, Mark Womack of the University of Tulsa, and, most recently and most particularly, Eleanor Cook of the University of Toronto.

I am grateful, too, to the patience and wit of my editors at the University of California Press: Katherine Bell, Michael Gauger, Juliana Cobb, Mari Coates, and Marilyn Schwartz.

This is the point in prefaces where I customarily say something nice about my wife. This time, however, I can't think of anything that even comes anywhere near doing her justice. Her name is Susan Patek Booth.

Berkeley, California
May 3, 1997

Introduction

KING: How well he's read, to reason against reading!
DUMAINE: Proceeded well, to stop all good proceeding!
LONGAVILLE: He weeds the corn and still lets grow the weeding.
BEROWNE: The spring is near when green geese are a-breeding.
DUMAINE: How follows that?
BEROWNE: Fit in his place and time.
DUMAINE: In reason nothing.
BEROWNE: Something then in rime.

Love's Labor's Lost 1.1.94–99

Any reader committed to reading and paying attention to the book that follows can profitably skip this introduction. Everything I want the introduction to do is done in the essays it introduces. I am writing an introduction only because experience has taught me that people who read academic criticism—usually authors of academic criticism—do not so much read critical studies as "check them out." Once such readers have a sense of a study's kind and/or its probable destination, they don't pay attention to what ensuing sentences are actually saying. For instance, the first thing I ever published was a long, dense essay on *Hamlet* ("On the Value of *Hamlet*" in *Reinterpretations of Elizabethan Drama,* ed. Norman Rabkin [New York, 1969]); the first thing the first section of that essay does is talk about how the first scene of *Hamlet* positions audiences in relation to the action that follows. The essay goes on to do a lot else (including an analysis of the "To be or not to be" soliloquy that I, who appear to be its only reader, admire immensely), but people who mention the

Hamlet essay to me or mention it in print almost invariably behave as if the essay as a whole were an essay on *Hamlet* 1.1.

The essays that comprise this book are at least as dense as the
Hamlet essay and have a lot more twists and turns. My fear for
the present essays, however, is not so much that each will be
treated as if the book's first point were its only point as that my
principal purpose in these essays will be mistaken to be what habit
may lead readers into assuming it to be. Even though each of the
following essays is laced with passionate disclaimers of interpre-
tational ambition, they are nonetheless likely to be assumed to
be telling their readers (1) that the Gettysburg Address, the Jonson epitaphs, and *Twelfth Night* are "really" other than what they
have seemed to be and (2) that they should henceforth be understood to say things they have not previously been suspected
to say. The assumption that analysis of literature and interpretation of it are always and necessarily synonymous is only an assumption, but it has been and remains very strong. At this point
in academic history, I persistently try and fail to open students'
minds to the possibility that one can say something about the details of a literary work that is not an assertion of hidden meaning in it. My hope in this introduction is to head off such mis-
conceptions as may be born of inattention or assumption or of
the two in combination.

In my experience, most students and many of their teachers
are also prisoners of the assumption that the purpose of literary
analysis must be to make analyzed works work better than they
have before—or at least differently. They take it for granted that
the analyst is trying to make them read or hear a given work in
a way other than the way they did before. I have no such ambition. (On the other hand, I would be delighted to substitute
the sort of comparatively modest, genuinely academic criticism
I offer in the body of this book for the kinds that pretend to an
ability to tailor readers' experiences to this or that neat pattern—
usually a pattern available in, but not at all exclusive in, the clut-
tered reality of an unmediated reading experience.)

Everything I do in studying literature in this book and elsewhere responds to the following two questions. What is it we value literature for (what we *do* value it for, not what we should value it for)? And what is it in the works we value most highly that makes us value them above others like them? My answer to the first question is that it is the experience—the two-hour experience of a play or movie or the two-minute experience of a lyric or a song.

This book works toward some of an answer to the second question.

The essential notion underlying everything in the book is that a great source, perhaps *the* great source, of the special appeal of highly valued works is that they are in one way or another nonsensical.

The purpose of this introduction is to illustrate the book's thesis by examining some small, beloved, humble works—popular nursery rhymes, children's songs, proverbs and stock phrases— things so simple, in such little need of an analytic middleman, and of so little cultural dignity that no one could mistake my analysis of them for efforts to interpret them, much less to make them work better than they do unaided. Most important, nursery rhymes and children's songs are not things in which I can reasonably be suspected of wanting to demonstrate flaws and lapses. I hope that my brief, quickly grasped discussions of the little things I talk about here in the introduction will go some way toward forestalling the easy, wrong impression that what I'm doing in the essays that follow is debunking the Gettysburg Address, the Jonson epitaphs, and *Twelfth Night,* revealing them to be unworthy of our admiration for them.

In the main this book discusses and asserts value in two distinguishable categories of nonsense—one substantive, the other not.

The first category, the substantive one, contains every sort of thing that one might label as nonsense: assertions or implied assertions that are silly ("The platform was already empty, although the train was not due to arrive for another hour"; ". . . why the sea is boiling hot and whether pigs have wings"); assertions contrary to fact ("Arabia is a lake"; "The sewers of New York City are full of alligators"); sentences that are syntactically chaotic; and so on. Although the essays that follow deal with examples of all the kinds of substantive nonsense, they deal almost exclusively with nonsense that is not perceived to be so. The essays that follow attempt to demonstrate that the Gettysburg Address, Ben Jonson's epitaphs on his children, and *Twelfth Night* are each to a significant degree composed of nonsense, demonstrable nonsense that, because each makes and always will make sense, is *merely* demonstrable. What is so interesting is that, if you look at them more carefully than readers and audiences ever have (or will, or ever should), it is hard to see how they can be understood at all.

As the lengths of the following chapters testify, the texts they describe and discuss are complex and require complex analysis. On the other hand, the nursery rhyme "Little Boy Blue," which exhibits just the sorts of nonsense that the Gettysburg Address, the Jonson epitaphs, and *Twelfth Night* do, can be analyzed quickly.

> Little Boy Blue,
> Come blow your horn,
> The sheep's in the meadow,
> The cow's in the corn.[1]

The presence of the cow in the corn is obviously just cause for the alarm the poem implies. But why should anyone make a fuss because the sheep is in the meadow—one of the places where one is most accustomed to finding sheep?[2] And why am I mak-

---

1. This, the one stanza of "Little Boy Blue" that is a fixture in the culture, exists in several variants. The same is true of most of the other things I discuss here. I quote "Little Boy Blue" and all other orally transmitted materials from memory.

2. As one of what I expect is a very small number of academic critics who have earned a merit badge in sheep raising from the Boy Scouts of America, I am embarrassed to have displayed what several people who read this book in typescript quite correctly took to be ignorance of the distinction between a

ing a fuss about "The sheep's in the meadow"? Because I want readers to mend their ways and take notice of their previous folly in letting context deafen them to the particulars of line 3? No. On the contrary, I celebrate the poem's ability to deafen us to the illogic of its assertion about the sheep, the poem's ability to let us understand something that does not make sense as if it *did* make sense, the poem's ability to free us from the limits of the human mind.

What I am going to say now may sound glib, a lot glibber than I think it actually is—or, I hope, than you will if you give it some thought.

What does the human mind ordinarily want most? It wants to understand what it does not understand. And what does the human mind customarily do to achieve that goal? It works away— sometimes for only a second or two, sometimes for years—until it understands. What does the mind have then? What it wanted? No. What it has is understanding of something it now under-

---

meadow (a field in which grass is grown and harvested for hay) and a *pasture*. A sheep in such a meadow threatens a potential cash crop. My surprise at our want of surprise at the alarm registered in "The sheep's in the meadow," however, remains valid, I think, because the distinction between meadowland and pastureland is and has so long been so generally forgotten. But in my embarrassment, I have nonetheless sought the comfort of company among writers with rural credentials at least as good as mine. In the seventeenth century, Margaret Cavendish concluded a poem called "Spirits" with reference to "*Sheep /* and feeding *Cattell* which in Meadowes keep." In the eighteenth century, John Dyer began "The Inquiry" by asking a "poor little sheep" if it had met his beloved Clio "On the mountain, or valley, or meadow, or grove." At the beginning of a poem called "Sports in the Meadows" the truly knowledgeable nineteenth-century "peasant poet" John Clare lists "sheep & cows . . . crowding for a share" of the flowers Maytime has brought to the meadows. My favorite in what is becoming a large collection of loose uses of "meadow" comes from a letter William Cowper wrote to Joseph Hill on April 15, 1792. In his translation of *Odyssey,* 9.518–19, Cowper had spoken of "wethers"—male sheep—that "bleated, by the load distress'd / Of udders overcharged." In the course of bemoaning his error to his friend Hill, Cowper casually wanders into mine: "It was a blunder hardly pardonable in a man who has lived amid fields and meadows grazed by sheep almost these thirty years" (*The Letters and Prose Writings of William Cowper,* ed. James King and Charles Ryskamp [Oxford, 1984], 4.54).

stands. What it wanted was to understand what it did not understand. I suggest that, by giving us the capacity casually, effortlessly to accept "The sheep's in the meadow" as self-evidently distressing news, "Little Boy Blue" does something comparable to the impossible: it gives us understanding of something that remains something we do not understand.

The second kind of nonsense that concerns me here, commoner in literary works than substantive nonsense, is nonimporting pattern, pattern that fits the "nonsense" label because and only because it does not ordinarily signify anything, is without import. Such pattern is familiar in effects based in repetition with variation: effects like rhythm, rhyme, and alliteration by which a literary construct gets a feel of coherence. Echoes and repetitions can make an artificial construct feel almost as inevitable—as obviously one thing and not a conglomerate—as an object in nature. Nonsubstantive nonsense is a category that includes the kind of incidental repetition that cannot reasonably be believed ever to have signified anything to anybody. The dogs that stud *A Midsummer Night's Dream* are a good example of the sort of insignificant (that is, nonsignifying) motif I'm talking about. So are slavery, furniture, and valuable refuse in Charles Dickens's *Our Mutual Friend,* where those substantively incidental topics thread across the thousand-page sprawl of the novel.

In the same category are submerged relationships among words and syllables that regularly share a common context entirely irrelevant to the context of the particular work or passage in which they appear. Consider, for example, the monumentally clumsy refrain of "Home on the Range":

> Oh give me a home where the buffalo roam,
> Where the deer and the antelope play;
> Where seldom is heard a discouraging word
> And the skies are not cloudy all day.

I think the song may derive some of its improbable durability from the presence of the word "heard" in that refrain in lines

previously focused on herd animals. The pertinence of the sound
of the word "heard" to buffalo, deer, and antelope is presumably
entirely inaudible to the conscious minds of readers and listeners. And, I suggest, is all the more powerful and valuable for being so. The available but unmade pun on "heard" and "herd"
gives a feel of rightness, naturalness, to lines that are *also* ludi-
crously form-driven. If one thinks about the lines, "seldom is
heard" and "discouraging word" seem to have been generated
for no reason but to rhyme with one another, and "the skies are
not cloudy all day" is a periphrastic pretzel pretty clearly designed
not for the purpose of noting the prevalence of sunshine in the
great plains but to place a rhyme for "play" where one is needed.
As I said, all of that is true of the lines *if one thinks about them.*
I suggest that the coherence the unmade "heard"/"herd" pun
brings with it helps one *not* to think about them, that it acts to
dissolve one's inclination to examine the content of the lines
or to notice their clumsiness and desperate obedience to form.
(So, I would add, does the unexploited contrariety of implication inherent in the meanings of the rhyming words "home"
and "roam.")

The transparent nonsignificance of the link between "heard"
and a collective noun useful for describing mammals that live
and travel in groups goes some way toward suggesting my reason for stretching the word "nonsense" beyond its usual function as a label for linguistic constructs that are meaningless or absurd and asking it also to cover varieties of unifying relationship
at most substantively incidental to—but usually substantively irrelevant to—the sense made and delivered by the passages they
inhabit. Unfortunately, however, the deer and antelope example
also goes a way toward evoking a response emblematic of the
ones I most fear and am writing this introduction to forestall.
Despite my protestations, readers are likely to bridle at what I
say. Habit will keep them forever suspicious that I am putting
forth a reading of "Home on the Range" that includes a pun on
"heard" and "herd" (and perhaps that I see irony in the union of

"home" and "roam") and make them eager to dismiss what I say because no such pun (and no such irony) can be believed ever to have been observed by any sane audience to the song.

I could seem foolish to force the available but idiomatically foreign sense "nonimporting" upon the common, garden meaning of the word "nonsense." By perversely using the word "nonsense" to designate things other than those it customarily designates, I risk the implication that I am about to launch a thesis that rests on a pun, rests on the linguistic accident of two senses of the word "sense." I'm doing no such thing. The risk of seeming to be, however, is worth taking because insistence on a kinship between what the word ordinarily describes—want of rational coherence—and what its elements are capable of describing—want of substantive import—can be useful in talking about kinds of coherence and incoherence in works of art. A principal tenet of the essays in this book is that in the works it discusses ideationally insignificant coherence often takes the place of, does the job of, the ordinary, substantive, syntax-borne coherence that we expect, demand, and do not notice is absent. The words "coherent" and "incoherent" are now most often heard in the metaphoric senses in which they say that this or that assertion or argument does or does not make rational sense. The nonsense I focus on in this book feels sensible because it participates in systems in which coherence is more literal, is like the coherence a snowball has, and in which incoherence is of the kind exhibited by a pound of granulated sugar.

I specified two *distinguishable* kinds of nonsense. That implied a categorical purity that does not exist among the nonsense examples I talk about here and in the book at large. Typically they combine wrongness in one dimension with rightness in another. For example, there is nothing truly nonsensical—unreasonable, ridiculous, illogical—in the substance of the lines I quoted from "Home on the Range." What is nonsensical—accidental to the import of the lines—is the interplay between the sound of "heard" and the herd animals that are its neighbors in the lines of the song. Similarly, the overlooked implications of its third line aside, what "Little Boy Blue" says is reasonable and ordinary. Moreover, the rhythm of the quatrain, the rhyme in "horn" and "corn," and the alliteration in "Blue" and "blow" give the lines substantively irrelevant extra coherence. Those lines get a more obviously nonsensical coherence from the presence in the sound of "Blue" of the sound of the past tense of the verb "to blow": "blew." They get another still from the presence of the sound "corn" (meaning "grain-bearing plants" and nothing else) in a poem much concerned with cornute animals. And, although few of the preschool children who are its usual audience are likely to know the terms "cornucopia" and "silver cornet," an adult English speaker—accustomed to hearing "cornucopia" and "horn of plenty" used interchangeably and familiar with the fact that cornets are horns—does not need etymologic lore to feel the far-off extra pull between "horn" and its rhyme.

In short, the process of perceiving "Little Boy Blue" is vastly more eventful than its paraphrasable substance implies. What I am suggesting is that "Little Boy Blue" is exciting for the mind that hears it and that the casual, effortless act of comprehending its simple substance is an act of considerable mental athleticism. I suggest, too, that, just because the act of perceiving the four little lines is so casual and so effortless, the act is godlike, as close to superhuman as anything we can do outside the experience of a work of art. We don't even notice how very many the systems of understanding are in which our minds casually participate.

Now I want to present a string of tiny examples of a great many variations on the kinds of unobserved verbal fireworks I have already illustrated. The examples are in no particular order. I wish they were. I would like to have grouped them by kind, but they resist categorization, and an effort to make categories and then argue the specimens into them would, I think, have inevitably resulted in an essay that seemed to give demonstration precedence over the demonstrated—that invited as much of a reader's attention to boxes as to what the boxes were built to assist them with. Consider the incidental troubles an author's presumably benign will to categorize has inflicted on readers of

Seven Types of Ambiguity and of the letter to Raleigh with which Spenser tagged the 1590 printing of the first three books of *The Faerie Queene*. Moreover, organizing the examples by kind would have swollen a brief introduction to chapter length.

I will begin with two particularly popular proverbs: "It's the exception that proves the rule" and "A friend in need is a friend indeed." Like "Little Boy Blue," the two proverbs are familiar small change in the currency of most English-speaking cultures. They apparently cause no more ripples in the consciousnesses of their users and hearers than "Little Boy Blue" does. They differ from it, however, in an important way. Each of the two proverbs has, I suspect, puzzled most English speakers—at least momentarily and probably in childhood. The idea that the exception proves the rule is customarily brought into conversations by someone supporting the validity of a rule questioned because it does not fit all cases.[3] It does not make sense that an exception

---

3. Note that I talk not about what the proverb means but about how it is used. I have heard cases made for "the exception proves the rule" as "really" meaning something other than what it is commonly used to mean (for instance, that to recognize the exception is to acknowledge the existence of the rule—whether the rule is valid or not). Such cases are obviously irrelevant to the fact that the proverb is in practice taken to say that exceptions to rules prove those rules to be valid. The most obvious and interesting corrective reading of the proverb takes note of "to prove" as a once-common synonym for "to test"— a sense that remains current in everyday English in such terms as "proving ground" and "printer's proofs." "It's the exception that *tests* the rule" makes fine sense, and one might guess that the improbable use we now make of the proverb drifted into being as "to prove" meaning "to test" drifted out of daily use. Surprisingly, however, back when "to prove" commonly meant "to test" in colloquial English, the proverb appears already to have been used as a contradiction in terms. Morris Tilley's *Dictionary of the Proverbs in England in the Sixteenth Century* (Ann Arbor, Mich., 1950) gives this from 1666: "The exception gives Authority to the Rule" and "the Latin says again, Exceptio probat regulam." The 1970 third edition of *The Oxford Dictionary of Proverbs* quotes Samuel Johnson from 1765: "The exception only confirms the rule." The proverb has evidently been brashly paradoxical for centuries. It may, however, have started life as an open play on the two senses of Latin *probare,* which like its English descendant meant both "to test" and "to show to be valid."

to a rule should be thought to prove the rule's validity. An exception to a rule may not disable it entirely, but an exception is certainly not to its credit. As to "A friend in need is a friend indeed," context dictates one meaning for it, standard usage another. The common adjectival phrase "in need" is ordinarily used and heard to mean "needy." But it is in no way probable that neediness should make someone seem a better friend than he or she would be if flush. The implications of the assertion thus belatedly tell us that "in need" must be the proverb's desperately contrary way of saying "when one is oneself needy."

As I said, the two proverbs are unusual among the buried nuggets of unreason on display here in being generally recognized as at least superficially paradoxical. The reason I bring them up here is that they are so perennially popular. These two are always among the first examples college freshmen call out when I ask them to give examples of proverbs. Their near ubiquity in our culture makes them evidence that taking pleasure in accepting nonsense as sense is usual among us. So is our delight in paradox and our fascination with oxymoron. Pointed paradoxes and oxymora display themselves to our minds as oddities, freaks of nature marked as such by their presentation in epigrammatic cages. Nonsense that lies hidden from consciousness is another matter. I suggest, however, that in contending that we take pleasure in nonsense concealed from our consciousnesses, and in contending further that nonsense that goes unobserved to consciousness can be a primary reason why we value some of the works we value most highly, I am only taking a new step along the already-established path that leads us to value open, self-assertive paradox.

Moreover, I contend here and in the essays that follow that the ordinarily unobserved effects I dwell on are of greater value to us, the satisfied clients of the works in which they lurk, than they would be if they were presented ostentatiously as puns or paradoxes or other witty whatnots. Puns, paradoxes, and all such self-conscious displays of simultaneously probable and improbable coincidence are like circus acts and sideshow menageries. Displayed as oddities to the minds that are audience to them, they reinforce our confidence in the norm with which they contrast and from which they are so efficiently isolated. The same is true of magicians' tricks. On the other hand, the feats of comprehension enabled by the phenomena I talk about here are not so much performed *for* their audiences as *by* them. We the readers and listeners are made capable of taking casual command of simple truths—that is, truths free of considerations foreign to them, uncontaminated by the muck of possibilities from which they rise up pure—that also cling still to inconvenient contexts and locally impertinent identities that would ordinarily force our minds to pause and reason them away. Whereas a pun or a paradox is just a pun or a paradox, the raw materials for a pun or a paradox are exciting to a mind that feels them and their energy, feels them and their energy raw, not diminished by having been fashioned into toys. The presence of the inert stuff of chaos is exhilarating to that mind when an ordered, ordinary play or poem or sentence brings with it the gift of casual superiority to a potentially baffling cacophony of ideational static unheard within it.

I want to talk now about the school-yard jingle "One for the money":

> One for the money,
> Two for the show,
> Three to get ready,
> And four to go!

Nothing in that quatrain violates reason, but neither does the quatrain make positive sense. "One for the money" sounds as if we understand it, but what do we take "for" to indicate? Do we take it to say "in order to obtain"? Maybe so. "Money" suggests so. But *what* money? And of what assistance might whatever it is that "one" refers to be to the obtaining? I don't think we ever know—or ever wonder. The one-two-three-four pattern and the rhythm take over and substitute nonsignifying articulation for substantive. Thus, by the time we get to "the show" in "Two for the show" we no longer care what "for" means in this context or notice that the context denies it the possibility of meaning anything at all.

At the same time, however, the lines vaguely and unsuccessfully beckon our minds in several directions obviously alien to the one in which one says or hears "One for the money." In the first line of a jingle used to insure a fair start for contestants in a race, "one" reaches toward its homonym "won" and is immediately seconded by the mere presence of "money"—a potential prize to the runner who is number one at the finish line. And any mind that heard "for" try to say "in order to obtain" in lines 1 and 2 will hear—and presumably fail to register—its echo in "to get" in "Three to get ready."[4] That echo is blocked from any listener's consciousness by "ready": the idea of obtaining a "ready" is ridiculous.

A quatrain charged in any event with gestures toward significances available only in other contexts gets a further charge of potentially bewildering energy for any present-day listener acquainted with the American racetrack terms "win," "place," and "show." A bet on the winner to win brings the bettor a large return. The horse that finishes second is said to "place"; a successful place bet—a bet that a chosen horse will come in either first or second—pays much less than a win bet. Betting a horse to "show"—to finish third or higher—gives a bettor three chances, but a winning show bet pays even less than a place bet does. For anyone familiar with "win/place/show," the line "One for the money" is a vague but straightforward echo of the hierarchical betting system. "Two for the show" is at once a considerably solider echo than "One for the money" was of the one-two-three of win, place, and show *and,* since the term for a third-place bet is paired with two and not three, all wrong.

---

4. Needless to say, the unobserved echo of "for" meaning "in order to obtain" is absent from the versions of the poem in which line 3 is "Three to *make* ready."

Experience of the "One for the money" jingle is further complicated, I think, by its patterned but unexploited play on "for" and "four" and on "to" and "two." Here is the quatrain as it might look if someone took conscious note of the pun potential and printed the 1-4, 2-4, 3-2, 4-2 pattern in such a way as to bring the shadow puns to light in our consciousnesses (and thereby rob the poem of the energy they bring it as dimly felt potential):

> One 4 the money,
> Two 4 the show,
> Three 2 get ready,
> And four 2 go!

What does all this strenuous analysis of signals and counter-signals in the jingle achieve? It demonstrates that, simple as the experience of "One for the money" is, it is also very complicated, very rich, and very demanding of mental agility we never notice ourselves to exercise. Such analysis, I think, goes a good way toward explaining why "One for the money," "Little Boy Blue," the exception/rule proverb, the "friend in need" proverb, and similarly standard cultural furniture persist when apparently comparable objects come and go.

We seem to value things that, like "One for the money," leave us thinking we understand what in fact we do not. A good example is the old campfire/nursery-school song "Go tell Aunt Rhody":

> Go tell Aunt Rhody,
> Go tell Aunt Rhody,
> Go tell Aunt Rhody
> Her old gray goose is dead.
>
> The one that she's been saving,
> The one that she's been saving,
> The one that she's been saving,
> To make a feather bed.

I find it fascinating that I—who lived through the 1960s in Berkeley, California, where my children's childhoods and those of their friends often seemed to me to consist principally of singing "Go tell Aunt Rhody" in groups—have never known anyone to wonder whether the news that singers order brought to Aunt Rhody is good news or bad. Think about it, and notice that you probably would not think about it unbidden.

I am similarly fascinated by the recently popular, apparently new idea of "getting one's ducks in a row"; people say that they or other people are getting their ducks in a row as a way to say that they are pausing briefly to arrange their affairs in preparation for efficient action. No one seems to wonder why one would want to get ducks into a row or why—since from birth onward ducks voluntarily form rows for travel—one would need to.

We seem particularly fond of things that are at once right and wrong, things like this:

> Roses are red.
> Violets are blue.
> Sugar is sweet,
> And so are you.

Red roses are red. And "rose" is the name of a color in the pink range. Violets are certainly bluer than they are red, but the label for their traditional color is "violet."

Some phrases seem to me to get special, extra energy from substantively unharnessed, usually unharnessable, relationships among their parts or between them and their contexts. "Fast food," a recently coined but now standard phrase, probably benefits as much from the unacknowledged presence in it of a label for abstinence from food—"fast"—as it does from alliteration in *f*. The operative sense of "civil" in "civil war" makes the term straightforward, but it is also a paradox: war and civility are ideas at odds with one another. And I suspect that the English language clings to the term "dry wine" precisely because, whatever else it is, it is oxymoronic.

Other favored phrases may be so because they embody relationships among their elements at once pertinent and entirely impertinent to the sense they are understood to intend. Take "horse's ass." Why that animal? Why not a cow or a pig or a moose? Because, I suspect, the term "horse's ass" refers—entirely unheard by the consciousnesses of its patrons—to a slave-master relationship between equine classes. I also suspect that some words that might be expected to be very rare in nonspecialized vocabularies are common because of sounds in them accidental to the words' etymologies, but pertinent to the contexts in which the words commonly figure. I am thinking in particular of "hierarchy," which contains the sound of "higher," and "exegesis," which has the sound of "Jesus" in it.

My current favorites among phrases that glow with unobserved energy are from popular music. Before he abruptly decided to have no name at all—he now insists on being called "the artist formerly known as 'Prince'"—Prince Nelson, who had dropped his surname for stage purposes, called his first movie (and one of its main songs) *Purple Rain*. I never heard any comment on the regal ramifications of "purple," traditionally the royal color, or the sound of "reign" in its homonym, but I think the title got energy from its unheard wit—much more than it could have had the title somehow pointed up its cleverness. More complex and more interesting is the experience of hearing the "Rolling Stones" as the name of the famous 1960s rock group (that is still going strong, though now composed of teenagers in their fifties). The wit and energy in the name is kept leashed by its open allusion to the proverb about not gathering moss. I suggest that, having acknowledged the allusion, minds feel no inclination to think further about the name and, by examining it, deaden the energy "Rolling Stones" gets from the unadvertised wit of using "stones"—*rocks*—with "rolling" in the name of a rock and roll band.

And so on through many more examples than I need bother with here.

I had one further reason for using little, undignified things to introduce a book on works that literary professionals take seriously enough to write about and teach to students. The sayings and rhymes and fragments I have just been talking about cannot, I think, be thought by any reader to have been trivialized by my analyses. They are already obviously trivial. And I doubt likewise that anyone will say that in talking about them I should properly have given at least some of my attention to their ideational substance, to what they say to us or demonstrate to us that we are gladdened to know or see. They are to the literature we honor as small coins are to great fortunes, and for that reason they present a particularly good background against which to take up the topic of literary value. I suggest that the one big difference between, on the one hand, "Little Boy Blue" and "One for the money"—each obviously valued in the culture but neither taken seriously—and, on the other, *King Lear, War and Peace,* the Gettysburg Address, and Jonson's epitaphs on his children is that the works in the latter list take up matters that matter to us, whereas nursery rhymes and the jingles do not.[5]

Readers who go on from here to read what I have to say about the Gettysburg Address, the Jonson epitaphs, and *Twelfth Night* will find that I give little honor and less time to the insights they provide or can be said to provide into their topics or the human condition or morality or society or politics. And readers who go on may well feel that in, for example, demonstrating that the Gettysburg Address is variously nonsensical I trivialize it.

I do not, however, believe that great literature is any more capable of trivialization than nursery rhymes are. As I have been saying in one way or another in conference papers, lectures, and

---

5. *Twelfth Night* probably belongs in the latter list too. One of the many unostentatious, substantively incidental patterns of repetition that unify it and give it its quasi-physical integrity is composed of phenomena that, looked at philosophically (that is, looked at in a way *Twelfth Night* never invites us to), put into question whether human beings should ever feel certain of anything. *Twelfth Night* differs from its listed peers in that the solemnity of that topic—the topic that gives it the kind of weight absent from nursery rhymes and urgently present in works on topics like premature death—is never brought forward in *Twelfth Night* for audiences to notice.

printed essays for the last several years, our fear that public display of some kinds of truths about literature will trivialize works we revere is born of our knowledge that literature is indeed trivial and that attention to it is essentially frivolous.[6] For as long as there has been a culture in the West, Western culture has felt a need to justify literature. The justifications have all, I think, been driven by a need to find a dignified function for an activity that, by all standards at all comparable to the ones we apply to other things we value, is frivolous—a need to find a function for literature that has the practical weight of the other things that matter to us, things like food, shelter, love, gods, children, and law.

There are lots of things people say to justify literature. We go through school and sometimes life parroting them and hearing them parroted, but none of them explains why we go to the movies, why we like some movies better than others, why we like some movies better than others that have the same themes, similar situations, similar philosophies. For an extreme case, consider *The Maltese Falcon.* The 1941 version, one of most movie lovers' favorite movies, is the second of two remakes of a good, relatively forgettable, now largely forgotten 1931 film, released both as *The Maltese Falcon* and as *Dangerous Female.* (The first remake, *Satan Met a Lady* [1936], was stillborn, stayed that way, and need not trouble us.) John Huston, the director of the 1941 *Falcon,* tinkered with the 1931 script, but minimally. Moreover, neither Huston's decisions as director nor the performances of his actors are ostentatiously different from their 1931 counter-

---

6. As I say, I have been making the points I am about to make in various places and in various ways for quite a while—since 1990 at least—most solidly in three printed essays: "The Function of Criticism at the Present Time and All Others," *Shakespeare Quarterly,* 41 (1990), 262–68; "Close Reading without Readings," in *Shakespeare Reread: The Texts in New Contexts,* ed. Russ McDonald (Ithaca, 1994), 42–55; and "The Coherences of *1 Henry IV* and of *Hamlet,*" in *Shakespeare Set Free: Teaching "Hamlet" and "1 Henry IV,*" ed. Peggy O'Brien (New York, 1994), 32–46. Bits and pieces of these last few introductory paragraphs are freely recycled from those essays.

parts. My point is that the kinds of reasons critics customarily give for why we value one work over another would not distinguish the 1941 *Maltese Falcon* from the 1931 one. *One cannot distinguish the two except by recourse to minor details.* One cannot distinguish the two except by admitting in effect that what we probably value in movies, stories, poems, and such is less dignified and spiritual than we would like it to be.

I contend that, although a great work may well be chock-full of spiritual nutrients, what we turn to it for and return to it for is the pleasure the experience of it affords us, the experience of a minute or so with a short lyric, a couple of hours in the theater, hours or days with a novel.

I submit that great literature is like spinach. I read somewhere that although spinach is indeed a valuable source of iron for human beings, only a small percentage of the iron that spinach contains is of a sort available to the human digestive system. I may be entirely misinformed about spinach, but what matters here is that, regardless of its accuracy, the analogy is usefully illustrative of the discrepancy between what a critic can say we see or learn from a work we value and what in fact we do value. Consider your own early experiences with the discrepancy between what introductions to classic works said they were and your own experiences of those works.

Fully as valuable as spinach as an analogy for the literature we value is ice cream. In the recent past, when milk products were still fondly believed to be good for people, advertisers and pop nutritionists in newspapers often gave the impression that what people liked about ice cream was its capacity to provoke and preserve good health. Absurd. The idea that we value the literature we find great for the insights it provides is equally absurd—but, as I will shortly explain, much more appealing.

Back when my work was first being rejected by editors and readers for university presses, the negative comments I got sniffed as if offended at what I wrote. They said, for example, that all I did was play head games or that I behaved as if great poems and plays were only head games. "Head games" was a popular term of academic contempt in the 1960s. Its opposite numbers, always vague but always solemn, were things like "profound" and "meaningful" and other terms redolent of spiritual or cultural or philosophical pith. Later, when I got things into print, one reviewer of my edition of Shakespeare's sonnets said (in a review I can't now find) that my fussing about moment-to-moment experience of succeeding syllables and their nuances was all very well, but that I needed to remember that Shakespeare's sonnets are more than that. My memorial reconstruction of what wanted to be and succeeded in being a cutting comment doesn't do it justice. I remember, too, that the review or some other said that I couldn't see the forest for the trees. I was appropriately stung by the criticisms. It was years before I realized that what the various negative commentators accused me of believing or seeming to believe was exactly what I did and do believe. The comments about head games and trees were unjust as *negative* criticism, but they were entirely just. I do indeed believe that great literature—at least what we principally value in it—can be justly called head games. And I do not think there is a forest, just so many trees—syllables that we perceive one by one as we read or listen, syllables whose relations to one another flicker and change as we and they progress to the end.

We care very much for the literary works we care for, much more than one would expect creatures to care who must service the serious, practical needs and fears and ambitions that human beings have to cope with. Nothing is likely to change that. I see no sense in finding or making up dignified excuses for our fondness. A behavior pattern that does not make sense is still a behavior pattern that exists. Reason not the need.

Let me end by quoting myself again. As I have said in print (in the essay on *1 Henry IV* and *Hamlet*), and say to students so often that their eyes glaze over, literature is different from all the other arts in that literature alone has for its raw material elements that appear to have been created only as means of transporting information from one mind to others: words.

Common sense says, therefore, that the value of literature must derive from the substance it delivers to our consciousnesses, from what it tells us.

Common sense is wrong. After all, as the physicist Percy Bridgman observed more than half a century ago, common sense is something that tells us the world is flat.

PART ONE

The Unobserved and All Observers:
The Gettysburg Address

The facts with which I deal here are mainly old and familiar; nor is there anything new in the general use I make of them. If there is any novelty, it will, I hope, be illusory—generated by inferences traditionally inherent in the kinds of observations I will present, inferences I reject. My general topic in this book is a ticklish one: remarkable but almost universally unremarked ideational and stylistic anomalies, contortions and perversities in well-known, well-loved works of literature. Can unnoticed literary effects be called effects—that is, have they any effect? And, if so, what kind?

My first major particular topic, Lincoln's Gettysburg Address, is a work I want to talk about because I love it, because most other people love it, because I so long wondered why, and because the Gettysburg Address is so short, so simple, and in such little need of the usual ministrations of an academic critic.

The version I work from appears to be the last one Lincoln made.[1] I choose it not because it came last but because it is the one that has lasted—the one usually cut into buildings, framed on school walls, parodied, memorized, and reprinted:

> Four score and seven years ago our fathers brought forth on this continent, a new nation, conceived in Liberty, and dedicated to the proposition that all men are created equal.

---

1. All Lincoln quotations are from *The Collected Works,* ed. Roy P. Basler et al. (9 vols., New Brunswick, N.J., 1953–55); since that edition is arranged chronologically, I will identify items only by place and date. The Gettysburg Address was delivered on November 19, 1863.

Now we are engaged in a great civil war, testing whether that nation, or any nation so conceived and so dedicated, can long endure. We are met on a great battle-field of that war. We have come to dedicate a portion of that field, as a final resting place for those who here gave their lives that that nation might live. It is altogether fitting and proper that we should do this.

But, in a larger sense, we can not dedicate—we can not consecrate—we can not hallow—this ground. The brave men, living and dead, who struggled here, have consecrated it, far above our poor power to add or detract. The world will little note, nor long remember what we say here, but it can never forget what they did here. It is for us the living, rather, to be dedicated here to the unfinished work which they who fought here have thus far so nobly advanced. It is rather for us to be here dedicated to the great task remaining before us—that from these honored dead we take increased devotion to that cause for which they gave the last full measure of devotion—that we here highly resolve that these dead shall not have died in vain—that this nation, under God, shall have a new birth of freedom—and that government of the people, by the people, for the people, shall not perish from the earth.

Although I will talk only about the Gettysburg Address and its particulars, I present it here as a representative of all works of literature that are generally recognized as both great and so simple as to be lovable. I intend this study and the studies of *Twelfth Night* that conclude the book as preliminary, necessarily inconclusive steps toward an investigation of the staying power of literary warhorses.

The Gettysburg Address is a highly complex document. It is also demonstrably bizarre. Before I get on with the demonstration, however, I want to insist on a radical distinction between kinds of literary fact. The Gettysburg Address seems simple and straightforward. Therefore it is so. Any close reading that said otherwise would lie. What is true of a work and what is demonstrably true of it—what is *only* demonstrably true of it—are very different things. When one reads a line, sentence, paragraph, scene, chapter, or complete work and then goes back and rereads, the second reading is a product of the first—not, as criticism seems often to suggest, a wholesomer substitute for it. Where there is anything puzzling in a work, the puzzle takes both literal and metaphoric precedence over any solution to it, and the puzzle is of the work in a way that a solution cannot be. It is unreasonable for a critic to change—or rather, pretend to change—the way we read a work.

The Gettysburg Address particularly recommends itself for my present purposes because it is a speech—conceived, like a play, to be spoken and heard—and because—unlike most classic orations and plays—its present currency continues in that form (most people who know the Gettysburg Address hear it before they read it). The Gettysburg Address also recommends itself because it lets me beg a question I very much want to beg, the question of second readings—investigative readings subsequent to the first, informed by knowledge of a word's, a phrase's, a clause's or a work's ultimate direction and places of ideational rest, readings often prompted by a desire to know how—and that—literary means accord with ideational ends revealed to a reader at what has proved to be the end of a syntactical unit—or of a larger logical one.

I do not mean to deny that such rethinkings of the particulars of literary units occur, but I doubt that close readings often occur outside classrooms or classroomlike situations—except for works that strike readers as puzzling during their first readings, works that present themselves as puzzles in the first place. I also think that the frequency of second readings by casual (by which I guess I mean "real") readers is exaggerated by noncasual readers for whom belief in the commonness of such exercises is prerequisite to acceptance of their own critical or scholarly theses. However, since experience of the Gettysburg Address has been and continues to be temporal (that is, one hears one syllable, then another, so that linguistic, ideational, and logical units emerge and dissolve as the speech proceeds), and since, aside from some juvenile trouble with *Four score and seven,* the Gettysburg Address

has not puzzled anyone but the occasional political scientist prob-
ing it for doctrine, my choice of example lets me admit to my
prejudice without danger that it will skew my analysis.

1 · THE GETTYSBURG ADDRESS
IN 1863

Since I am aware of another danger, the danger of seeming to
bite the hand at the end of my own arm, let me hasten to modify the foregoing assertions. There is ordinarily an exception to
the rule that says it is unreasonable to change or try to change
the way we read a work—a huge exception, one that for most
literary scholars is bread and butter. It is altogether fitting and
proper that a commentator enrich a work with such specific richness as it has lost in translation from one time or dialect or audience to another. If, like a responsible anthropologist, I properly
assume that the Gettysburg Address, like any work chronologically or culturally foreign to my audience, includes what it was
when written and first read, I do not add to or change the Gettysburg Address if I adjust my own audience in an effort to make
it correspond more nearly to Lincoln's.

Thus I may usefully remind a socially secular twentieth-
century audience that, for our great-great grandparents, Lincoln's
carefully archaic phrase *Four score and seven years* would have carried pertinent resonances of "threescore and ten," the phrase
from the Ninetieth Psalm by which the normal human life span
was specified—a phrase still useful in graveside ceremonies.
That reminder does not so much throw light on Lincoln's phrase
as reillumine it.

The same is true of reminders to twentieth-century readers of
the special urgency that the phrase *all men are created equal,* the
Declaration of Independence generally, the declarers, July 4 of
1776 and July 4 of 1863 had for Lincoln's audience in November
of 1863. The Declaration and that particular phrase from it had
been staples of the decade of formal and informal debate that
preceded the Civil War and continued into it. So too had been

the word *fathers* in reference to the framers and signers of the Declaration and the Constitution.[2] As to the two Independence Days, reference to July 4, 1776 is inherent in the substance of Lincoln's first sentence and in the phrase from the Declaration quoted in it. Reference to July 4, 1863 was inherent in the occasion of the speech. July 4, 1863, less than five months before Lincoln spoke at Gettysburg, was the day on which Lee withdrew his beaten army from Gettysburg and on which the northern cities heard the news that Vicksburg had fallen to Grant. In the speech preceding Lincoln's, Edward Everett had noted and decorously milked the poetic potential of the elegant coincidence of the great victories of the preceding summer with the Fourth of July.[3]

I put the pertinence of July Fourth to the Gettysburg Address into a list of innocuous scholarly supplements to a modern reader's consciousness. It belongs there, but, unless the information is cradled very carefully, it can distort a modern reader's understanding. (In observance of what might be formulated as an academic Gresham's Law—"*New* old knowledge drives out *old* old knowledge"—I take it as a fact of historical criticism that even

2. See, for example, Lincoln's Cooper Institute speech of February 27, 1860. He begins by quoting Stephen Douglas on "Our fathers, when they framed the Government under which we live"; he then goes on to work the word over for several pages. Edward Everett used *fathers* in that sense in the Gettysburg address that preceded Lincoln's.

3. See p. 188 of the transcript of Everett's oration in Louis A. Warren's *Lincoln's Gettysburg Declaration* (Fort Wayne, Ind., 1964). At the end of his account of the battle, Everett refers to Lee's activities on July 4: "That day—sad celebration of the 4th of July for an army of Americans—was passed by him in hurrying off his trains" (Warren 199). Lincoln was, understandably, possessed by the Declaration and the supposed events of July 4, 1776; they are constant topics throughout his career. Had he needed any prompting to mention the Declaration, however, he could not have had it from Everett's speech. Lincoln's allusion to the Declaration occurs in the drafts written before he left Washington, and he could not have seen Everett's speech until he got to Gettysburg. The common belief that Lincoln had (and was photographed with) an advance copy of Everett's speech is authoritatively exploded by David C. Mearns in "Unknown at This Address," in *Lincoln and the Gettysburg Address: Commemorative Papers,* ed. Allan Nevins (Urbana, Ill., 1964), 118–33.

slightly arcane knowledge enlarges in the awareness of its pos-
sessor where it threatens to obliterate other pertinent data.)
The pleasure Everett took in the coincidences of July 4 can be
rekindled in twentieth-century students who, newly delighted
with the coincidence of dates, can find themselves assuming
that that coincidence loomed as large in the minds of Everett's
and Lincoln's audience as in their own newly illuminated consciousnesses.

On July 4, 1863 that audience had surely been very conscious
of a poetic justice, but on November 19 that awareness was at
least dormant enough for Everett's manner to suggest that he expected to be considered solemnly witty in ringing changes upon
the historical accident of the date of the battle. I suspect that the
dim suggestions of the two Fourths of July gave Lincoln's first
sentence an extra feel of truth and feel of pertinence to its occasion, but no more—even though Lincoln's hearers were less
than an hour from Everett's overt rhetorical exploitation of the
coincidence. I would do my readers disservice if I let them believe that Lincoln's first sentence directed his audience's conscious attention to the complex and manifold pertinences of the
Fourth of July and the occasion of the speech.

In that same, first sentence, *nation* calls for a simpler but similarly treacherous scholarly augmentation. In its political sense,
nation still had some of its etymological meaning. As a label for
the United States—a nation only in the metaphoric political
sense of the word—*nation* still had the propagandistic force that
the propagandists' success has lost for it; *nation* still asserted tribal,
racial unity for the United States, the very unity that the United
States so notably lacked. One might also point out gingerly that
nation still had enough of its etymological meaning so that—as
"a thing born"—it both extends Lincoln's natal metaphor and
brings it down to a base of near literal solidity. However, Lincoln
is using the word in its political sense—the sense in which we are
used to hearing it—and a commentator must not allow his readers the fun of thinking that he and everyone else in this century
has been misunderstanding *nation* in the Gettysburg Address.

Of the phrases that need or can stand historical reillumination, the touchiest and most interesting is *under God,* the phrase Lincoln inserted in the last sentence of the Gettysburg Address between the time of writing the drafts and the time of delivering the speech.[4] In the context where Lincoln put it, *under God*

4. The insertion seems to have been impromptu. The phrase first appears in stenographic transcriptions from Gettysburg and is awkwardly inserted between *shall* and *have* (see note 5 below). The insertion was probably made on the platform and may have had its seed in Everett's speech. Lincoln must have listened closely to Everett. In *The Gettysburg Address* (New York, 1963), Svend Petersen reports that "twice Everett inadvertently said 'General Lee' when he meant to say 'General Meade.' The President corrected him in a loud voice both times, but the orator evidently did not hear him the first time. When he was set right the second time, he made a correction" (20). Everett used the expression "under Providence," a periphrastic variant on *under God* and meaning "as a factor second only to Providence": "Victory does not always fall to the lot of those who deserve it; but that so decisive a triumph, under circumstances like these, was gained by our troops, I would ascribe, under Providence, to the spirit of exalted patriotism that animated them, and the consciousness that they were fighting in a righteous cause" (Warren 199). The conjunction in this one sentence of two idiomatic uses of "under"—"under circumstances" and "under Providence"—might have helped nudge Lincoln's mind toward the idiomatic use of *under God* that has since become standard. As a self-conscious rhetorician, listening to an acclaimed orator and fresh from touching up the speech he was himself about to deliver, Lincoln had reason to take note of the potential of the word *under* and the phrase *under God.* Everett's ample preamble—the first two thousand words of his oration—plays insistently, but gracefully and subtly, with the primary physical fact of graveyards. Listen to him evoke, and yet resist exploiting blatantly, the paradoxes with which Gettysburg invests "up," "down," "high," and "low," and their various kinds. This is the first sentence of Everett's address (particularly note the two uses of "beneath"): "Standing beneath this serene sky, overlooking these broad fields now reposing from the labors of the waning year, the mighty Alleghenies dimly towering before us, the graves of our brethren beneath our feet, it is with hesitation that I raise my poor voice to break the eloquent silence of God and Nature" (Warren 185). Everett continues to exercise the word "beneath" in succeeding paragraphs. He goes on loosing notions of physical position in a dense series of metaphors until he gets to the first of his major topics, a detailed account of the Battle of Gettysburg, and, when he reaches that, he immediately introduces the first of his contextually inevitable military uses of the word "under"; he refers to the Army of the Potomac under General Meade (in fact this first mention of Meade may well have been one of the two points where Everett's tongue slipped and the attentive Lincoln corrected him). (In *Lincoln at Gettysburg* [New York,

must always have meant exactly what it means to us now.[5] *Under God* says "guided by God" and—colored by specialized implications of *under*—"in the [quasi-military] service of God" and "under God's protection." However, when Lincoln used it that way in 1863, the phrase may have had something like the energy puns have. *Under God* was already a stock phrase in patriotic contexts, but its stock use was as a parenthetical disclaimer of patriotic idolatry and acknowledgment of the danger of forgetting or seeming to forget that God's authority supersedes man's and that allegiance and gratitude to the American political system take second place to allegiance and gratitude to God. The phrase was a parenthetic acknowledgment of God as the first cause of whatever effect a speaker was about to ascribe to some particular and apparent earthly agent. Louis Warren, who does not seem to notice the difference between Lincoln's Gettysburg use of *under God* and Lincoln's and his contemporaries' usual use of it, gives examples from a book popularly believed to have been a favorite of Lincoln's: Mason Weems's *Life of Washington;* for instance, Weems says that the American people were used to looking up to Washington "as, under God, their surest and safest friend" (*Lincoln's Gettysburg Declaration,* 112). When the Gettysburg Address was new, Lincoln's unusual use of the phrase *under God* probably carried some dim acknowledgment of the pertinence of its standard use to a speech that rises idolatrously above the topic of the Christian dead. At the same time, the phrase appropriated for the speech the appropriate ceremonial, religious considerations that the speech omits to include overtly. In doing that, *under God* is like *shall not perish from the earth.*

1992], Garry Wills rejects the idea that Everett's "under Providence" prompted Lincoln's *under God* [298, note 29], but the basis of that rejection appears to be Wills's rather arbitrary rejection [293, note 6] of the possibility that Lincoln revised his speech during the two hours of Everett's.)

5. There can have been no question about the matter for the audience that heard Lincoln at Gettysburg. There he said, "the nation shall, under God, have." In the versions he wrote out and allowed to be published soon after, he wrote the now-familiar "this nation, under God, shall have."

Like the first phrase of the Gettysburg Address, the last, *shall not perish from the earth,* is a biblical echo—but a complex one, one so complex that a critic who points it out is in danger of becoming infatuated with his own just perceptions and doing injustice to his own readers. The phrase "shall perish from the earth" occurs in Job 18:17: "His remembrance shall perish from the earth." No reference to any part of a book as much read as Job can be called arcane, but I think it unlikely that any of Lincoln's audience would have tied his final phrase to the words of one of Job's comforters. Rather, both phrases echo Moses' formulaic warning to Israel about breach of the law: "Ye shall soon utterly perish from off the land whereunto ye go over Jordan to possess it" (Deuteronomy 4:26). Variations on those words recur throughout the Bible.[6] What is most interesting about their echo in the Gettysburg Address is that they concern a chosen nation and a promised land. *Shall not perish from the earth* has the potential to confirm and sanctify Lincoln's assumption that the welfare of the living nation both supersedes and includes the welfare of the dead men whom Lincoln and his listeners had come there to celebrate. On the other hand, the locally pertinent words *perish* and *earth* cause the phrase, spoken about the nation, to allude to and specifically embrace the superseded topic of the soldiers who perished from the earth and lie beneath it at Gettysburg. Moreover, in the mere fact of sounding biblical (and continuing the more vaguely religious cast of the whole address), *shall not perish from the earth* appropriates the topic of the heavenly (rather than national) life hereafter so that Lincoln seems to have made the Christian graveside assertion he never makes (but which he taps for much of the optimistic energy in the body of the speech, energy available because any listener to a cemetery speech is ready to hear about the life to come).

6. For instance, Deuteronomy 11:17, Joshua 23:13, Psalms 10:16, Ezekiel 25:7, Micah 7:2; also see John 3:15, 16. Like Job 18:17, Esther 9:28 and Isaiah 26:14 connect echoes of Moses' threats with the topic of enduring memory.

As to the cast of the whole, the phrase "new birth of free-dom," which appears in company with "under God," also con-tributes to the speech's religious "feel": Garry Wills points out that, behind the new birth Lincoln foresees, "there is the bibli-cal concept of people 'born again' (John 3.3–7)" (*Lincoln at Get-tysburg,* 88). Also note the last phrase of John 3 : 16, the famous verse that follows shortly after the passage to which Wills directs our attention: "For God so loved the world, that he gave his only begotten Son, that whosoever believeth in him should not per-ish, but have everlasting life." Like the "born again" elements in John 3 : 7, "begotten son" in 3 : 16 resonates with *new birth* and the other supernatural birth references in the Gettysburg Ad-dress. And the context of *new birth* endows Lincoln's *shall not per-ish from the earth* with distant echoes of John's "should not perish, but have everlasting life."

The difficulty in dealing with the relation of *shall not perish from the earth* and the Bible is that the specificity of the evidence can overwhelm its presenter and lead him to posit an audience as finely tuned to biblical echoes as his research has recently and temporarily made him. (In fact, a searcher might fall into a su-perficially persuasive source study if he came upon Isaiah 26 : 12 – 21—a passage that, for an eager student of Lincoln, is so star-tlingly reminiscent of the language and topics of the Gettysburg Address that such a student could come to believe that the Get-tysburg Address is, was, or should have been reminiscent of *it* when heard by someone other than an eager student of Isaiah 26 : 12 – 21.)

Snatches of the Gettysburg Address are so familiar to modern readers that they can feel about it as people do who find *Hamlet* quite good, but too full of quotations. A critic can perform a useful service if he tells such a reader that to some extent the speech must always have seemed full of quotes. It contains one real quotation, the one from the Declaration. It also repeats and echoes formulas that Lincoln used regularly (for instance, this sentence from Lincoln's speech on the *Dred Scott* decision sounds like a casual parody of the Gettysburg Address but was delivered more than six years earlier, on June 26, 1857: "Three years and a half ago, Judge Douglas brought forward his famous Nebraska bill"). Lincoln scholars have long hoped to find a specific source for the prepositional triad in *government of the people, by the people, for the people;* they have not found one,[7] but the number of similar locutions they have come up with testifies both to the cause and the justice of their search. (Warren presents a selected catalogue of analogues proposed by scholars "attempting to find an early combination of these three prepositions" [116]. The most notable and most popular candidates are a sentence from Justice Marshall's decision in *McCulloch v. Maryland* [1819][8] and a fragment from Daniel Webster's Reply to Hayne [1830].[9] Marshall or Webster or both could have inspired Theodore Parker's definition of a democracy as "a government of all the people, by all the people, for all the people" [1850].[10] Actually, the strongest

7. Mark Womack points out to me that *The Columbia Dictionary of Quotations* (New York, 1993) gives the following s.v. "Bible": "The Bible is for the Government of the People, by the People, and for the People" and cites its source as the "General Prologue to the Wycliffe Translation of the Bible (1384)." The Columbia Dictionary's confidence about the date and its apparent indifference to the distinction between the early version of the Wycliffite Bible and the later one are surprising. I have not found the quoted sentence in any printed text of any of the Wycliffite prologues.

8. "The People's government; made for the People; made by the People; and answerable to the People."

9. "The government of the Union . . . is, emphatically and truly, a government of the people. In form and in substance it emanates from them. Its powers are granted by them, and are to be exercised directly on them, and for their benefit."

10. The quoted passage is from "The Slave Power," a speech to the New England Anti-Slavery Convention, Boston, May 29, 1850. All my quotations from Parker are from the Centenary Edition of his works [16 vols., Boston, 1907–11]; the "all the people" passage is from vol. 11 [n.d.], 250. Parker regularly used variations on the phrase; I count eighteen printed instances. The most notable of those for tracers of the lineage of Lincoln's "of-by-for" phrase is in a sermon Parker preached on July 4, 1858. This is from the Lincoln biography first published in 1889 by Lincoln's abolitionist friend and law partner William Henry Herndon, a regular correspondent of Parker's: "On my return [from a trip to the East Coast] . . . I brought with me additional sermons and lectures by Theodore Parker, who was warm in his commendation of Lin-

confirming echo behind the triad is probably the form and substance of the last clause of the Lord's Prayer: "For thine is the
kingdom, and the power, and the glory, for ever.")

More important, the speech is so meticulously repetitious that
within its own brief course it becomes its own authoritative base.
Most important, the distinction between Lincoln's audience and
us is effectively erased by a phenomenon that also figures in the
modern identities of such things as *Hamlet,* "Kubla Khan," *The
Rime of the Ancient Mariner,* and the Song of Songs: phrases from
the Gettysburg Address have so far invaded American consciousness that even a child first hearing it hears it strengthened and
confirmed by echoes of itself. At this point in its history, the par-

---

coln. One of these was a lecture on 'The Effect of Slavery on the American
People,' which was delivered in the Music Hall in Boston, and which I gave to
Lincoln, who read and returned it. He liked especially the following expression,
which he marked with a pencil, and which he in substance afterwards used
in his Gettysburg Address: 'Democracy is direct self-government, over all the
people, for all the people, by all the people'" (William H. Herndon and Jesse W.
Weik, *Abraham Lincoln* [2 vols., New York, 1909], 2:65).

The key word in Parker's many uses of the formula was "all." Parker commonly used the phrase in contexts where he was contrasting the principles asserted in the Declaration to those inherent in any government that tolerated
slavery. For instance, what follows the paragraph defining democracy as "a
government of all the people, by all the people, for all the people" in "The
Slave Power" is a paragraph beginning, "That is one idea; and the other is, that
one man has a right to hold another man in thraldom." And this is the original
context of the sentence Lincoln is said to have marked in the 1858 Music Hall
sermon: "Theocracy, the priest power; monarchy, the one-man power; and
oligarchy, the few-men power—are three forms of vicarious government over
the people, perhaps for them, not by them. Democracy is direct self-government
over all the people, for all the people, by all the people." Lincoln's variant on
Parker's formula leaves out "all." It matters a lot, I think, that, by echoing an
abolitionist formula Lincoln both espoused the idealism of Parker and other
single-minded prewar champions of freedom for slaves (people loud in their
impatience with any suggestion that slavery might be tolerated a few years more
for the sake of saving the Union, people whose indisputably noble policies
were inherently divisive) and, by omitting the pointed insistence on *all,* pro-
duced a phrase that really unifies, one that implies no distinction, moral or
otherwise, between former slaves and former slave owners or, in the future, between former enemies in the Civil War.

ticulars of the Gettysburg Address itself have taken over the en-
riching functions of the now-unheard allusions and echoes that
vouched for its breadth, profundity, and respectability in 1863.

2 · PERVERSITY

However cautiously one manages the business of historical reillumination, the fact remains that what is restored by a scholar
is not of the modern reader's ordinary experience of the work,
and—in the case of classics still vital in the everyday experience
of casually bookish people—was presumably not a part of the
early experience of the illuminating scholars, who presumably
knew and loved such works before that knowledge and love led
them to know, show, and tell all about them. Such works have
the capacity to hold an audience unfit and many. Such works
may be buffeted by time and fashion, but they persist; they may
be sustained by accidents of curriculum, but they survive when
those supports are withdrawn. Why?

I do not pretend to a right to answer that question here, where
I will call so few works in witness. I have, of course, looked at
and thought hard about a lot of works that have the same sort of
apparently special staying power as the Gettysburg Address and
Twelfth Night—the most (and most consistently) popular Shakespearean tragedies, nursery rhymes comparable to the ones I
talked about in the introduction (the few everybody knows, as
opposed to the many always included in collections but rarely
remembered), "Kubla Khan," *Pride and Prejudice,* the Song of
Songs, and so on. That reading and thinking draws me toward
the following generalizations, which I do not so much propose
as admit to harboring.

Great works of art are daredevils. They flirt with disasters and,
at the same time, they let you know they are married forever to
particular, reliable order and purpose. They are, and seem often
to work hard at being, always on the point of one or another
kind of incoherence—always on the point of disintegrating

and/or of integrating the very particulars they exclude—always and multifariously on the point of evoking suggestions of generally pertinent but locally impertinent auxiliary assertions and even saying things they cannot want to say, things irrelevant or antipathetic to their arguments or plain untrue. For instance, Lincoln's patriotic context keeps *conceived in Liberty* in check, but, because of the conjunction it makes between a word with potential to refer to sexual engendering and a word that regularly means "license," the phrase strains toward impertinence.[11] I think also that dangerous energy derives to *from these honored dead we take increased devotion to that cause for which they gave the last full measure of devotion* from the pairing of "to take" and "to give" and from the almost infinitely distant idea of grave robbing, an idea that cannot be imagined ever to have emerged to the consciousness of an auditor or reader.

Works of the caliber of the Gettysburg Address often include half-formed relevant assertions that dissolve in passage. When Lincoln says that *The world . . . can never forget what they did here,* the next phrase, *It is for us the living,* sets off into—and thus can

---

11. See John Hollander, *The Figure of Echo: A Mode of Allusion in Milton and After* (Berkeley and Los Angeles, 1981), 66:

> "Four score and seven years ago our fathers brought forth on this continent, a new nation, conceived in Liberty . . ." is seldom considered an allusive text. . . . But the implicit contrasts set up a powerful pair of tropes, and either lack of appropriate access to scripture or exigetical *pudeur* has passed them over. They might be sketched out as follows: (1) "*Whereas in the beginning, at Our Father's command, the earth brought forth grass* . . . (Genesis 1:12), a mere fourscore and seven years ago brought forth on this piece of earth a new nation" and (2) "Whereas man is *conceived in* sin, this nation was conceived in liberty." The rhythm of "fourscore . . . forth" makes us notice the ellipsis of 'fore(—fathers), but the ellipsis itself makes the forebears into secular forms of *pater noster.* Thus the two tropes make a new, but no longer young, nation into a natural, unfallen, new-Adamic being. In the Gettysburg Address, even the word *nation* is accompanied by biblical resonances.

In a note Hollander adds "perhaps the canceled words *upon this continent* in the first draft of the Gettysburg Address indicate Lincoln's awareness of the biblical tradition."

carry us into—the assertion that "It is for us the living that they did it." (*For* there ends up having meant "incumbent upon," but—even though the phrase reads "It *is* for us" and not "It *was* for us—*for* can momentarily and provisionally say "on behalf of.") And for a fraction of a second, the fraction before *in vain,* the speech actually says *we here highly resolve that these dead shall not have died.*[12]

What my tentative generalizations point to—and what most of the rest of this book will talk about and recommend for your approval—is perversity. That is not surprising. After all, all the standard devices of literary art—devices like alliteration, rhyme, meter, and metaphor—have perversity as a common denominator. Each of them adds a usually gratuitous and potentially distracting and counterproductive extra system of coherence that rivals—and advertises the limitations of—the narrative, po-

---

12. Lincoln's speeches suggest that he was aware to a degree unusual even in writers of his caliber of the fact that sentences emerge one syllable at a time to the minds of their hearers and that sentences therefore can carry with them traces of shadow sentences that bloom in passage and vanish. Consider the following examples.

The reminiscence of Mark 3:25 from which Lincoln's "House Divided" speech (Springfield, Illinois, June 16, 1858) gets its nickname occurs about a hundred words in: "A house divided against itself cannot stand." What I want to consider are the two sentences that immediately follow that one. The first starts with a momentarily complete assertion: "I believe this government cannot endure." As a result the completed sentence ("I believe this government cannot endure, permanently half *slave* and half *free*"), carries with it a dire warning from which it *also* retreats. And this is the next sentence as it would have been without its last word, the word "divided": "I do not expect the Union to be *dissolved*—I do not expect the house to *fall*—but I *do* expect it will cease to be."

The emphasis and punctuation here are those of the most authoritative surviving text of the speech, that of the *Illinois State Journal.* It is apparently Lincoln's own. In his anthology of Lincoln texts, *Abraham Lincoln: His Speeches and Writings* (1946; New York, 1962), Roy R. Basler says "Horace White's account of the printing of this version, as given by Herndon, specifies that the *Journal* text was set up from the manuscript and the final proof read by Lincoln himself" (381). The emphasis and punctuation matter because the comma after "endure" suggests that Lincoln paused in a deliberate manner after "I believe this government cannot endure" and because stress on "cease" before "to be" would have promised continuation.

lemic, or other ideationally essential organization of the work. The extra systems, counterproductive to a work's substantive purpose, are commonly and wonderfully productive of that work's larger essence, wonderfully productive of the simultaneously easy and complex experiences that the works we value enable in us.

It should not be surprising either that I pay attention to perversities that do not call for attention. All criticism, casual, deliberate, amateur, and professional, has traditionally valued works in which substantively incidental devices are unobtrusive, works that seem—and therefore are—straightforward.

The simple, straightforward Gettysburg Address is full of small gratuitous stylistic perversities that complicate—but do not weaken—our perceptions of the continuity and connection that syntax, logic, and phonetic patterning assert. Ostentatious repetitions in the Gettysburg Address are simultaneously ostentatiously imperfect, and related words (like *take* and *gave* in *take increased devotion to that cause for which they gave*) appear in paired constructions but are used in senses that are not immediately related. Similarly, very different phrases are illogically related. For instance, the word *dedicate* always has potential as a muted, bizarre, and complex oxymoron: a verb indicative of purposeful beginning that could be—and that novices in the English tongue sometimes mistake for—a synonym of "to kill," "to make dead"; in the Gettysburg Address the first syllable of *dedicate* echoes and is echoed in the word *dead* and in the idea of dying at the same time that Lincoln is exploiting, extending, and insisting on the full measure of the word's forward-looking optimism.

For a related example, consider the beginning of the second sentence of paragraph 3: *The brave men, living and dead, who struggled here.* The parenthetically asserted inclusion of the living among the brave men whose deeds at Gettysburg are unforgettable and the latent ambiguity of *thus far* in *the unfinished work which they who fought here have thus far so nobly advanced* give the speech a genuinely mystical aura that has all the advantages that orators on similar occasions always fail to get in overt hyperboles by which the dead are said to go on fighting in their surviving comrades. Moreover, but in another dimension of understanding, the allusion to the Battle of Gettysburg is more vivid than it would be if the word *struggled* were not in company with *living and dead;* that parenthetical modifier presents a pair of opposites, and—although the terms of opposition are not those in which warring armies are opposed—the mere fact of opposition enlivens *struggled.* In the same sentence the phrase *to add or detract,* as specifier of *our poor power,* carries extra testimony of poverty because the pair echoes and suggests a related idiom describing a particularly humble power, the power "to add and subtract," the arithmetical skill of a grammar-school child.

In the next sentence *little note, nor long remember* echoes the physics of the larger processes by which Lincoln equates opposites in the same actions that assert distinction between them. The phonic relations of *little note, nor,* and *long* are an emblem of those processes: the unifying alliterative pattern is chiasmic *l, n, n, l.* Similarly, but in another dimension, *little note,* a negative idea expressed positively, is in parallel with *nor long remember,* a negation of a positive idea (the smooth operation of the parallel is probably largely enabled by the presence in *note* of the ideationally dormant sound of negation, which is echoed in both the sound and the sense of *nor*). *Little* and *long,* likened by alliteration and by the negating action of *nor* upon *long,* are distinguished semantically (they are not quite parallel opposites; one measures mass, the other extension; here, where both are adverbial and metaphoric, *little* measures abstract degree, and *long* measures duration). The paired halves of *little note, nor long remember* also relate ideationally (and therefore primarily) in yet another set of terms—action (*note*) and duration of action (*long remember*).

The most effective and efficient agents for extra actions and counteractions in language are the little words indicating function, relationship, or ideational equivalence. They can unobtrusively suggest that there is more to be designated—suggest so even as they successfully complete the function of designating a selected and closed relationship among a selected and exclusive group of things. They do their job of constructively blurring the distinctions they establish (thus making a genuinely and effectively particular assertion reach for infinity) by means of only subliminally perceived improprieties or quickly abandoned temporary gestures toward other assertions.

The various uses of the syllable *for* in the Gettysburg Address are a good example. If Lincoln cannot be said to be dedicated to the preposition *for,* he is dedicated to its sound. The *fors* are so strong at the start of the speech that it is often remembered as beginning "Four score and seven years ago our *fore*fathers brought forth." As the sense of the words that surround the word *fathers* dictates its particular, specialized sense, so the sounds of *Four* and *forth* can press the sound of "forefathers" upon the memory.

After the first sentence the sound *for* recurs seven times, and never to quite the same effect. The *for* of *forget* is obviously foreign to the preposition, as is the *for* sound in *before* (which echoes the theme of the first clause of the speech and specifically echoes the "fore" that is ideationally present but phonetically absent in *fathers*).

Of the five prepositional uses of *for,* two are semantically identical and mean "incumbent upon"—so clearly identical that they are used in ostentatiously twin constructions: *It is for us the living, rather, to be dedicated here to the unfinished work which they who fought here have thus far so nobly advanced* and *It is rather for us to be here dedicated to the great task remaining before us.* On the other hand, the likeness of the two phrases is countered by an equally eloquent unlikeness. The elements of the first are repeated in the second, but the duplication is muted by internal chiasmus. *It is rather for us* echoes but incidentally contorts *It is for us . . . rather.* And *here dedicated* replaces *dedicated here.* The general process continues when *unfinished work* is and is not repeated in *great task remaining before us.*

The other three uses of the preposition are variants of *for* meaning "in behalf of." The first indicates the possessors of the graves: *final resting place for;* the second indicates the cause in behalf of which the honored dead died: *that cause for which they gave;* the third is *government . . . for the people.* The three different kinds of relationship between benefit and benefited act with the three different but related benefits in the three phrases (*resting place for those* [*who died*], *cause for which* [*they died*] and *government . . . for the people* [*shall not die*]) to pull the phrases together and apart so variously that a reader or hearer is casually and unconsciously a mental acrobat in casually comprehending them as incidental in the linear flow of easy exposition.

Before I go further, I should acknowledge that the rhetorical energy to be had from repeating words and from repeating them in different senses has been obvious for centuries. Most of the different kinds of repetition have several different, impressive, forgettable, and confusing names. The only difference between the effects I discuss here and those that rhetorical manuals talk about is that the rhetoricians ordinarily concern themselves only with noticeable effects, effects that call attention to themselves and to their authors' aesthetic or rhetorical intent.

It would take a handful of such terms to describe the activities of the word *that* in the Gettysburg Address. The thirteen *that*s help to integrate the speech, working much the way alliteration would.[13] The thirteen *that*s are all concentrated in two parts of

13. Lincoln took a lot of trouble with his *that*s. One cannot be sure which of the two extant early drafts is the earlier, but the one that differs most from the two transcriptions of the speech as delivered and from the three copies Lincoln wrote out later has "it" instead of *that field,* has "that the nation" instead of *that that nation,* has "This we may in all propriety do" instead of *It is altogether fitting and proper that we should do this,* and has "highly resolve these" instead of *highly resolve that these.* The other draft has its full measure of *that*s except for *of that field,* which first replaces "it" in the three copies Lincoln made of the speech after it had been delivered at Gettysburg. The preliminary drafts also show Lincoln experimenting with placement of the words *here* (which appears eight times in the middle of the final version of the address) and *for*

the speech: seven occur just after the beginning—in the last phrase of sentence 1 and in paragraph 2; six occur just before the end of the last sentence. The two clumps thus participate in the simultaneous contrasts and equations of the beginning and end of the speech and the past and future of the nation. The *that*s are also persistently—though quietly and inefficiently—disintegrative because the same insistently repeated sound has different functions.

The readiest example of simultaneously identical and nonidentical *that*s is *that that nation might live* near the end of paragraph 2. The preeminent example is the progressively dynamic activity of the last three *that*s in the last sentence:

> We here highly resolve *that* these dead shall not have died in vain—*that* this nation, under God, shall have a new birth of freedom—and *that* government of the people, by the people, for the people, shall not perish from the earth.

Each of those three *that*s acts straightforwardly to introduce a clause specifying a particular resolution. However, although the second and third of the trio act to that end straightforwardly, they do not act to that end exclusively. The second, the *that* of

---

(in one of the drafts he tried out "final resting place of those who," but he scratched out *of* and wrote *for* above the line).

I need hardly say that the fact that Lincoln cared about and fussed with the incidental little words of the Gettysburg Address does not make reading the speech any different than it would be if the number and positions of the *that*s, *here*s, and *for*s were as they are by accident rather than design. It is presumably also unnecessary to say that, although Lincoln surely knew what he was doing when he selected and arranged the substantively minor elements that support and connect his nouns and verbs, I do not suggest that he would have analyzed his results in the way I do. I do not ask you to imagine Abraham Lincoln sitting down on the train with his early drafts on his lap and saying to himself, "Let's see if we can't get a few more *that*s and *for*s into this speech." Study of the drafts is only valuable to a critic in that it helps one notice the kind of richness that goes unnoticed in the finished versions. Such study is dangerous to critics if they let their audiences forget that such richness does, did, and always will go unnoticed and/or if they let their audiences believe that the speech is, was, or can be enriched by conscious awareness of its unobserved but efficient effects.

that this nation, acts twice on a listener's understanding: (1) to introduce appositive, alternate specification of what is to be resolved and (2) to introduce a desired result of the first resolution. It simultaneously acts to say "as follows" ("We . . . resolve . . . that this nation . . . shall have"), and to say "so that" ("We . . . resolve that these dead shall not have died in vain *so that* this nation . . . shall have a new birth"). The third, the *that* of *and that government of the people . . . shall not perish,* does even more. It has both of the functions the previous *that* had: it continues the sequence of fulfillments of the syntactic needs of *resolve* ("We . . . resolve . . . that government . . . shall"); and, like the *that* of *that this nation,* simultaneously specifies a desired result of the first suggested resolution ("We . . . resolve that . . . *so that* government shall"). Unlike the *that* of *that this nation,* however, the final *that* has a supplementary adjectival action beyond its two conjunctional ones. In echo of and response to the syntax of *that these dead* and in echo of and response to both the syntax and the substance of *that this nation,* the *that* of *that government* acts as a demonstrative adjective, pointing back to the United States (*this nation* in the preceding clause), and specifying it as "that government [which is] of the people, by the people, for the people."[14] In effect, then, the *that* of *that government* functions three times simultaneously: "We resolve that . . . so that that government."

14. In fact, the final phrase is often quoted as if it came from a context in which the whole phrase, from *that* to *for the people,* were a noun phrase like *these dead* and *this nation.*

Note that the process I describe only confirms (and complicates perception of, and suggests a natural, a quasi-organic, truth in) an assumption inherent in the speech because of its speaker, audience, and situation. Even if this last of the last three *that* clauses were first (if the sentence read "resolve that government of the people, by the people . . . ," so that the juxtaposition of *resolve* and *that* and the absence of *this nation* as a potential antecedent for the demonstrative sense of *that* limited it to its conjunctive function)—an audience would still take the general definition for all democracy as simultaneously a very specific reference to the United States. As the clause is in fact placed, however, it has absolute generality and absolute particularity, each of which is urgent and neither of which is modified or diminished by the other.

It is interesting—and typical of this speech—that the third and last *that* in the sequence dependent on *resolve* is the one fullest of meaning. As the signals of sequence and parallelism indicate increasing limitation on the functions of the *thats*, their functions become less and less limited. The last *that*, the one whose primary syntactical function is most immediately obvious, performs more extra actions than any other word in the whole speech.

The combination of increasingly sharp focus evoked by repetition and increasing expansiveness also occurs on a larger scale in the pattern of the clauses that make up the single, repeated, and progressively more sweeping assertion about the duty of *us the living*. The first assertion (*It is for us the living, rather, to be dedicated here to the unfinished work which they who fought here have thus far so nobly advanced*), is repeated in the complicated echoing clause I have already described (*It is rather for us to be here dedicated to the great task remaining before us*), but the second clause suddenly expands when two subordinate and variously parallel *that* clauses are tacked on to it; in turn, the second of those subordinate clauses (*that we here highly resolve*) has not two but three appended subordinate clauses, and the third of those suddenly swells to include the modifying triplets *of the people, by the people, for the people*.[15]

The speech is not only wittily perverse in specifics; it is wittily perverse in its gross conception—and is much less remarkable for that wit than for managing not to flaunt it.[16] As Lincoln

15. Note the obverse relationship and reverse rhetorical effect in *little note, nor long remember* (double) and *never forget* (single).

16. Perversity was Lincoln's stylistic stock in trade. So was the deep, quiet perversity I talk about here.

On February 22, 1861, eighteen days after the founding of the Confederate States of America, Lincoln spoke in Independence Hall in Philadelphia about the Declaration of Independence adopted there. He said nothing about the new confederacy of southern states, but he took gratuitous pains to mention that the Declaration of 1776 declared a "separation of the colonies from the mother country," and, incredibly, he referred to the Union as "this Confederacy."

For a different sort of example of Lincolnian perversity, consider his use of the "this too shall pass" story. The story was apparently introduced to Europe

says, he and his audience came to the battlefield at Gettysburg to
dedicate a portion of that field as a cemetery; but he archly refuses to do it. First he flirts with his assigned topic by using *dedicated* to describe the nation; then he announces that his task can
not be done: *we can not dedicate . . . this ground;* then he dedicates
the audience rather than the field. He achieves a rightness in the
speech by teetering on the edge of wrongness in what it conveys. The speech ends up rededicating the nation and thus repeats the action described in its opening clause. Lincoln thus
implies identity between the nation's chronological past and its
chronological future—an identity that is not literally possible.
He simultaneously duplicates that physical paradox in the structure of the literary object that asserts the union: the beginning and the end of the speech are opposites—are so in several
dimensions—but the last forty-eight syllables (the last three
clauses) echo not only the topic of the first forty-eight (the first

---

by Warren Hastings, who in 1795, when he was at last acquitted of charges of
official malfeasance as governor-general of India, is said to have told friends that
he had taken comfort from it during his years of trial. Lincoln tells the story
at the very end of the speech to the Wisconsin State Agricultural Society (Mil-
waukee, September 30, 1859) and immediately concludes by applying it to a
purpose exactly contrary to the one it embodies. This is the last paragraph of
the speech:

> It is said an Eastern monarch once charged his wise men to invent him
> a sentiment to be ever in view, and which should be true and appropri-
> ate in all times and situations. They presented him the words, "*And this,
> too, shall pass away.*" How much it expresses! How chastening in the
> hour of pride; how consoling in the depths of affliction! "And this, too,
> shall pass away." And yet, let us hope, it is not *quite* true. Let us hope,
> rather, that by the best cultivation of the physical world, beneath and
> around us, and the intellectual and moral worlds within us, we shall se-
> cure an individual, social, and political prosperity and happiness, whose
> course shall be onward and upward, and which, while the earth endures,
> shall not pass away.

Also see the casual-sounding confusion between Washington the city and
Washington the man at the end of the Cooper Institute speech (February 27,
1860).

sentence) but their ideas, metaphors, and diction—most of which have dropped away during the body of the speech (consider *brought forth / new birth; this continent / this nation; continent / earth; new nation / new birth; conceived in Liberty / birth of freedom; all men are created equal / of the people, by the people, for the people*).

All the perversities I have mentioned and those I will get to later justify generalization: the farther Lincoln gets from a topic in the Gettysburg Address, the closer he comes to it; and the more limited and specific his locutions are, the more expansive and general. Those generalizations point toward these. The variously circular actions of the Gettysburg Address give it identity, independent being, a being that is independent of other physical or ideational things because it is itself a thing—an object, a quasi-physical fact marked out in time as a building or a fenced field is in space—and also a being independent of the persistently exercised limitations of the still-unthreatened systems that define it—reason and syntax, the very tools by which its outlaw identity is carved out. Its objectivity—the pseudophysicality of the literary object—vouches for the validity of Lincoln's assertions, much as the inherent suggestions of other and variously incompatible assertions vouch for and suggest superhuman breadth and depth in the meager assertions it does make.

Having now reached as much of a conclusion as I mean to reach for, I want to push my luck by going back to the first and last sentences of the Gettysburg Address to talk about more bizarre and even less noticeable elements in the speech and to suggest that they are like the other phenomena I have described and also contribute to the grandeur of the Gettysburg Address.

I will start cautiously with a fact of the Gettysburg Address that has indeed been remarked—its pervasive concern for birth. This is Robert Lowell, speaking in the auditorium of the Interior Department Building in Washington in 1963: "Last spring I was talking about the Gettysburg Address to a friend who is also a man of letters. He pointed out to me its curious, insistent use of birth images: 'brought forth,' 'conceived,' 'created,' and finally, a 'new birth of freedom.'"[17]

Actually, of course, the insistent use of birth images in graveyard speeches is not curious at all; the coincidence of one kind of death and another kind of birth is a rhetorical dividend of Christian theology. And yet Lowell and his friend were right to use the word *curious*. What is curious is that the birth images, so obviously plentiful and paradoxical when pointed out, could have elicited surprise in two men of letters raised on the Gettysburg Address. In reporting the phenomenon, Lowell sounds like a man telling his listeners something they didn't know—or, properly, didn't know they knew. He seems to find the perception striking, to have found it striking the previous spring, and to have heard it from a friend who presented it as a surprise for Lowell.

An audience of students would assume that I am in the process of mocking Robert Lowell and his friend. I am not. The curious thing about Lincoln's use of birth metaphors is that, despite their density, they are recorded by their audience as atrophied metaphors would be. In the first sentence the idea of birth in *brought forth* has little more vitality than the idea of "heart" has in "recorded."

At this point, the same student audience would assume that I am debunking the Gettysburg Address. I am not. By critical tradition, atrophied metaphors are bad, and, if a work is said to be good, its metaphors will be, or will be said to be, vivid and vital.[18]

The tradition is well-founded, but we need not follow it superstitiously. I suggest that the dormancy of the birth metaphors

17. *Lincoln and the Gettysburg Address: Commemorative Papers,* ed. Allen Nevins (Urbana, Ill., 1964), 88.

18. A similarly conditioned reflex probably accounts for the numerous assertions that the Gettysburg Address is terse. Although probability says that a speech both admirable and brief will be concise, the Gettysburg Address is luxurious in its expense of words unnecessary to the overt utilitarian aims of the sentences.

in the Gettysburg Address is a specific source of its greatness and is like the other specific sources of its greatness. The speech is sublime in all Longinus's senses of the word. It is also sublime in an etymologically dubious sense that lurks invitingly within it, but, though often endorsed, has always been suspect: a sense that can suggest the kind and location of the elements by which a writer's greatness of spirit comes to echo in the previously diminutive spirit of his readers. "Sublime," which derives from Latin *sublimis* ("uplifted"), a word probably unrelated to *sub limen* ("below the threshold"), could be a cousin of "subliminal" in fact as well as appearance. And, since I am pushing the proposition that the sublimity—the elevation—of elevated works can inhere in ideationally significant effects that do not signify and in demonstrably insignificant ones that do, the dubious but temporarily helpful etymology can encapsulate and clarify my contention that what one does not notice in great literature—what does not literally import and is not literally of its matter—is, in the metaphorical senses of those words, what is most important and matters most.

In the first sentence of the Gettysburg Address, the birth metaphors are demonstrably present, and specific reference to the two Fourths of July demonstrably is not. I suggest that the two are similar in their similarly nebulous action. They and the ultrapertinent but muted, casual echo of Psalm 90 act as tokens of infinity. By their agency a sentence understood as a simple assertion about the founding of the United States also includes an assurance of special and extra pertinence of the sentence to the occasion and an acknowledgment of a cloud of unformulated potential alternative or auxiliary assertions that give the sentence a feel of limitless and absolute truth. All the specifically available topics that the narrow assertion shuts out are also let in by the particulars that make it up; for example, take the appearance of *dedicated* in the first sentence, a sentence that is ostentatiously failing to get to the business at hand: dedicating a cemetery. The physics of the first sentence's action are, I think, these. The paraphrasable content of the sentence is solid, specific, and tells no one anything everyone does not know. The message conveyed is not only absolutely true but familiar and unquestionable: the United States was indeed founded in 1776 and, at least in theory, was founded on the principles enunciated in the Declaration of Independence. Since the sentence says no more than that, its freight of misty grandeur gets the benefit of mundane, factual solidity while the mundane assertion has the feel of a grandly comprehensive, philosophically pregnant utterance by which a listener apprehends more than cool reason ever can.

An underlying idea in the notion of pregnant utterances is that their vitality is there and theirs but not delivered to the apprehending mind. When we say that pompous, obviously highflown ceremonial assertions sound as though they conveyed more than they do, we are usually and properly faulting them. I suggest that the same can be justly said, not against, but to the credit of treasured literary objects in which we feel extraordinary energy and truth.

3 · PLAIN NONSENSE

I have so far talked mainly about ideationally potent elements that do not in any ordinary sense exercise their semantic potential. I want now to move on from undelivered sense to plain nonsense.

The Gettysburg Address has not undergone much detailed analysis. There have been some pedantic exercises in taxonomy (for instance, Wills [174] quotes a 1917 essay by Charles Smiley, who identified "six antitheses, six instances of balanced sentence structure, two cases of anaphora, and four alliterations"). Wills himself devotes most of a chapter to Lincoln's style in general, is particularly illuminating on the ending of the First Inaugural, but is very brief about the Gettysburg Address itself. He gives most of his attention to Lincoln's use of repetition as a unifying device (171–75); what he says is good; this is a fair sample of the kind of point he makes: "By repeating the antecedent as often as possible, instead of referring to it indirectly by pronouns like 'it' or 'they,' or by backward referential words like 'former' and 'latter,' Lincoln interlocks his sentences, making of them a constantly self-referential system. This linking up by explicit repetition amounts to a kind of hook-and-eye method for joining the parts of his address" (172).

But most detailed study of the Gettysburg Address has focused on its first phrase and on *government of the people, by the people, for the people,* one of its last. As I said earlier, the beginning and end of the Gettysburg Address have a special relationship to one another. They also have a common denominator in the fact that *Four score and seven* and the *of-by-for* trinity call for the attention they receive. Those phrases are the only ones that advertise the artifice of the whole, the only points where one hears rhetorical sweat. Their chief function is as boundary markers, isolating the speech as an island apart from everyday prose. Their chief attraction for commentators is that they can bear explication.

The attention given *Four score and seven* is mostly oral, amateur, and juvenile; it is deserved because at some time quite late in every modern English speaker's early life he or she does not know that "a score" is twenty. There is satisfaction in learning that and more satisfaction in passing it on. The pleasure is a kind of starter set for the sort of mentality that will later know the joys of telling a friend that (and how) *Utopia* and *Erehwon* mean "nowhere," learn to translate sailboat words out of and into English, and/or acquire the key particulars, private and public, by which to penetrate Pound, Eliot, Yeats, Joyce, and Wordsworth.

The *of-by-for* cluster is a different matter. Hearing or casually reading the speech, no English speaker would notice that he or she does not precisely see the specified distinction among *of the people, by the people,* and *for the people* or know the specific meaning of the whole urgently meaningful definition of democratic government. Most people are and have been content simply to understand the phrase as a triple drumroll saying and celebrating "American democracy." Some social scientists have felt a professional obligation to explicate *government of the people, by the people, for the people,* and most have ended up dismissing it (with bless-

ings on its head) as "rhetoric."[19] Some of them have, however,
first looked at it closely.[20]

19. For instance, see Giovanni Sartori in *Democratic Theory* (Detroit, 1962),
27: "The truth is that Lincoln's words have stylistic impetus rather than logical meaning. As they stand they constitute, strictly speaking, an inexplicable
proposition. But this is precisely its purpose and its value—and I am not being paradoxical, for to use 'democracy' in its literal sense opens a prescriptive
discourse whose very nature is to remain unfinished, to go on *ad infinitum* as
well as *ad indefinitum.*"

20. The potential (but efficiently inactive) ambiguity of *of the people* is particularly popular with political scientists. Sartori (26–27) analyzes the phrase
in detail, and Bertrand de Jouvenel brushes it aside as a tautological truism:
"The first term [in Lincoln's formula] stresses a 'necessary' feature of Government, for the lack of which a Government has no claim to that name, does not
exist as such" ("What is Democracy?" in *Democracy in the New States: Rhodes
Seminar Papers* [New Delhi, 1959], 29). These narrowly literalistic readings,
both—significantly—by non-native speakers of English, evoked strenuous
clarification in a *New Yorker* essay (September 8, 1975, 42–60) by Mortimer J.
Adler and William Gorman. They concentrate on de Jouvenel's sentence. They
announce that *government of the people* contains "a deliberate double genitive."
Thereupon they spend two columns saying, essentially, that the phrase can mean
both "that which is the governor of the people" (the one sense apparent to de
Jouvenel) and "the government belonging to the people" (the sense contextually evident to English speakers). Although I doubt the deliberateness of the
ambiguity, that does not matter here. The explication *as* explication does not
matter for a different reason: the double meaning Adler and Gorman reveal is
not apparent until looked for—and was not looked for until two political scientists were cornered by a literal-minded French speaker. When the triad is
heard by someone who has never heard it before, its first element probably registers momentarily as a reference to the enterprise of governing the citizenry
(says what Parker's "over all the people" says and continues to say as the phrase
goes on), but the next two elements, *by the people* and *for the people,* are so obviously active modifiers (as opposed to tautological extensions of meaning already inherent in the word *government*) that they entirely override any understanding of *government of the people* as a long-winded way of saying *government.*
Although the tautological sense is not efficient as an alternate reading of *of the
people,* it does, I think, operate in the completed triad; it operates *after* it has been
dismissed by the defining pressures of its two successors, and it can thus give
what feels like almost witty—clever-seeming—extra emphasis to the already
emphatic declaration that this democracy is literally a people's government,
emphasis derived from the now-established philosophical pertinence of the very
fact that *government of the people* read as "government that governs the people"
is tautological: "government belonging to the people, in which the people
themselves are the governors of the people and govern for their own benefit."

My sole purpose in going into previous analyses of phrases in the first and last sentences of the Gettysburg Address is to establish that those sentences have been scrupulously looked at and found strange by students of widely differing interests and sophistication. And my sole purpose in establishing that is to point out that two more remarkably strange things about those sentences have not been generally remarked—if indeed they have been remarked at all.

(1)   Fathers—males—give birth in the metaphor of sentence one. (It has been suggested to me that *fathers brought forth* makes physiological sense if one takes it as a metaphor from midwifery, a metaphor in which the fathers are likened to an obstetrician. That explanation seems the product of desperation. In any context of parenthood the idiom "to bring forth" is so firmly associated with the action of the mother [e.g., Matthew 1:21, 23] that any other understanding of it in context of *fathers* is highly improbable, except after the fact and in answer to a critic-evoked need to make sense of the phrase.)

(2)   The last sentence can be demonstrated to be syntactically incomprehensible.

Before anyone goes hunting in the last sentence to see what can possibly be structurally amiss, in a sentence that has never seemed amiss let me remind you, as I have previously reminded hypothetical students, that I am only talking about the unnoticed paternal prodigy *because* it is unnoticed and is therefore not part of what the sentence says—not part of the sense delivered by, and carried away from, the sentence. Similarly, I am neither finding fault with the last sentence, nor mocking previous readers for their folly in finding it syntactically clear; nor—and this is what matters most—do I mean to suggest that since the sentence is demonstrable nonsense it therefore was, or should henceforth be apprehended as, nonsense. All that one can see *in* a work is therefore *of* it and of its action on a mind capable of perceiving it, *but* not all of that is, or should be said to be, part of what a work delivers to the conscious understanding. I insist on a distinction between, on the one hand, what a work comprehends (what it holds within it and what is thereby included within our perception of it) and, on the other, what we apprehend from it (what we pick up and carry away from it, what we know it to have told us).[21]

Now to the syntax of the last sentence. Looking at the sentence in isolation, and knowing that it makes sense, and always has made sense, one can—if one looks hard enough—see a quite reasonable syntactical relationship between the main clause, *It is rather for us to be here dedicated to the great task remaining before us,* and the two succeeding *that* clauses; both *that from these honored dead we take increased devotion . . .* and *that we here highly resolve . . .* could be appositive to *task: great task remaining before us—* [*namely*] *that . . . we take increased devotion . . .* Nonetheless, I think it unlikely that anyone ever actually understood the sentence that way. My reasons are these. (1) An appositional relationship between a concrete noun like *task* and a noun clause specifying its particulars is unusual; there is no idiomatic impetus toward hearing such an apposition here. (2) The habits of the English language do not prepare us to hear the taking of increased devotion—or vowing of any kind—labeled a *task; task* usually implies effort of some duration; we are used to hearing *task* refer to something that requires sustained physical or mental labor in its performance (keeping a vow may take that, but vowing does not). (3) When we hear *the great task remaining before us* in the Gettysburg Address, it is itself in apposition—in apposition to, and therefore already specified by, *the unfinished work which they who fought here have thus far so nobly advanced;* the *task* is necessarily and obviously "winning the war"; the following *that* clause

21. When I made this distinction between "apprehend" and "comprehend," I thought I was merely adapting the one Theseus makes in *A Midsummer Night's Dream* 5.1.4–6, 18–20. However (and predictably), Shakespeare there manages to make a clear, efficient, memorable distinction and also to use the two terms almost interchangeably.

does not invite us to understand it as an appositional definition of the already firmly defined *task*.

On the other hand, the *that* clauses following *task* are, as I will argue shortly, in effective apposition to the *whole* main clause. In fact, the whole last sentence is a series of increasingly expansive appositional fulfillments of *It is for us the living, rather, to be dedicated here to the unfinished work which they who fought here have thus far so nobly advanced.* Since *that from these honored dead we take increased devotion* is so obviously in general apposition to the clauses that precede it, it is easy to assume—or assume one has assumed—that the *that* clause is in apposition to *task*—the one element in the preceding clause to which it could be in syntactic as well as effective apposition.

If *that from these honored dead we take increased devotion* is not appositive to *task,* how does the *that* of *that from these honored dead* relate to, connect syntactically with, *It is rather for us to be here dedicated*? An answer is obvious: the *that* of *that from these honored dead* is understood as "so that."

I will come back to "so that" in a moment. First I want to say that I think that what is signaled syntactically—"so that"—and what we understand from the construction are different. I suspect that, regardless of syntax, a listener or reader apprehends the substance of the sentence as if it read, "It is rather for us to be here dedicated to the great task remaining before us—it is for us to take, from these honored dead, increased devotion to the cause for which they gave the last full measure of devotion—it is for us highly to resolve that these dead shall not have died in vain. . . ." In my awkward reconstruction of the sentence, the second and third clauses of the original (*that . . . we take* and *that we resolve*) become infinitive phrases parallel with *to be here dedicated.* If I am right in saying that the recast sentence only provides syntactical cause for the general effect of the original, then why and how does the original smoothly achieve an effective logical relationship demonstrably denied by its syntax?

Complexly and multifariously.

First of all, again regardless of syntax, the substantive words in

that from these honored dead we take increased devotion suggest, and
are ideally suited for, an appositive restatement of *It is rather for
us to be here dedicated to the great task remaining before us: take . . .
devotion* echoes *be here dedicated* ideationally; *dead* echoes *dedicated*
phonetically; *that cause for which they gave the last full measure of devotion* restates *the great task remaining before us* (as that phrase had
previously restated *the unfinished work* in the preceding sentence).
Moreover and simultaneously, the propriety of the second clause,
the one beginning *that from these honored dead,* is vouched for by
its mention of the *honored dead* who *gave the last full measure of devotion*—a topic missing from the first clause but prominent in the
preceding sentence, the sentence to which that first clause is itself so pointedly appositive; the second clause not only echoes
the substance of the first but completes that clause's apposition
to the last part of *It is for us the living, rather, to be dedicated here to
the unfinished work which they who fought here have thus far so nobly
advanced.* Furthermore—and by still another logic—the second
clause of the last sentence seems not only an alternate way of saying what the first does but also a better way, a stronger way; the
third clause is stronger still: the three clauses build in intensity
from the unmodified verb in clause 1 (*be here dedicated*) to the
comparative proposition of clause 2 (*take increased devotion*) to the
effective superlative of clause 3 (*highly resolve*).

I said that the reason the second clause overrides its syntax and
is understood as appositive to the first is "first of all" the likenesses between the substantive words of the two. In saying so, I
meant that the substantive diction is first in importance. What is
literally first of all in relating the two clauses is *that* in *that from
these honored dead.* How—at the moment it is heard or read—
does the *that* of *that from these honored dead* function? As I implied
earlier, I think that, at the moment it is heard or read, it is understood as a conjunction meaning "so that." Lincoln has twice
said what "it is for us" to do; *that* seems to introduce a reason why we should do it. But to dedicate oneself to a task for
the purpose of taking increased devotion to that task would be
nonsensical.

However, the phrase *from these honored dead* intervenes between the briefly probable "so that" reading of *that* and *we take increased devotion,* the subject and verb of the clause. The variously pertinent intervening phrase gives the nonsyntactical logics of diction and sound time enough to assert themselves and lets us forget the logic of the syntax. By the time a listener or reader gets to *devotion,* to the word by which the substantive unreason of the apparent "so that" construction is revealed, the ideational parallelism and phonetic likeness between the two clauses has emerged, and one understands a connection between the clauses other than the one the syntax presents. If I am right about the way the sentence works, then the temporarily evident "so that" construction is a momentarily necessary and only momentarily available syntactical bridge that sustains the mind until it is ready to progress without the syntactical support we expect—support that here collapses without our noticing at all.

The *that* introducing the third clause of the last sentence (*that we here highly resolve that these dead shall not have died in vain . . .*) is a slightly different matter. It is syntactically free-floating almost as soon as it is heard. A listener's mind can momentarily respond to another gesture toward a "so that" construction, but the blurring process by which we lost consciousness of the promised "so that" construction in the preceding clause presumably diminishes our expectations of a "so that" here. Moreover, even if the order of the second and third clauses were reversed and a "dedicated so that" construction were positionally possible, the absence of an intervening phrase like *from these honored dead* between *that* and the subject and verb would make the nonsensical redundancy of the "so that" reading immediately and disturbingly evident: "It is rather for us to be here dedicated to the great task remaining before us so that we here highly resolve . . ." would be a proposition so immediately improbable that the mind would almost surely balk long before the sustaining logics of dictional and ideational parallelism could substitute for syntactic logic. As the clauses do stand, however, the fact that the third clause is not even momentarily anchored to the main clause is no more evident than the more complexly blurred syntactic incompatibility of the main clause and the second. The third clause is appositive in every way to the second—or rather, to the second as it turns out to be after we have forgotten about the "dedicated so that" syntax on which we were carried into it. The third clause matches the second, and, if we do not blink at the relationship of the second to the first, we will surely not pause to worry about the relation of the third to the first.

Above all, the sentence's syntactical failure to accommodate *that we here highly resolve* goes unnoticed because it begins with *that;* the semantic gesture the word makes is logically impertinent to the sentence, but its sound—as sound—is ultrapertinent. As the first of the six *that*s in the sentence—the *that* of *that from these honored dead*—is the source of the difficulty I am demonstrating, the other five help to neutralize it—to render it only a hypothetical difficulty, one that *requires* demonstration if it is to be observed at all. In particular, the adjectival *that* of *that cause* vouches for the wholeness, the coherence, of the sentence while also and simultaneously acting—like any antistasis (any repetition of a word in a different sense)—to question the very continuity it asserts.

I have already talked about the multiple actions of the two final *that*s in the Gettysburg Address. Here it is worth also noticing that they have a complex effect comparable to the simpler one I have just described in discussing *that cause:* in incorporating the idea of "so that," they echo the momentarily signaled "so that" which turned out to be substantively inappropriate and had to be discarded in the course of listening to *It is rather for us to be here dedicated . . . that . . . we take increased devotion.*

I earlier recast the final sentence of the Gettysburg Address in a way that made its subordinate clauses syntactically pertinent to its first clause. That reconstruction was accurate enough, I think, as a paraphrase of what listeners or readers understand, but the reconstruction is obviously not accurate as a chart of the physics by which they understand it. I suspect that the clause beginning *that we here highly resolve* enters the mind as if the word *that* were not there at all, as if the word *that* had no specific logical conjunctive power at all, as if the clause were independent, were the speech-act of resolution previously recommended: "We here highly resolve. . . ." At the same time, the word *that* is obviously present, heard, and active. In fact, since *that we . . . resolve* echoes "Resolved that . . ."—a standard phrase by which resolutions are proposed—the presence of the word *that* is probably vital to the process by which this syntactically subordinate clause can register as an independent act of resolving. More important, the presence of the word *that* in *that we here highly resolve* is inevitably an assertion of formal and logical continuity. It asserts continuity both phonetically and as a false syntactic gesture of logical subordination to the first clause.

In short, the identity of the *that we . . . resolve* clause is multiple. As one hears it, one hears it in several independently signaled, syntactically incompatible, but nonetheless coexistent, relationships to the clauses it follows: (1) the *that we . . . resolve* clause repeats the form of the clause it immediately follows (the *that from these honored dead* clause), and the substance (a) of that clause, (b) of the first clause of this final sentence, and (c) of the whole of the sentence that precedes this one; (2) it is a syntactically subordinate continuation of the syntax begun in clause 1; (3) it is effectively a syntactically independent unit—the promised act of resolution. The act of understanding the clause is paradoxical (the clause is not paradoxical, but the act of understanding it is). One's mind easily and casually masters more than common sense says it is possible for a mind to master or the clause contain. The act of comprehending the clause and apprehending its simple, clear sense is a metaphysical act—easy, casual, but beyond the apparent limits of our faculties.

That mental act is all the more satisfying for not only effectively apprehending a single syntactical gesture—one syntactical identity—as two that are mutually exclusive, but also apprehending other temporary identities that turn out to be syntac-

tically incompatible with their contexts and substantively incompatible as well. For example, the tentatively signaled and instantly rejected "so that" construction momentarily inherent in
they gave the last full measure of devotion—that we here highly resolve
. . . can add a shadowy, syntactically illicit suggestion of "they
gave the last full measure of devotion *so that we would* highly resolve"—an assertion never made, never heard, and unjustified
by the probabilities of military motives, but one that pertains to
and supports Lincoln's implied assertion that the survivors owe it
to the dead to continue the fight for which they died.

Such signs of shadow dimensions are valuable because they
increase the *trueness* of the literary object that contains them.
They add to the speech's logically, syntactically, and phonetically
achieved impression that its topics all pertain necessarily—naturally—to each other (the impression we testify to when we say
that a work of art is an organic whole). Such a hint of extra dimension is also valuable as one of many token inclusions of potential considerations, assertions, and grammatical constructions
that, as a purposeful and successful artifice, the speech excludes.
By letting our minds touch momentarily on irrelevancies—irrelevancies at once *defined* as such by a logic and syntax that cre-
ate a context that exists only to exclude them and *evoked* by that
same logic and syntax—the Gettysburg Address gives the impression that—even though it is obviously a special arrangement
of specially selected truths—it is a comprehensive embodiment
of all truths that could impinge on its chosen territory. The
speech goes beyond the limits of its own insistent and effective
precision. It lets us have our cake and eat it too. By virtue of the
simultaneously efficient and inefficient—precise and imprecise—operations of tools by which our experience is mediated,
the Gettysburg Address makes us seem temporarily to be as we
would be if we could master *un*mediated experience.

No successfully assimilated irrelevancy is quite so valuable and
satisfying as one that dimly or momentarily suggests a line of
thought that, if it emerged fully in an audience's consciousness,
would undercut the assertions among which it lurks. The mere

ridiculousness of the unsaid shadow sentence implying that soldiers might die for the specific purpose of evoking a resolution
that they did not die in vain has that kind of value. And so has
fathers brought forth. The literal sense of that phrase is compre-
hended within the assertion and within the experience of hearing it or reading it, but is not part of what one apprehends from
it. The ridiculous metaphor is really only an exaggerated version
of any metaphor, and its value is of the same kind, but greater—
greater because the assertion of oneness among distinctly separate entities is made without purposeful recourse to the link of
likeness—a link that admits and asserts (as links in real steel
chains do) that the unity it makes exists only by virtue of that
single connection—admits and asserts that the unit is not a unit
but a federation of otherwise and essentially separate elements.
Where a simile or a logically acceptable metaphor connects things
by virtue of a likeness between them, *fathers brought forth* and (in
a more complicated way) the muddle of *that*s at the end of the
speech make an amalgam, a substance more urgently *it*self than
its parts are *them*selves.

I submit that the sublime, traditionally contrasted with the
ridiculous, gets its sublimity by including the ridiculous—that
the ridiculous is of the essence of the sublime here and every-
where else where sublimity is perceived.

In talking about assertions and implications that are present
and available to the eye and ear but to which the consciousness
of an auditor or reader is insensible, and in talking about assertions and implications that are senseless (are ridiculous) but are
apprehended as sensible and straightforward, I am talking about
nonsense. That is not necessarily the same as talking nonsense,
but it is not easy to make and keep the distinction evident. I have
repeatedly insisted that Lincoln's failures of precision are valuable
only because they increase the scope of an obviously orderly, rational, purposeful, exposition—and only because they are not
consciously noticed. However, it takes so much time and energy
to demonstrate the presence of nonsense in a straightforwardly
sensible work that students are liable—nay, eager—to think that

in asserting the preciousness of nonsense in things that have made simple sense, do make simple sense, and will continue to make simple sense, one is asserting the preciousness of nonsense generally, asserting its general superiority to sense, and encouraging them to believe that what was clear before is unclear now and is therefore better than things that are clear.

Students are conditioned by the classroom norms they have known since grammar school. For instance, when teachers deal with stylistic elements, they usually point only to things unusual in ordinary speech. One can insist endlessly that a literary effect need not be unique, or even unusual, to be present in—and contribute to the unusual goodness of—an unusually good work; and one can insist endlessly that what matters is the density, variety, and inconspicuousness of elements that enrich a work with ideational static rather than the nature or the presence of any particular element; and students will still say that one's argument leads to the conclusion that any sentence that uses the word *that* twice and in two different senses is a masterpiece, or dismiss commentary on elements like Lincoln's *that that nation* by saying that that sort of thing happens even in their own sentences. Moreover, since so much of classroom literary analysis has so long seemed accusatory—a process in which the student is demonstrated to have missed a thousand ships—students either insist that analysis of the unobserved in literature is invalid because "*I* didn't see any of that" or insist on filling with shame because "I didn't see *any* of that." Academic critics are by tradition explicators, and their audiences therefore assume that anything said to be true of a work is presented as something readers should notice and should take meaning from.

The heart of this whole problem is the special quality of language that distinguishes it from all the other materials in which artists work. The problem does not, for example, exist at all in considerations of the humblest and most sophisticated of the arts, interior decoration. Language, however, exists to convey ideational substance (that is, the word *dog* seems to have been brought into existence only to enable abstract reference to the animal it labels). Common sense says therefore that what is valued in things made of words must be the ideational substance its audience takes away from it. We all know that common sense is wrong. However, we cannot act decisively on that knowledge because common sense is not *altogether* wrong. *King Lear* is better than "Jack and Jill" and is probably so not only because of its physical size but because its ideational matter matters to us. Still, the currency and obvious justice of the stock notion that works lose something in translation testify that not all value in literature resides in the substance one takes away with one when one finishes reading. Nonetheless, the obvious purpose and always primary function of language leaves us all with an all but instinctive fear that a critic who talks about the nonsensical elements in literature must be talking nonsense, must be tempting us to take his observations about a work for that work as previously observed. Students are therefore relieved and teachers pleased whenever substantively incidental elements like alliteration or rhythm are imitative of, or at least auxiliary to, the substance discussed or asserted. It is no accident that a whole generation of American schoolchildren was taught Masefield's "Sea Fever," by which they got the comforting notion that the purpose of rhythm in verse is to induce sea sickness in stay-at-homes.

I must admit that I am myself comforted by an irrelevant awareness that the various meanings of the sound *for* have a special aptness to Lincoln's topics and assertions; the sound pertains to the Fourth of July, birth (bringing forth), purpose, sacrifice, and duty. I find similarly dubious encouragement in the pertinence of the literary physics of the Gettysburg Address to the ideas of *e pluribus unum,* civil war, and forming a "more perfect union."[22]

22. The essentially biographical incidentals presented in notes 10 and 12 are similarly irrelevant to the validity of what I say about the Gettysburg Address. However, I find the existence of other examples of Lincolnian perversity reassuring. I admit also to taking illicit, logically contemptible, but nonetheless real comfort from Lincoln's concern for the ideational small change with which I am concerning myself. The comfort is vaguely akin to the com-

It is hard to break habits that have become nearly instinctual. Take, for another example, the notion that literary analysis is always intended to make a work work better, that the critic's purpose is always to heighten his reader's experience of the work, and that a critic's function is thus comparable to that of the work he or she describes. Once again the Gettysburg Address is ideally suited to my purposes. No one in this culture can be insensible to the charm of a spurious irony that sparkles like a zircon in any analysis of the Gettysburg Address: my analysis is several dozen times longer than the work analyzed. We can perfectly understand why it takes an anatomist a volume to explain what the muscles of a hand do when it picks up a pen; we do not suspect the anatomist of thinking that his analysis improves or could improve the action he describes. Such is not the case with literary critics, but it should be.

Leonardo da Vinci dissected cadavers in an ultimately futile search for the seat of the human soul. I suspect that the soul of great literature may be found by examining what one of my students has, with merciless precision, called "literary chickenshit." The search may be as futile as Leonardo's, and its laboratory reports will sadly lack charm and belletristic grace, but the enterprise will be nonsensical only if it is assumed that the purpose of the dissection is to increase the vitality of the objects studied. If we as academic critics can resign ourselves to answering academic questions, and if we can once get shut of the general assumption that our purpose is inevitably and exclusively to explicate and to supplement, then we will no longer be slandered from our different and humbler duty, but rather dare to do our duty as we would be wise to understand it.

---

fort collectors of modern art in the 1950s got from being able to assure their bemused acquaintances that Jackson Pollock was, and could if he wished again be, an enormously able draftsman.

PART TWO

Failure and Success in Ben Jonson's Epitaphs for His Children

Any poem generates two separable responses. We have a sense of the poem as poem (does it impress us? is it clever? is it like other poems on the subject? is it elegant? is it smooth? is it learned? are we jealous of the poet's talent? . . .). We also develop an attitude toward the matters the poem treats (do we judge of the topic presented as the writer appears to want us to?). The distinction is obvious, but rarely thought about in those terms. Ben Jonson did think about it in just about those terms—as did the classical theorists he translated and paraphrased. This, his translation of lines 99–100 of Horace's *Ars Poetica,* is one of many places in his work where he points to the distinction:

> 'Tis not enough, th'elaborate Muse affords
> Her Poem's beautie, but a sweet delight
> To worke the hearers minds, still, to their plight.
>
> (140–42)

This essay is generally concerned with the interrelation of various kinds of poetic failure and various kinds of poetic success, but its principal particular thesis is that the two Jonson poems I mean to talk about make improbably subtle and improbably efficient rhetorical use of Jonson's success or failure in exercising his craft—that is, that the poems make use of the sense they generate of themselves *as* poems to shape and direct our sense of the subject matter they present.[1]

---

1. Note that I say "poems make use," not "Jonson makes use." The ensuing discussion inevitably invites questions as to the extent to which Jonson calculated the particulars of the effects I describe. Those questions, however valid,

Of the two poems I will talk about, one, "On My First Son,"
is a very good poem:

> Farewell, thou child of my right hand, and ioy;
>   My sinne was too much hope of thee, lou'd boy,
> Seuen yeeres tho'wert lent to me, and I thee pay,
>   Exacted by thy fate, on the iust day.
> O, could I loose all father, now. For why
>   Will man lament the state he should enuie?
> To haue so soone scap'd worlds, and fleshes rage,
>   And, if no other miserie, yet age?
> Rest in soft peace, and, ask'd, say here doth lye
>   Ben. Ionson his best piece of *poetrie*.
> For whose sake, hence-forth, all his vowes be such,
>   As what he loues may neuer like too much.

The other, "On My First Daughter," is a great poem:

> Here lyes to each her parents ruth,
> Mary, the daughter of their youth:
> Yet, all heauens gifts, being heauens due,
> It makes the father, lesse, to rue.
> At six moneths end, shee parted hence
> With safetie of her innocence;
> Whose soule heauens Queene, (whose name shee beares)
> In comfort of her mothers teares,
> Hath plac'd amongst her virgin-traine:
> Where, while that seuer'd doth remaine,
> This graue partakes the fleshly birth.
> Which couer lightly, gentle earth.[2]

---

are biographical—are questions about the poet rather than the poems; and I
therefore feel both free and obliged to beg them. Although I do not suggest
that my account of the poems is an account of Jonson's thinking about them, I
am personally inclined to believe that Jonson always knew just what he was doing and just how. But that, and speculations like it that are similarly irrelevant
to the validity of my accounts of the poems themselves, I reserve to notes.

2. "On My First Son" is number 45 in Jonson's *Epigrams;* "On My First
Daughter" is number 22. These and all other Jonson texts are quoted from
C. H. Herford and Percy and Evelyn Simpson, *Ben Jonson* (11 vols., Oxford,
1925–52—hereafter abbreviated as H&S). The poems quoted here appear in
Volume 8 (1947), on pages 41 and 33 respectively.

H&S attempts rather precise typographical approximations of the first

1 · "ON MY FIRST SON"

"On My First Son" is an *interesting* poem. Its first line contains a satisfying diversion: the riddle of *child of my right hand.* That is an odd epithet. Why *child of my right hand?* Owners of a Geneva Bible—which, among those of Jonson's contemporaries who had had any schooling, was effectively everybody—were acquainted with the pleasures of knowing the etymological roots of given names, and could puzzle out the epithet as a translation of "Benjamin"—which the Geneva "table of the interpretations of the proper names" glosses as "sonne of the right hand." [3] Editors and

---

printed texts of the two poems, those in Jonson's 1616 folio *Works* (for instance, H&S uses several different sizes of small capitals). I reproduce the texts here in a simplified typography (for instance, like most modern editors, I replace small capitals with lower-case letters).

Moreover, in the course of my discussion, incidental references to words and phrases from the two poems are casually modernized wherever modernizing is unlikely to result in distortion—and wherever duplications of orthographic peculiarities of the 1616 text would be clumsy, purely pedantic gestures of superstitious textual piety. (I say that even though Mary Thomas Crane has persuasively suggested that the typographical variations in Jonson's *Epigrams* may be purposeful, designed to make the printed poems resemble inscriptions chiseled in stone ["'His Owne Style': Voice and Writing in Jonson's Poems," *Criticism,* 33 (1990): 39]. However useful Crane's suggestion may be in contexts other than this one, the typography of the two epitaphs does not pertain here.)

The confusion likely to derive from inconsistency between my formal and informal citations is, I believe, more likely theoretical than it will be in fact.

By retaining the H&S texts, I avoid seeming wantonly to suppress orthographic invitations to interpretive ingenuity in twentieth-century critics conditioned to modern, logically informative punctuation and accustomed to looking for nuances of meaning in nuances of spelling. (Editorial suppressions only make such orthographic invitations more inviting and that much more hazardous to common sense. For an example of the kinds of invitations I mean, consider the commas that surround *less* in line 4 of "On My First Daughter.")

And by modernizing citations in the course of my discussions of the poems, I can quickly and efficiently acknowledge readings that seem to me to be obvious and effectively exclusive without denying readers easy access to possible evidence that what seems obvious to me may be so only because of a personal, peculiar lapse in my perception.

3. This is the Geneva entry in full: "Benjamin, sonne of the right hand who was first called Benoni the sonne of sorow." The naming of the newborn Benoni by Rachel and his renaming by Jacob are in Genesis 35:18; this is the

classroom teachers now get to decode this bit of what Jonson elsewhere scornfully calls "herald's wit."[4] The pleasure of decoding it and explaining the arch etymological pedantry by which, in line 10, the child is the senior Ben Jonson's *best piece of poetry* may account for the poem's current popularity as an object of classroom analysis. (Over the years that I talked about "On My First Daughter" in Freshman English at Berkeley, I had regularly to contend with helpful teaching assistants who ran off copies of "On My First Son" for the students or attempted otherwise to help out by getting us off colorless little "On My First Daughter" and onto its more demanding and critically rewarding brother.)[5]

Geneva version: "Then as she was about to yelde up the goste (for she dyed) she called his name Ben-oni, but his father called him Beniamin." Geneva's list of etymologies appears to have been well known in Jonson's time (perhaps because it provided something nonreligious to read on Sundays), and Jonson's first readers might have heard the sad irony by which the son of Jonson's right hand had become the son of sorrow.

Herford and Simpson note that in addition to its literal meaning, "the Hebrew Benjamin" meant "fortunate" or "dextrous" (11.9). And Don W. Der, talking about Jonson's first readers, says that "'child of the right hand' would cause them to remember that the Latin *dexter,* which literally means 'on the right side' or 'right,' figuratively means 'dextrous,' 'skillful,' or 'lucky'" (*Explicator,* 44 [1986]: 17).

4. See line 12 of "To the Memory of . . . Lady Jane, Eldest Daughter to Cuthbert, Lord Ogle: and Countess of Shrewsbury" (H&S, 8 : 394). These are lines 1–3, 7–12 (since the "original" orthography of this particular poem is particularly and inconsequentially cumbersome and since I quote the poem only incidentally, I have casually modernized both spelling and punctuation):

> I could begin with that grave form, *Here lies,*
> And pray thee, reader, bring thy weeping eyes
> To see who it is. . . .
> But every table in this church can say
> A list of epithets and praise this way.
> No stone in any wall here, but can tell
> Such things of every body, and as well.
> Nay, they will venture one's descent to hit,
> And Christian name too, with a herald's wit.

5. The teaching assistants spoke for the literary establishment. The fullest treatment of "On My First Daughter" is an essay by Ann Lauinger called "'It makes the father, lesse, to rue': Resistance to Consolation in Jonson's 'On my

There is similar, though less elaborate, cerebral fun in the ostentatiously artful financial metaphor (*lent, pay, exacted, just day*) in the second couplet. And, although the commentators I know of have let it slip by them ungarnished, the poem's diverting display of wit is even more extravagant in line 5, where *O could I lose all father now* awkwardly stretches idiomatic English to come up with *all father,* which context glosses as "all fatherly emotions" and which is the price Jonson pays for a play on "the mother," the old medical term for "hysteria." [6]

Nonetheless, there is a great deal to be said in favor of "On My First Son," which, however debilitating its showy effects may ultimately be, also has capacities comparable to those that make "On My First Daughter" great. Those capacities largely derive from effects that are hardly more than gnats to the con-

---

first Daughter'" (*Studies in Philology,* 86 [1989]: 219–34)—an essay with which at several points I disagree profoundly and which I nonetheless recommend to everyone interested in the two epitaphs. Lauinger, whose modest ambition in the essay is to say that "while not necessarily greater" than "On My First Son," "On My First Daughter" is "at least more interesting than it is usually considered" (219), begins her essay by saying this: "For any reader of Jonson's *Epigrammes,* comparisons between the two epitaphs "On my first Daughter" (Ep. XXII) and "On my First Sonne" (Ep. XLV) are probably inevitable. That "On my First Sonne" is the greater poem is a judgment from which few readers would dissent. . . ."

Lauinger says "few *readers* would dissent," but the consensus she reports is not of readers but of twentieth-century professionals, academic critics whose product is explication and whose preferences tend to be for poems that can be shown to need analysis in order to function fully. I think it says a lot about the two poems that in the seventeenth century—when the two epitaphs were new and were read rather than studied—the poem extensively alluded to and imitated was "On My First Daughter," not "On My First Son."

In his notes to a strenuously interpretive essay called "To Write Sorrow in Jonson's 'On My First Son'" (*John Donne Journal,* 9 [1990]: 149–55), Lauren Silberman gives a valuable, succinct account of previous commentary on "On My First Son."

6. Jonson's fondness for playing on the medical sense of "mother" was all but inexhaustible. See his plays on "Fits o'th' Mother" in line 40 of "An Epigram on The Court Pucell" (H&S 8:223) and "Sicke o' the uncle" in *Epicoene,* I.1.143, to which Herford and Simpson (10:8) compare Robert Burton's "the sonne and heir is commonly sicke of the father."

sciousness of a reader—effects whose energy and life span are comparable to those of a quark (and whose existences are as hard to demonstrate as the existences of quarks)—effects like the ones described in the next five paragraphs.

In line 4, *by thy fate* is delicately and insignificantly ambiguous. The phrase permits the mind to apprehend the same information in two different ways at once. The word *by* at once personifies Fate as a creditor by whom the debt is exacted and establishes a concurrent construction that sustains the financial-legal metaphor in quite another way and makes the same general point as its alter ego: "according to the terms of thy fate."

In line 5, the 1616 text gives *loose* where we would print *lose*. Renaissance texts make no systematic orthographic distinction between the two related words, but there is no reason to believe that Renaissance readers spent any more time deciding which sense "lose" or "loose" signaled than we do when we see "the bow" and decide whether it refers to an archer's implement (pronounced to rhyme with "toe") or the front end of a ship (pronounced to rhyme with "plough"), or than we do when we see "to bow" in the stock phrases "to bow one's neck" and "to bow one's head." Context tells us. And context surely told any Renaissance reader which word *loose* signaled in the Folio's *O, could I loose all father, now.* But—if it is understood that I am not proposing the presence of active, substantively informative ambiguity of the sort close readers are wont to propose—I do suggest that, in the fraction of a second during which seventeenth-century minds were open to either identity, the ideas of letting loose and of looseness entered their consciousnesses where the two ideas complemented both the hysteria of the exclamation about losing all father (the speaker lets loose his fatherly emotions in a paradoxically passionate wish to lose them) and the new looseness in the relationship between the couplet form and the speaker's sentences.

I would argue similarly about the word *Will* in line 6 (in *why/ Will man lament,* which means "why does mankind *persist* in lamenting" and nothing else), and about the word *yet* in line 8

(in *And, if no other misery, yet age,* where the function of *yet* is almost purely emphatic and its nearest synonym is "neverthe-
less"). Both words appear here in sentences that preclude the
time-related senses they commonly have, but they appear here
in the general context of a poem held together by the constancy
of its various appeals to a reader's sense of time—and in close
proximity to *now, soon,* and *age* in the poem's central four lines.

Similarly, the verb *To have* in line 7 turns out to be a mere
auxiliary to *'scaped,* but appears in context of the topic of possession and loss and in a line where, until the construction is
defined by *'scaped,* the phrase *To have so soon* can fleetingly say
"So early to have possessed."

And in line 8, the sense to be taken from the phrase *no other
misery* is dictated by context, but a potential sense inadmissible
in the syntax of line 8 is urgently pertinent to the substance of
the sentence in which it appears: "no further misery."

I want now to go through the poem and talk about the interactions of its flashy, self-congratulatory effects and little ones like
those I have just described.

My harsh comments on the glitter of "On My First Son" are,
I believe, warranted, but they are insufficient and are to that extent unjust. My accounts of the cold, trivializing conceits imply
that the lines are merely cold and trivial, but they are not. The
first two couplets are saved from brittleness by things like the
prose-simple artlessness of line 2 and the humane clumsiness of
the phrase *and joy,* which—as an unexpected and anticlimactic
appendage to a perfect nugget of etymological wit in a neat, complete octosyllabic line—feels as if it is there only because what it
says is true—is there only because the child *was* his father's joy.[7]

---

7. That sense of artless simplicity is, I think, pure—even though *child of
my . . . joy* offers its readers' minds a potential aftertaste of "product of my sexual pleasure" and of "child of my beloved wife." Note, too, that—though
loved boy (the syllables that stretch line 2 to match the decasyllable *and joy* made
of line 1) can feel to readers like metric filler particularized by the poet's need
to rhyme *joy*—the expansion of line 1 itself is a very different matter. That expansion feels artless because *and joy,* the substantive and rhythmic afterthought

Moreover, and surprisingly, I think the assertions in the first two couplets feel like more than vehicles for displays of crafts-manship—feel true—because each is sustained by an extra witty fillip over and above the relatively brazen wit of the etymology of "Benjamin" and the earnestly sustained financial metaphor of lines 3 and 4. (One of the most curious things about wit is the metamorphosis that an extra twist can bring about in the essence of the experience of perceiving and responding to a conceit or to a joke. When a speaker shows us a surprising connection be-tween two objects or contexts, we are likely to dismiss the union as a toy; but, when we perceive two independent points of acci-dental or contrived junction between two disparate things, their improbable union comes to feel real—comes to feel like a super-natural fact of nature. Consider the difference between our re-sponse to a joke and the sense of spiritual exultation engendered by a "topper" for it. The independent arbitrary unions that me-ter and rhyme make in, say, an iambic pentameter couplet can interact similarly to transform an artificial union into a unit—a thing, a whole perceived as an identity stronger than the identi-ties of its distinguishable parts.)

In line 1 of "On My First Son" the mere wit of *child of my right hand* coexists with an equally trivial suggestion of honor, importance, and usefulness that comes with *right hand,* a term id-iomatically familiar in the notion by which a great man's second in command is his "right hand" (the *Oxford English Dictionary* cites this from 1581: "that arch-Papist Edmund Campion, the Pope his right hand")—and daily repeated in the Apostles' Creed ("[Jesus Christ] ascended unto heaven, and sitteth on the right hand of God the Father Almighty"). As the English words *child of my right hand* "miraculously" say "Benjamin," so both the honor inherent in the phrase *right hand* and the notions of father, son, and immortality in heaven inherent in the most famous con-

---

at the end of line 1, is the first indication we get that the line will not be an octosyllable and occurs before we know what rhyme sound the poet will com-mit himself to.

text of *right hand* also miraculously fit a context in which a father considers the premature death of a son. Play on those connotations of *right hand* is only potential—and is most effective for being so. I suggest that the potential lies just behind the consciousness of a reader (whose mind is as a mind is just before it seizes on a witty connection between disparate things), and that the felt potential for unexploited wit gives a feel of rightness that exploited potential (like that in "Benjamin" and its etymology) loses by virtue of the advertisement of artifice that the action of making the openly witty—and thus openly arbitrary—connection brings with it.

Ultimately, I think, the rhetorical failure of the first couplet—the failure inherent in the fact that we attend more to its etymological cleverness than to its substance—outweighs and overwhelms the effects that can be justly said to militate against that failure. The same is true of the second couplet:

> Seuen yeeres tho'wert lent to me, and I thee pay,
> Exacted by thy fate, on the iust day.

That couplet fails for a reader who, like me, objects that it sweats too much in elaborating the analogical symmetry of the loan metaphor—a metaphor traditional since classical times, but rarely used with so cool a display of craftsmanlike thoroughness. The couplet fails, I think, even for a reader who takes pleasure in noticing and admiring the fullness of the metaphor. In either case the couplet—the artist's immediate, palpable product—is the object of a reader's attention and not the couplet's substance.

I want, however, to consider a different sort of rhetorical failure in the second couplet, a failure that makes for rhetorical strength. The interaction of exploited and latent energies in the second couplet is far more complex than that in couplet 1. Like the first, the second couplet is at once ostentatiously, extravagantly tenuous *and* possessed of effective suggestions that there is mysterious underlying validity to the speaker's line of thinking. The key element in the couplet, the one that lets us accept it without stopping to evaluate its justice, is its appeal to the idea that one cannot fight fate—specifically to the idea that some people are fated to die young. However, most of the energy of the lines is devoted to invoking another tradition, one that is both appropriate and inappropriate, and one that is a means whereby an easy, platitudinous gesture acknowledges considerations capable of revealing the insufficiency of the narrow, arbitrarily conceived consolation it offers. The couplet's inclusion of reminders of uncomfortable ways of thinking about the child's death gives a still-platitudinous and simplistic gesture the feel of a philosophy that has been tested and found sufficient.

Let me explain.

Most of the energy of the couplet goes into the analogy between a life span and the stipulated term of a loan—an analogy proverbially familiar in notions such as "owing God a death" and "paying one's debt to nature," and therefore, by a logic comparable to the precedental logic of common law, automatically persuasive. There is an obvious justice to the analogy; and, since its currency augments that justice, a gesture toward it can be efficient—even though the analogy fits a normal life span of three score and ten and is desperately impertinent to the death of a child.[8]

In the second couplet of "On My First Son," however, Jonson disables the persuasiveness that we are culturally conditioned to accept from the analogy. Jonson's self-assertive display of financial terms calls so much attention to the "poetic" justice of the analogy that it calls attention to the fact that application of the analogy is arbitrary, the product of the poet's decision to "look at it this way." (After all, any simile or analogy asserts its own inadequacy; the mere fact that it must be invoked advertises the fact that what it makes evident is not evident in the given sit-

8. The analogy appears to similarly comfortable effect in the second couplet of "On My First Daughter," where its logical action is only to say that the child would have died anyhow, but where it also carries a logically illicit implication that the death in question was in the nature of things just as death at seventy would be.

uation as normally perceived.) In this case, moreover, Jonson brings the brevity of the dead child's life into the analogy (*Seven years thou'wert lent to me*), and challenges his own device in *on the just day,* which asserts the desired conclusion so openly as to advertise the injustice of applying the analogy to this situation. The obviously ameliorative analogy thus *also* aggravates the sense of injustice that a child's death evokes. Sheltered as it is by the easy efficacy of the couplet's gesture toward fatalism, Jonson's financial analogy actively generates exactly the response to the poem's occasion that the debt metaphor generically signals its desire to combat.

I suggest that there is positive rhetorical value in reminding the poem's reader of the arbitrary narrowness of the premises from which the conceit offers consolation. No conceit for dealing with the death of a child can succeed. No way of thinking about the death of a child can make it feel other than wrong. And, except where speaker and audience are genuine fanatics, that includes conceptions based in the transparently sufficient comforts of Christianity. Genuine belief in death as a benefit cannot—and never could—combat knowledge that death is an evil.[9]

Comfortable and uncomfortable conceptions of death ordinarily live side by side in the mind, and ordinarily they do not

9. Many students and some of their teachers are given to starting for a historical rabbit hole when confronted with poems like this one. They announce that "in those days" the faith of Christians was so intense and so literal that they could think of a dead child in paradise much as a modern parent thinks of a child away at a fashionable boarding school. No one can deny the depth and sincerity of Christian faith during any period, but "in those days" no less than in our own the number and the urgency of reminders from friends, clerics, and poets of the metaphysical truth of the situation testify loudly to the need for such reminders and to their insufficiency. Although the analogy is far-fetched and coarse, I suggest that to accept Christian protestations that the deceased is lucky as straightforward historical evidence of the general prevalence of the state of mind they so strenuously promote is logically comparable to taking the "No Spitting" signs that festooned the United States in the first half of this century as evidence that in the first half of this century Americans did not spit in public places.

effectively touch.[10] In this second couplet of "On My First Son"—a couplet that includes connotations of *the just day* that pertain to the premature death of a child and do not pertain to the loan analogy—a fanciful and contrived escape from the responses premature death inevitably elicits is openly fanciful and contrived. In admitting the frailty of the conceit, in acknowledging the consideration it is designed to exclude, the couplet admits—includes, lets come in—the very facts and responses that evoke the need for consolation. That substantive admission augments the implication of breadth and scope that the couplet has by virtue of its double conception as a familiar statement of fatalistic resignation and as an application of the equally familiar analogy between death and paying a debt. By acknowledging the existence of considerations beyond both of its strictly limited frames of reference, the simplistic, pathetically eager little couplet takes on some of the authority of a genuine panacea. The rhetorical weakness of a particular tactic, the debt analogy, makes the couplet rhetorically stronger and more capable of providing consolation.

10. And, when they do touch, they do not *efficiently* touch, do not effectively crash into one another and do damage to one another. Occasions when minds notice the discrepancy between what they sincerely believe and what they actually think and feel are likely to be comfortably comic. Consider, for example, Feste's proof that Olivia is a fool for mourning the death of a brother she knows to be in heaven (*Twelfth Night,* 1.5.52–67), and Friar Laurence's speech to Juliet's grieving parents on the day they had expected her to marry Paris:

> The most you sought was her promotion,
> For 'twas your heaven she should be advanced;
> And weep ye now, seeing she is advanced
> Above the clouds, as high as heaven itself?
> (*Romeo and Juliet,* 4.5.71–74)

Both the fool's trick and the friar's strike us as just that—tricks, clever pieces of choplogic that are amusing because the matter-of-fact practical consolation the speakers quite logically presume is unthinkable for even the most devout of Christians.

(Here and throughout, I quote Shakespeare in the revised Pelican text, ed. Alfred Harbage et al. [Baltimore, 1969].)

There is still more to be said about elements in the second couplet that are foreign to its overt strategy and purpose. At the same time that *on the just day* triumphantly continues and adds a disconcerting final flash to the loan analogy, and at the same time that the idea of justice disables the comfort of that analogy, the components of the phrase introduce a free-floating, "accidental," suggestion of the day of judgment—an idea irrelevant to the neat, narrow loan analogy but urgently relevant both to death and to efforts to comfort survivors. The suggestion is evoked by the context in combination with the verbal echo of "day of judgment" and, more actively, its common synonym, "day of account." [11] Here, as with *right hand* in the first couplet, a verbal hint of an unexploited line of thinking vouches rhetorically but illogically for the validity of the alien proposition in which it occurs. It quietly dissipates one's sense of the arbitrary narrowness of the line of thought that is pursued, and it beckons one's mind toward collaborating with the speaker and saying "not only that, but . . ."

A similar effect occurs in this same couplet in another dimension entirely. The couplet points toward, but does not pursue, an alternate conceit—one that, if exploited, would have been both more just than the loan analogy and perfectly unjust as well. The length of the child's life, seven years, is accidentally the traditional term of an apprenticeship. Since the departure of an apprentice after seven years is of the nature of the system in which it occurs, the analogy between a father bidding resigned farewell to a prematurely dead child and a craftsman regretfully but cheerfully discharging a "right-hand man" whose indenture is fulfilled is, in one way, a much stronger persuasion to sanguine acceptance of the child's death than the loan analogy.

However, where the natural span of an apprenticeship is seven years, that of a human life is seventy. So, although the appren-

---

11. Jonson himself uses the term in *Discoveries;* see H&S 8:603 (lines 1282–84): "When the great day of Account comes . . . there will be requir'd of him a reckoning. . . ."

ticeship analogy offers a desirable sense of rightness in the death, the falseness of the analogy would be transparent if it were applied overtly. As the couplet is, the unexploited, latently present apprenticeship analogy is both more effective than its full development could have been *and*—because it comes to us as if of the nature of the situation—more effective than any open (and therefore openly purposeful, calculated, and arbitrary) request that we "think of it this way."

Although the slick, determinedly detached intellectuality of the first two couplets is undercut, it is nonetheless extreme. The next four lines—the exclamation in line 5 and the lurching syntax that trails off from it through line 8—present themselves as a frustrated reaction to the preceding neatness:

> O, could I loose all father, now. For why
>   Will man lament the state he should enuie?
> To haue so soone scap'd worlds, and fleshes rage,
>   And, if no other miserie, yet age?

Now the surface is hysterical—all passion. But, as the boxlike orderliness of the two earlier couplets was sabotaged by metric and ideational loose ends, the desperate flailing of these two loose middle couplets is countered by the cold dexterity of Jonson's play on *all father* and "the mother." The actions of that conceit make it an emblem of the physics of the whole poem: as a mere witty device—a word-trick that steps aside from tragedy to play—the *father*/"mother" conceit is counteractive to the emotional tone of the line *and,* since the substantive "point" of the squalid little gimcrack is to conceal and then reveal a reference to hysteria, the conceit *also* cooperates with the exclamation and with the variously informal syntax that follows it.

That syntax coexists with the formal couplet pattern—overlies it—but mirrors it neither grammatically (as it might if the completion of syntactic units coincided with line ends), nor logically (as it might if the completion of each proposition coincided with the rhyme that completes the formal identity of each couplet). As a result, the loosely connected outpouring of propositions in lines 5–8 has the random feel of ungoverned emotion. However, from *For why* on, the substance expressed in those four lines is not only rationalistic but the stuff of traditional efforts to reason one's way out of grief. The stuff of those four lines is the stuff of the classic, clichéd, sanctimonious choplogic Feste echoes in his transparently arbitrary, transparently valid, and transparently irrelevant comic proof that Olivia is a fool for mourning a brother in heaven—and of the equally inefficient, traditional arguments that the shorter one's passage is through this vale of tears the better (see note 9 above).

Those middle four lines enact a paradox: hysterical intellectualization. And, like the whole poem—in which the two modes of response have so far fought each other to a draw—those four lines point toward despair. The situation is equally invulnerable to emotional and to rational mediation.[12]

And the new couplet in lines 9 and 10 begins by giving up: *Rest in soft peace*—the *requiescat in pace* of tombstones—a dignified formula that had already come to suggest "so much for that." However, just as he had done in his previous sorties, Jonson disables his new tactic—giving up, dismissing the matter as finished—in the very act of executing it. The word *soft*—which introduces a very gentle, perfectly undemanding pun on *in* indicating condition (as in plain "Rest in Peace") and *in* in its most literal sense, indicating location (as in "rest in bed" or "rest in soft sheets")—particularizes the formula, revitalizes it, and (like the more explicit bed metaphor at the end of "On My First Daughter"), demands our awareness of the physical fact of a human body bedded down in earth.

---

12. The words "lose" and "father" in "O, could I loose all father, now" at the beginning of the third couplet bring it a substantively irrelevant feel of simultaneous "wrongness" and "rightness" that makes it casually emblematic of the stalemate of competing considerations and realities in the speaker's mental situation. A father lamenting a loss wishes for a loss; what he has lost is a son, and what he now wishes to lose is "all father." On the other hand, no two words are more pertinent to the poem's topic than "lose" and "father"—no two are "righter" for this poem.

Rest in soft peace also opens the way for a further complication by echoing a phrase "spoken" by a gravestone.

> Rest in soft peace, and, ask'd, say here doth lye
> Ben. Ionson his best piece of *poetrie*.

The conjunction of *Rest in soft peace* and *and asked say* initiates a confusion among three of the four parties to the poem—a vastly complex confusion, even though, because each signal so perfectly pertains to one of the systems in which the poem is organized, it does not effectively confuse the fourth party, the reader.

When a gravestone "says" "Rest in Peace," it addresses the deceased, and we consciously understand it to be delivering a message from the stone's sponsors. The second gravestone formula in the couplet is different. When a gravestone "says" "Here lies . . . ," it addresses passersby, and, though we know that any sign speaks for a human being who set it there, we think of the sign as we would if it were autonomous; we do not think of any "they" who are trying to get the information to us.[13] *Rest in soft peace* is spoken by the father/speaker directly to the child (who has been addressed throughout—expressly addressed in the first two couplets and, by inference, still auditor to the outburst in the second two). Line 9 addresses two instructions to the child: *Rest* and *say*. The first instruction echoes a gravestone's stock wish for the deceased who lies beneath it, and—since the poem presents itself as if it were an inscription on a gravestone—*Rest in soft peace* here is both the stock phrase and a witty revivification of it. The second instruction, *say* (in *and, asked, say*), is just an ordinary imperative, addressed by the speaker to a listener capable of obeying it. The action of understanding *say* thus inci-

---

13. The difference in our senses of the relation between these two messages and messengers is comparable to the difference between the way we think about a sign that says "No Parking" and the way we think about a sign that says "Bush Street." Compare "Trespassers will be prosecuted" and "Trespassers W," ancestral home of the Piglets.

dentally involves—and thus casually, effortlessly assumes—the revivification of the child whose death is the poem's occasion. A split second later, the speaker tells the child what to say. The logic of the sentence presents *Here doth lie / Ben Jonson his best piece of poetry* as words the child is to say. But the child is dead. The only physically available speaker for the prescribed response to askers is the stone on which the poem is engraved and which thus fulfills the injunction the syntax addresses to the dead and speechless child. Moreover, the words echo words ordinarily "spoken" by a gravestone legend of the sort this poem adopts as a sort of persona.

There is nothing even theoretically difficult about reading *Rest in soft peace:* the speaker speaks words that a gravestone would ordinarily permanently repeat for him. But one does not ordinarily think of "Here lies . . ." as a message in which the deceased identifies himself in the third person. Yet the "Here lies" formula "belongs" here (because this is a gravestone poem) and "belongs" in this particular line (which begins with a gravestone formula). The various ways that "Here lies" belongs overwhelm the probability that we will pause to realize that, asked, we could not say just what the particulars are that we so easily comprehend as we move across line 9—a line that, however much and however justly I may analyze it into nonsense, remains perfectly easy to follow, so easy that editors do not bother to explain it.

What line 9 gives its readers is what the whole poem has sought to provide: an ability to comprehend—to grasp as one can a physical object—ideational substance that exists in more than one physics and does not, except in the purely verbal simplicity of this line, quite exist in any single one.

At the end of line 9 we know, as we always did and always will, which is the father and which is the child; and we know the differences among what the father says, what tombstones say, and what the child may be fancied as saying; but in the action of understanding this easily understood line our minds have behaved as they would if we confused a dead child with a living one, a dead child with his gravestone, and a father (who is writing a poem for a gravestone) with the gravestone.

Line 9 ends before it completes the formula *here doth lie* begins and promises to fulfill. No matter what the first words of the next line might have been, any reader would have tried to understand them as the name of the deceased: "Here lies *name.*" And line 10 does indeed begin with a name: *Ben Jonson.* The poem momentarily asks us to understand that the poet—the antecedent for *My* in the title of this epitaph he is writing on another person— is the deceased, is the person in the grave. That, of course, is impossible. One's first, momentary response to *Here doth lie / Ben Jonson* is likely to be a momentary suspicion that one has misread. In fact, we are indeed mistaken; and the poem contains two quite separate, mutually incompatible demonstrations of the error. One precedes the error: the solution to the elegant puzzle in line 1 told us that the child's name was Ben Jonson; so we did not misread the "Here lies" formula; we only misunderstood it. The other demonstrator of error is the word *his,* the word that signals a syntax capable of accommodating *best piece of poetry* (and thus redefines a whole clause and renders consideration of the son's name obsolete and pragmatically irrelevant): these lines are not trying to say "Here lies Ben Jonson" but "Here lies Ben Jonson's . . ." This genitive construction in which "his" does what "s"—or in recent times "'s"—ordinarily does was a literary fad among language-conscious Elizabethans.[14] Although Jonson's contemporaries would have been familiar with the affectation and modern readers are not, I think the four centuries between us and the long-forgotten fad has only intensified, and lengthened the

14. Renaissance genitives in proper name-plus-*his* are principally found in self-consciously elegant, learned, and pompous writing. My guess is that the affectation arose from an ignorant belief that *his* represented the pure, uncorrupted state of a construction that had degenerated into *s*. In fact, the apostrophe by which we now indicate the inflected form may well have gained currency from the same linguistic speculation: it may have been understood to be a sign of ellipsis.

duration of, an effect that was always there: all readers have always been offered the potentially complete assertion *Here doth lie Ben Jonson* before coming upon the modification provided by *his*.[15]

Similarly, a reader's mind can for an instant take hold of a potentially sufficient assertion ending with "his best peace" before the phrase expands into *his best piece of poetry*. Jonson's contemporaries, not conditioned to orthographic distinctions between homonyms,[16] were presumably opener to *piece* as an echo of *Rest in soft peace* than we are, but even eye-governed modern readers probably hear a connection between *here doth lie Ben Jonson his best piece*[17] and *Rest in soft peace*—a connection that vaguely confirms and further complicates our sense that these lines require us actively to reject unreasonable suggestions that the poet himself is dead. The lines momentarily contain vague, unanchored reference to the traditional notion of death as a way to peace—of death as desirable for such traditional reasons as are rehearsed in the preceding couplet.

As *his* made us put aside momentary considerations about *Here doth lie Ben Jonson,* the last two words of the couplet, *of poetry,* require us to put aside any transitory awareness of the general pertinence of the sound of "peace" in *piece*. Only one sense of that syllable is now locally pertinent. Once again, however, the new element that narrows and clarifies our understanding introduces a new challenge. This one is overt: what lies in the grave is a child's body, not a poem. Everything I have said about this couplet demonstrates that, as one reads the sentence begun in line 9, the phrases and their interactions repeatedly and variously tease one toward consciousness that the sentence delivers

15. In context of *asked, say,* and a succession of transparently artificial efforts to assert resignation to the will of heaven and/or fate, it is possible also that a reader's consciousness may be momentarily tickled by the momentarily justifiable "Here Ben Jonson tells falsehoods" in *Here doth lie / Ben Jonson.*

16. *OED* reports "peace" as a spelling for the word also spelled "piece" from the fifteenth to the eighteenth centuries. It gives examples of Renaissance spellings common to both words.

17. Compare the construction of *Antony and Cleopatra* 2.3.41: "In the East my pleasure lies."

its simple message in a perverse, unreasonably confusing way. The arch etymological play (on poet as maker and poem as thing made) and the just but creaky analogy between child and poem[18] differ from the other peculiarities of the couplet principally in being showy and demanding: we have to work out—and applaud and congratulate ourselves on solving—the puzzle; we have to see not only *that* this apparently strange statement is only a strange locution, but *how.*

I submit that, however trivial and distracting the glitter of its final conceit, this couplet puts us through a tiny but real experience of seeing justice in a series of bizarre events (here merely verbal events); the experience of reading "Rest in soft peace, and, asked, say here doth lie / Ben Jonson his best piece of poetry"— the experience of reading the sentence *as* sentence—is comparable to the larger, more desirable, unattainable mental experience of perceiving the secret logic of the mind of God. The couplet—as couplet, whatever its content—is a box; the word *poetry,* its second rhyme word, closes it. The same word completes a noun phrase that allows us to brush away the last of the tiny, fleetingly misleading incidental signals that heighten our mental achievement in finally seeing the justice of the lines—in seeing that *Ben Jonson his best piece of poetry* equals "my son."

From its first line on, this poem has offered to substitute the satisfaction of discovering the logic of its anomalous verbal events for the desired satisfaction of discovering a logic behind the unreasonable fact of a child's death. A reader's "Oh, I see" about the *piece of poetry/*child puzzle substitutes for the fully informed concurrence both speaker and reader would like to have in the divine logic by which a child is dead. We are urged to walk away from the grave as contentedly as we can now walk away from one of these easy little couplets.

18. The ostentatiously surprising etymological quibble is quietly sustained by the "brainchild" tradition, the tradition in which poets speak of their works as their children. For famous examples, see the metaphors in the first sonnet of *Astrophel and Stella,* the introductory letter Sidney prefaced to *Arcadia, Amoretti* 2, and Shakespeare's Sonnet 76.

Although completion of the phrase *piece of poetry* gives us a moment of triumphant clarity and simplicity derived from the final, satisfyingly solvable puzzle, the end of this couplet is not the end of the poem. Moreover, the word *poetry*—the word that closes the couplet and cuts off further concern about what the lines mean to say—is *also* specially suited to keep us uneasy— not consciously uneasy about our conclusions, but uneasy about the conclusiveness of the miniature triumph of solving the *piece of poetry* puzzle. What we are reading here *is* a piece of poetry (that lies before us on a page and presents itself as a gravestone inscription). Moreover, the couplet that concludes with *piece of poetry* calls attention to its dutiful obedience to Procrustean metric demands. Thus, like so many earlier effects in the poem, the couplet reminds a reader that even the limited mastery the poem offers is arbitrary and artificial—is of the couplet rather than of the situation it deals with. We have been reminded that this is verse. We are reminded, first, because neither the formula "Rest in Peace" nor the formula "Here lies . . ." is quite present in line 9: one has an extra syllable, *soft,* and the other is *doth lie* and not the traditional "lies"; these are not gravestone formulas but echoes of them, echoes puffed out to fit the meter. Second, we are made aware of the poem as poem—the poem as artificial buffer between its audience and the realities that occasioned it— because, even with the syllables added for metric regularity, the meter of line 9 is rough anyway, made so by its insistence upon the two syllables of *ask'd, say* (which both invite stress), rather than the metrically predictable "askèd, say."

The satisfying finality that comes with our arrival at the word *poetry* is further diminished when the next couplet—the sixth and last—turns out to be a syntactic continuation of the one *poetry* so neatly ended:

> Rest in soft peace, and, ask'd, say here doth lye
>   Ben. Ionson his best piece of *poetrie.*
> For whose sake, hence-forth, all his vowes be such,
>   As what he loues may neuer like too much.

And, oddly enough, the new couplet—which the pronoun *whose* makes so openly dependent on the preceding syntax—so quickly generates an independent identity that it feels as tight, neat, and self-contained as the first, second, and fifth do.[19]

The paradox by which the last couplet is and is not separate from the couplet that precedes it is worth noting only because, in its own tiny way, it requires a reader—or, better, enables a reader—to perceive in a way typical of the means—and crucial to the ends—of both the couplet and the whole poetic enterprise of "On My First Son." The independence of related things—knowing where one thing ends and another begins—is of the essence of the dilemma that the epitaph attempts to handle. The stylistic paradox relates to the general situation: the body is dead / the soul lives on; the child is gone / the body remains; the child is dead / the father lives on.

The paradox of the last two couplets' disunity and unity, their simultaneous independence and interdependence, also relates to the inherent function of any epitaph: an epitaph perpetuates the memory of the deceased *and* is an act of dismissal, a final assertion after which no more need be said. An epitaph is a means of going on and leaving what is "dead and done with" behind. As an act of conclusion, an epitaph's chief asset is conclusiveness. The quality we label in the word "epigram" is similar; we say that something is epigrammatic when it encloses a large complex matter in a quick, final-sounding, summary pellet of language. The things we call epigrammatic are gestures toward forestalling further consideration of their topics. Epigrams seal the elements of a topic in one relationship to one another by presenting that relationship in a way that seems organic—of the nature of the topic. Their chief means are ideational and/or phonetic patterns

---

19. In support of the proposition that the last couplet seems like a self-sufficient logical-syntactical unit, I offer the testimony of editors who have prepared modernized texts for student anthologies. I have not attempted an exhaustive study, but a majority of the repunctuated texts I have seen retain the period that appears after *poetrie* in the 1616 Folio.

that are superimposed upon their topics so that the identity established by the patterns of presentation (for instance, rhythms, rhymes, puns, polyptotonic kinships, alliterative series), fuses with the propositions they present. The reality of the amalgam is simultaneously strengthened by persuasively neat correspondence between elements of the topic and elements of the particular sentence that presents it (for instance, between proposition and analogy or proposition and metaphor).

The thing-like, pseudo-organic identity of an epigrammatic proposition is peculiarly self-sufficient—peculiarly immune to modification or correction from other considerations and points of view—because its special identity is internally established—is due more to the affinity its own elements have for one another than to a correspondence between the proposition and the facts to which it is addressed. However, the ostentatious neatness of epigrams *calls attention* to the fact that they shut out inconvenient considerations—that, although they are all-encompassing in manner, they are not so in matter but exclude the very considerations that lead one to want a topic managed once and for all in a single summary pronouncement. The inherent advertisement and admission of their own arbitrariness and narrowness is, I think, the root source of the benign contempt with which epigrammatic utterances are treated; we know they are "just epigrams": not as just as they momentarily seem to be.

My description of the first ten lines of "On My First Son" has been designed to demonstrate the ways in which those lines offset the limitations of their own epigrammatic neatness without losing their epigrammatically engendered feel of summary completeness. The last couplet—to which the issues of finality and completeness are most urgent—generates the same sort of double identity, but does so more successfully than any other section of the poem.

The final couplet is splendidly final: "For whose sake, henceforth, all his vows be such, / As what he loves may never like too much." I assume that readers go away from the poem having understood those last two lines as the poet's vow never again to

make the mistake of being too fond of what he loves. That assumption derives first from my memory of my own response to
the couplet and secondly from the negative evidence of various
editors who annotate the poem. No editor I know of explicates
the last couplet. I take the general silence as evidence that, like
me, the editors find the sense of the couplet so clear that their
readers will not need help; and, if the couplet does not need explaining, then the only sense readily adaptable to the context is
the vague one I offer. My statement of what I think readers take
the couplet to be saying is many mental steps from the readings
syntactically signaled for the actual phrases on the page, and I
will shortly take up the relation between readers' experiences of
the words on the page and those readers' vague, easy, contextually inferred understandings of the couplet. Before I do that,
however, I want to talk about the one element of the couplet that
is not entirely transmuted in my capsule summary of the general
purport of the lines: the witty, ideationally central distinction
expressed by *loves* and *like* in the last line.[20]

Whatever else may also be true, *what he loves may never like too
much* is straightforwardly paraphrasable as "what he loves may
never be too pleasing." The use of "to like" as a simple synonym
for "to be pleasing" is now obsolete, was never very common,
but usually is (and presumably was in the past) obvious in context; see, for instance, the last line of Jonson's prologue to *The
Devil is an Ass:* "If this play do not like, the Devil is in't." As
scholarly annotators have long recognized, this last clause of "On
My First Son" duplicates the essential elements of the last line of

20. The first critic I know who found it worth his while to gloss the word
like in this line is L. A. Beaurline (in "The Selective Principle in Jonson's Shorter
Poems," which first appeared in *Criticism* [8, Winter 1966]; I cite Beaurline's
essay in the revised form given in *Ben Jonson and the Cavalier Poets,* ed. Hugh
Maclean [New York, 1974], 516–25). Beaurline does a full and splendid job,
but—although he acknowledges that "most readers think that *like* is a weaker
form of love, and they imagine that Jonson ends with a cynical turn of thought:
he vows he'll not love as intensely in the future" (519)—he is much more
confident than I am that the complexity of dealing with *like* in this context is
purely the product of the four-century gap between Jonson's English and ours.

an epigram by Martial (VI.xxix, on the death of a friend's servant boy): *quidquid ames, cupias non placuisse nimis,* "you should desire that whatever you may love may not be too pleasing."[21]

In Martial's stoic caution against allowing oneself to become in any way dependent upon anything prey to the vicissitudes of fortune and time, the distinction between what is loved and what is pleasing is considerably more prosaic than it is in Jonson's version.[22] Where Martial used the Latin verbs *amare* and *placere,* Jonson uses "to love" and "to like"—two verbs that, as near but imperfect synonyms, commonly distinguish distinct kinds and degrees of affection notoriously difficult to distinguish from one another (moreover, since "love" and "like" are phonetically similar and phonetically very different, their sounds are an accidental mirror of their complex semantic relationship). The wit of Jonson's line—the "punch" it has as a concluding and conclusive-sounding flourish—derives from the pointed juxtaposition of *loves* and *like* in a context that, since the line does indeed concern a contrast between related emotional responses, activates the more familiar contrast between loving (*what he loves*) and another and more nearly parallel sense of "liking" ("what he likes").[23]

Although a good deal remains to be said about the activities of *loves* and *like* in line 12, I want, for the moment, only to say that by activating a locally casual extra contrast between "to love"

---

21. This and all subsequent citations of Martial are to Walter C. A. Ker's Loeb Classics edition (2 vols. [London and Cambridge, Mass., 1919, rev. ed., 1968]).

22. The principal wit in Martial's line is in the use of the verb *cupire.* The context ultimately requires that *cupias* be understood as "you should wish" (the Loeb editor translates the line "Whate'er thou lovest, pray that it may not please thee too much"), but the verb *cupire,* which here follows immediately upon a use of the verb *amare,* usually describes not wishing but lusting. Another sense of *cupire,* one irrelevant to Martial's particular syntax, is "to be well disposed to," which pertains to Martial's general context of a benevolent master and a servant eager to serve.

23. In fact, a modern reader who does not recognize "to like" as a synonym for "to be pleasing" may very well take *like* in this line as the imperfect synonym of "to love" and arrive at the sense of the clause by reading it as an ellipsis for "what he loves [he] may never like too much."

and "to like," Jonson generates opacity in a clause that is also and simultaneously altogether clear and straightforward. The experience of reading such a clause is of a piece with a reader's continuing experience of clearly distinguishing between absolutely distinct entities (speaker and topic, father and son, poem and gravestone, and so forth)—that also drift toward interchangeability. The experience of reading the clause is also, I think, a miniature, purely literary, approximation of the *kind* of unified, easy, common-sense apprehension of metaphysical and physical truth that is so very unavailable to a particular bereaved Christian thinking about the premature death of a particular child— a child released from the vicissitudes of life into the better life beyond and *also* a victim of fate, its parents' loss, and a pitiable corpse.

The other "effects" of the last couplet are not noticeably witty. They are comparable to the *loves/like* contrast, but, where the last clause is a demonstrably clear and straightforward one that is incidentally and wittily clouded, the rest of the syntactic units of the couplet are exactly the opposite: demonstrably opaque, but apprehended as prose-clear. I suggest that in apprehending those units readers understand what they still do not understand—see sense in what does not make sense. And much the same claim that I made for the experience of reading the last clause can be made for its rhetorical obverse: the paradoxical failures of logically unassailable arguments of Christian comfort.

What mourners need, and what a comforter attempts to provide, is an effective harmony between what the mourners feel and the comfortable things available for them to think. A mourner's sense that death is unjust and unreasonable derives from logics altogether immune to invasion by comforting conclusions based on consideration of such "facts" as the inevitability of mortality, the painfulness of life, the immortality of the soul, and the reunion of body and soul at the Last Judgment. Therefore the ambition of poems like this one and of any other saying of "comfortable things" is to enable a mourner to do the impossible, to understand what remains beyond understanding. The couplet repeatedly presents us with impossible challenges to the under-standing, challenges that we casually surmount without noticing that we have gone beyond limitations inherent in our expecta-tions about language and the human mind.

The number and diversity of easy obstacles to comprehension in the last couplet are so great that there is no obvious efficient way to describe them. I propose merely to quote the last third of the poem again and then present a piecemeal description of its many genuine but curiously nonobstructive hurdles.

Please bear in mind that I insist on the presence of the diffi-culties I am about to describe only because they do not give us anything like the difficulty common sense suggests they should. In reading the lines we go beyond common sense. Bear in mind too that, however great the likeness between this analysis and in-genious arguments for "new readings," I have no ambition to reinterpret, or even interpret, these lines. They do not need in-terpretation—do not need an agent between them and a reader; that is precisely the fact of this final couplet that prompts me to discuss it. The following analysis is designed to be literally in-consequential: it does not, and does not hope to, lead a reader to new responses to the couplet. I beg you, however, not there-fore to assume that the following paragraphs are inconsequential in that word's metaphoric sense.

What I am trying to do is demonstrate a reader's achievement in easily comprehending the couplet and justify the assertion that what the lines allow our minds to do with their self-generated, merely literary challenges becomes a surrogate for the mental mastery over the fact of a child's death that both speaker and reader seek. I believe that poems are enabling acts. They free their readers from mental limitations comparable to the limi-tations of physics. Although such analysis as that which follows is joyless, its ambition is to point toward the sources of the joy poems give.

Here again, then, are lines 9–12 of "On My First Son"—the last couplet and the one from which its syntax emerges:

> Rest in soft peace, and, ask'd, say here doth lye
>   Ben. Ionson his best piece of *poetrie*.
> For whose sake, hence-forth, all his vowes be such,
>   As what he loues may neuer like too much.

To begin with a relatively easy example of the ease with which we meet and master demonstrable, but only theoretically potent, challenges to our understanding, consider the matter of how and when we recognize that the prescribed speech introduced by *say* in line 9 has concluded. At some point during the poem's last line, the logic of the situation makes it obvious that the whole of the last couplet must be understood as spoken by the poet-father in his own person. But, as we read line 11, *whose* can as easily refer to the senior Ben Jonson as to his *best piece of poetry,* the newly clear synonym for "my son." And the structural and ideational likeness between *his vows* and *his best piece of poetry* suggests that the child's answer is still in progress. The drift in our understanding continues and complements the previously generated indistinctions among father, son, and gravestone inscription.

There is a valuable, though nonsignificant, hint of scope, of sweeping validity, in the word *For,* the word that introduces the last couplet and suggests its relation to the ten preceding lines. Its function is instantly defined by *whose,* the word that follows it, but it occurs in a context where the conjunctive function it had in line 5 (where it introduced a reason for wishing "to lose all father") would be welcome, a context of necessarily inadequate effort to respond to a need for explanation, a need for a reason why a seven-year-old should have died. As a momentary gesture toward explaining, the word *For* includes a suggestion of that action in the nonexplanatory clause it introduces.[24]

24. Note that Jonson's first readers were used to hearing the word "for-why" as a synonym for "because." For them, the last two syllables of line 5, heard or read before the poem gives any sign of the rhetorical question that emerges in line 6, would presumably have, for a moment, actually said "because," would have promised some sort of explanation to follow. The simultaneous presence and absence of "because" there would thus once have given the

Once one understands that *whose* refers to "my son," the phrase *For whose sake* presumably presents itself as preface to some sort of pious vow, a grieving father's resolve for some future virtuous action to be dedicated to the memory of the son. So far, then, this next-to-last line appears to be a vow. The following nounphrase, *all his vows,* confirms that impression by actually mentioning *vows,* but that confirmation is also something of a surprise: this is a vow about kinds of vowing. That is a strange topic for vows. And yet, this poem has previously been self-conscious about its identity as poem, a verbal product of its speaker, a professional poet; moreover, the general, generic likeness of vows and poems is quietly underscored both in the superficial structural likeness between *all his vows* and *his best piece of poetry* and in the relation between *vows* and the literal reference of *whose* (an altogether improbable and altogether impractical literal reading of the line could be "For the sake of his best poem . . . may all his vows be equally excellent poems").

So the introduction of *vows* as the topic of this line is at once variously a continuation of previous local patterns of the last lines of the poem and a surprising departure from them. In that respect the relation of the word *vows* to what precedes it is comparable to that between the last two simultaneously interdependent and independent couplets, and, as I will explain shortly, between the topics and considerations of the preceding ten lines and those of this couplet.

What interests me most about the next crisis of this couplet, the "be such as" construction, is the telling fact that the modern editors from whose omissions I have already concluded so much do not gloss it. For a modern reader, the "such as" formula presumably signals a kind of construction incompatible with the phrase *such / As* introduces here—a construction such as this one (in which the formula introduces an example, "this one," and "such as" functions as "like" might), or a construction like

---

poem one more fillip of doubleness and let its readers experience one more instance of contrariety.

"be such as would do him credit" (where "such as" means "of a kind which"), or one like "be such as you would want them to be" (where "such as" means "what"). The easily demonstrable but evidently inaudible challenge of the "such as" construction is unusual here because, like the challenge of "to like" meaning "to be pleasing," a pennyworth of scholarship will dissolve it: this use of "such as" is an example of a once-standard idiom in which "as" performs the function "that" would perform for us; fully spelled out, *such / As* here means "of a kind to ensure that." [25] Jonson was particularly fond of the idiom. Among the modern editions of Jonson's poems, William B. Hunter's (in the Anchor Seventeenth-Century Series, New York, 1963) is the most scrupulous about explaining idioms unfamiliar to twentieth-century nonspecialists. Hunter glosses "as" meaning "that" in lines where its sense is much more readily apparent than it is here, [26] but neither he nor editors of general student anthologies (such as *The Norton Anthology*) explain the "such as" construction in "On My First Son." Once again, I take the omission not as a sign of editorial laxity but as another sign that the puzzles of this demonstrably—but only demonstrably—incomprehensible couplet do not ordinarily puzzle anyone. Here, evidently, the force of context is so strong that modern readers entirely unfamiliar with the idiomatic use of "such as" to mean "such that" read the couplet with the casual competence of people who have heard and used the idiom all their lives.

I want now to return to the incidental activities of the word *like,* the word so pointedly distinguished from *loves* and so close to being indistinguishable from it. As I said earlier, the substan-

25. Even though Jonson's contemporaries would have been familiar with the idiomatic use of "such as" for "of such a kind to ensure that," the particular example of that idiom in the last couplet of "On My First Son" must always have allowed a reader's comprehension of the sentence to float free from his moment-to-moment apprehension of the words on the page: the necessary idiom is only finally signaled by the verb *like* in the middle of the final line.

26. See, for example, Hunter's glosses on "as" meaning "so that" in *Epigrammes* 35 (line 5), 67 (line 4), and 102 (line 17).

tively operative sense of "to like" here is "to be pleasing," and the juxtaposition of *like* with *loves* colors that sense with suggestions of "to like" meaning "to have a liking for." However, the senses carried by three other, often overlapping, groups of "like" words also pertain to matters Jonson considers in the poem and to the experience of reading the twelve lines. One group indicates similarity, likeness (for instance, the common prepositional and conjunctional uses of "like"; the verb "to liken" and, in Jonson's time, the verb "to like to," meaning "to compare [something] to," "to liken [something] to"; and the always-rare "to like" meaning "to make a likeness of" [*OED* gives this example from 1622: "Her lily hand (not to be lik'd by Art) / A pair of pincers held"]). Another group corresponds to the various forms and derivatives of the word "thrive" (for instance, the verb "to like" in this *OED* example from 1601: "Trees generally do like best that stand to the Northeast wind"; and the noun "liking" in this *OED* example from 1590: "I have one sheep . . . that's quite out of liking"). Yet another group of "like" words indicates probability, likelihood (for instance, the verb in *Much Ado About Nothing* 5.1.115: "We had liked to have our two noses snapped off") and, in particular, promise of success (as in "a likely lad" and in "a fellow of no mark nor likelihood" [*1 Henry IV* 3.2.45]).

Talking about the broad pertinence of those locally impertinent senses of "like" is a touchy business because it can either invite foolishly ingenious fresh interpretations—alternative paraphrases—of what the couplet is telling its readers or invite levelheaded and justly suspicious readers to suppose that I myself am trying to sell them on an alternate reading of the lines or on the presence of some paraphrasable latent meaning in them. Carefully, then, "to like" meaning "to be promising" is even less likely than "to like" meaning "to be pleasing"—the sense that fits the syntax—ever to have immediately proposed itself for inclusion in a sane English speaker's sense of the purport of a line that so pointedly pairs *like* with the verb "to love." But the thwarted promise of a hopeful child is naturally pertinent to the general topic of premature death—and was overtly introduced into this poem in line 2 when the poem momentarily focused on the idea that a child's death may be divine punishment for a parent's sin: *My sin was too much hope of thee, loved boy.* Similarly, although *like* in *what he loves may never like too much* cannot reasonably be said to say "thrive" and is most certainly making no reference to similitude, the idea of thriving obviously pertains to a poem about a child who perished, and the idea of likeness between the senior and junior Ben Jonsons has been a constant and insistent incidental element in the poem ever since the etymological fuss about their shared first name in line 1.

To see yet other aspects of the complex relationship between the words on the page and the purport one carries away from them, consider what happens to the phrase *For whose sake* and the words *henceforth* and *vows* as one progresses from line 11 through line 12. Here for reference are those two lines again:

> For whose sake, hence-forth, all his vowes be such,
> As what he loues may neuer like too much.

As a reader comes upon the "for . . . sake" construction, it carries an implication of benefit to the antecedent of *whose*. But that implication—present in a reader's understanding at the moment of reading and generally appropriate to the speaker's situation (a grieving father might reasonably vow to dedicate some future action to his deceased son)—is irrelevant to the kind of vows we do in fact hear about—vows that, to the degree that we can conceive of them as vows rather than hopes or prayers, are vows to minimize emotional vulnerability. How can a father's vows to protect himself be thought to benefit a dead child? (The couplet's overt logic can color a reader's perception of it with a suggestion that no future object of the father's affection will supersede this child, but—however appropriate that suggestion is to the speaker's situation—it is *only* a suggestion.)

If, having read through to the end of line 12, one were to go back to *For whose sake* to see just what logical connection it makes between the preceding couplet and the substance of this one, one would see that the phrase must be glossed "on account of whom," "because of whom," and works as "therefore" would. That gloss is contextually dictated (I know of no other use of the "for . . . sake" idiom so completely devoid of implication of benefit).[27] Moreover, that gloss is effectively irrelevant to a gloss on the whole couplet because the phrase itself is also ultimately irrelevant to a reader's final sense of what the lines are saying. The idea of benefiting the child vanishes, but not before it has made a gesture that the completed sentence cannot reasonably be thought to make. The child is beyond any human help but prayer, but *For whose sake* colors the experience of reading about the father's future welfare with an illogically comforting, fleeting implication that such help is possible, that the child's welfare is like the father's—still susceptible to actions of the human will.

As to the word *henceforth* in this last couplet, its action does not have substantively vital reverberations, but, to the extent that the process of understanding it is one in which a reader's mind leaves the quasi-physical limitations of syntax behind, a reader's experience of *henceforth* is comparable to the experience of *For whose sake. Henceforth* operates as if it appeared twice: "may all his vows from this time forward" *and* "that whatever he loves from this time forward may never . . ."

---

27. One prominent instance of the "for . . . sake" idiom used to mean "on account of" is *Othello*, 1.3.195–98. There "For your sake" first signals "for your benefit," but the developing sentence ultimately allows the phrase to deliver only "on account of you." Brabantio says this to Desdemona: "For your sake, jewel, / I am glad at soul I have no other child, / For thy escape would teach me tyranny, / To hang clogs on them."

The closest thing I can find to another instance of "for . . . sake" used simply to mean "on account of" is Herrick's use of the construction in line 54 of "The Dirge of Jephthah's Daughter" (and even there the idea of benefit remains):

> No more, at yeerly Festivalls
>   We Cowslip balls,
> Or chaines of Columbines shall make,
>   For this, or that occasions sake.

(This and all subsequent citations of Herrick are from the Oxford Standard Authors edition, ed. L. C. Martin [Oxford, 1965].)

The vowlike opening the phrase *For whose sake* gives to line 11 probably always dictated that *vows* be understood as a twentieth-century reader understands it. In a suitable context, however, the word "vow" was used like its French and Latin cognates to mean "prayer" or "wish" (*OED* gives this illustration from 1563: "So when those thynges whyche we have desyred, do fall oute accordinge unto oure mynde, wee saye we have oure wishe or vowe"). And just such a suitable context emerges in line 12. As I suggested earlier, once line 12 tells us what these vows will be designed to achieve, it becomes evident that they are prayers or hopes or wishes. Of course, since the ultimate meaning of *vows* is contextually evident, awareness of the now-forgotten archaic sense of "vow" (which editors and commentators do not—and do not need to—mention), does not much clarify one's understanding of the means by which this couplet has meaning. However, the mere fact that our understanding of *vows* shifts in the course of the sentence—the fact that the word *vows* has one sense at the moment it is read and another by the time the couplet is complete—*does* matter because it adds one more mental victory over physics to our experience of the poem. Once again, one thing is two things.

I began discussion of the final couplet by pointing out its simultaneous dependence on the syntax that precedes it and independence from it. A comparable paradox occurs on the larger scale in which the couplet continues and completes the poem as a whole and—in *vows,* the syntactic focus of lines 11 and 12—introduces a wholly new matter for consideration. The words *henceforth all his vows be such / As what* can justly be said to be merely a satisfactory, though vaguely disorienting, substitute for "he vows that henceforth," a substitute that fills out the meter of the couplet, provides a convenient rhyme word, and—since, although the noun "vow" was regularly used to mean "prayer," the verb "to vow" was not used to mean "to pray"—enables the incidental metamorphosis in which a reference to pledging becomes a reference to wishing.

And yet the words on the page are undeniably there and do make *his vows* the couplet's syntactic focus rather than the vower or what is vowed. The idea of resolution—determination to go on and determination of a future course—is generically and emotionally pertinent to the resolution of a funeral elegy. Furthermore, the fact that the focus on vows diverts readers from the track of particulars they have followed coexists with the fact that vows, as real but purely verbal actions, relate by a sort of ideational alliteration to a poem that has been a series of efforts to make altogether just assertions supersede an unjust situation.[28]

Everything I have talked about in the final couplet and in the poem at large has been a manifestation of the interplay of closedness and openness. That is true even of the puzzles on "Benjamin" and "the mother." Closedness manifests itself in syntactic and semantic precision and is regularly complemented by syntactic and semantic imprecision in exactly the same phrases (for instance, *Here doth lie Ben Jonson* in lines 9 and 10) and words (for instance, *henceforth* in line 11, *like* in line 12, or, in line 1, *Farewell*—an incidental emblem of the whole poem, a word that is always a gesture of finality *and* is an imperative for the future welfare of the person addressed). Closedness manifests itself in the formal identity of the individual couplets and is countered by substantive and/or syntactic continuity between couplets. Closedness manifests itself in the identities of the poem's princi-

---

28. One could, I guess, work out a connection between vows and the possible play on "here doth tell untruths" in *here doth lie* in line 9. Or one might point out a connection between vows and the legal bond in the second couplet. Less far-fetched, but still in sorry need of fetching, is the connection between the last couplet and line 2 (*My sin was too much hope of thee, loved boy*), a line and a line of thought that are not directly related to the body of the poem. *Loves* and *like too much* echo *loved boy* and *too much hope,* but the echo is chiasmic, must carry over eight intervening lines, and—since one must extrapolate a link to *vows* from *hope* (for instance, through the idea of a father confidently planning his son's future and vowing to secure such and such advantages and opportunities for him)—so vague that the connection would strain the understanding even if the first and last couplets stood alone as a four-line poem.

pal creatures (father, child, gravestone inscription) and is regularly and variously complemented by their tendency to become casually and momentarily confused.

The interplay of the two principles is visible in the overall sentence structure of the six couplets that make up the whole (a structure that makes the poem—the poem as object—a physical emblem of its speaker's efforts to achieve his object, namely, to get his feelings and his philosophy into a single closed box). The last couplet both does and does not complete the pattern (the first and second couplets are closed, syntactically and logically independent units; the four middle lines spill logically and syntactically across formal divisions of line and couplet; the fifth couplet is a neat, self-contained unit; the last couplet is not syntactically independent but feels isolated and, in its substance, is so).

Similarly, the poem seeks relief in alternative ways of thinking about the child's death—ways alternative to one another and, above all, alternative to the ordinary, heartbroken way natural to the situation: one can retreat into a verbal therapy that remains merely verbal (as in lines 1–4); or one can attempt to substitute logic for emotion (as in 7–8 and the "For why" question in lines 5 and 6), but the logic has power only where its premises operate in convenient, arbitrary, fragile isolation from the premises to which the poem responds. The verbal escapes are variously undercut by the poem's own inconvenient appeals to logic (for instance, why bother with etymological games? what is just about a premature death?), suggestions of emotion (for instance, *and joy*), and gratuitous confusions (for instance, *Here doth lie Ben Jonson*). And the efforts to reason away grief are disabled by the frantic, spastic syntax that mocks the passionless formality of line and couplet divisions in lines 5–8.

The last couplet reaches the poem's extremes of epigrammatic tightness, formal control, determined rationalism, and summary dismissal and *also* of syntactic, logical, and ideational openness. The paradoxical nature of both the poem and the situation it treats appears at its largest in "what he loves may never like too much," the poem's simultaneously cold and heartbreaking last clause—arbitrary, witty, self-sufficient, ideationally isolated, *and* the poem's most evocative reminder of the preciousness of the lost child and the persistence of the grief that occasioned the poem and that the poem seeks to allay.

The accomplishment of the final couplet is to give (not *assert* but *give*) infinity to what is finite and to put limits on what remains boundless. That is an immense accomplishment, one toward which the whole poem aspires but one that the poem as a whole fails to achieve. My opening objection holds true: the poem is overwhelmed by the glittering cleverness of its etymological tricks. Above everything else, the poem engenders admiration for itself. Even for the most casual reader, the primary pleasure of "On My First Son"—the one that dominates because it must precede the operation of the poem's other effects—is critical, is the pleasure of translating *child of my right hand* and *piece of poetry*. One might persuasively argue that the poem's fancywork and its ostensible substantive ambitions complement one another (a piece of poetry on a page *is* the child of the hand that writes it out); and etymology itself pertains to the poem's topic (a father and son are an original and a different creature derived from that original). But the fancywork remains fancywork. Confusions of identities do enter the poem, but only syntactically. And by the time they do, the poem is already in the shadow of its own surface brilliance and asking to be dismissed as clever.

2 · "ON MY FIRST DAUGHTER"

One's overall sense of "On My First Daughter" seems to me likely to be altogether different from one's overall sense of "On My First Son." The clevernesses of "On My First Son" insist that its readers engage with it—if only as an exercise in wit. Indeed, it is so busy and so successful in its insistence that, ironically, it has taken me almost twice as long to give an account of the operations of "On My First Son" as it will to do the same for its humble sibling, the poem I champion as worthier of the two. "On My First Daughter" invites us to dismiss it as dowdy, casual, and ineffectual—as just another rehearsal of traditional words of comfort. The invitation is metrically underscored by the inherently chipper octosyllabic couplets. Where the decasyllables of "On My First Son" can feel like needlessly expanded octosyllables and therefore have the dignity of enforced slowness, these lines trot along with an easy glibness that implies a like ease and lightness in what the poem says.

> Here lyes to each her parents ruth,
> Mary, the daughter of their youth:
> Yet, all heauens gifts, being heauens due,
> It makes the father, lesse, to rue.
> At sixe moneths end, shee parted hence
> With safetie of her innocence;
> Whose soule heauens Queene, (whose name shee beares)
> In comfort of her mothers teares,
> Hath plac'd amongst her virgin-traine:
> Where, while that seuer'd doth remaine,
> This graue partakes the fleshly birth.
> Which couer lightly, gentle earth.

The poem only once comes close to demanding attention to its wit, and even then—in the speaker's parting instructions to the earth that covers the child's grave—the conceit is such as to seem merely sweet, an ornamental ruffle that calls attention to its easiness, artificiality, and perfect incapacity to redefine either the facts of the situation or anyone's perception of them. There is undeniable wit in Jonson's uses of *safety* in line 6 and of *virgin-train* in line 9, but, although the business of explaining those effects to a modern reader can seem to make them comparable to the showy and demanding little puzzles in "On My First Son," there is nothing in "On My First Daughter" to make a reader aware either of the poet's brilliance or the poem's effectiveness in enabling its reader's mind to perceive the fact of the child's death in a single set of terms (the poem) that recognizes and subsumes all the pertinent but mutually exclusive terms available (for the most obvious instances, those of grief and those of Christian comfort).

The wit of "On My First Daughter" is undemanding, apparently natural to the English language and the topic. It is a kind typified by the play on *on* in the title of this poem, of "On My First Son," and of innumerable other epitaphs; in the particular case of "On My First Daughter" its first phrase, *Here lies,* abruptly changes the meaning of *On* in the title from "on the subject of"—"about"—to "over"—"on top of." Play on *on* indicating topic and *on* indicating location is so common, so much an accident of the language, and so contextually just in both of its applications in epitaph titles that even to label it wordplay is to exaggerate its intensity and its impact upon a reader's conscious perception. Although the paragraphs that follow will attempt to demonstrate great complexity and subtlety of effect in "On My First Daughter," I want it understood in advance that the fact of that complexity and subtlety coexists with the fact not only of the poem's genuine simplicity but with the fact of its genuine vapidity. Whatever else and however grand "On My First Daughter" may be, it is also as insipid as this poem, the most vapid of Herrick's several pallid imitations of it:

> *Upon a child*
> Here a pretty Baby lies
> Sung asleep with Lullabies:
> Pray be silent, and not stirre
> Th'easie earth that covers her.

The first line of "On My First Daughter" is altogether matter-of-fact: a flat statement, interrupted by "to the sorrow of each of her parents" (an interruption by which the fact of the parents' grief becomes syntactically indivisible from—and as unalterable as—the fact that "here lies Mary") and further augmented by

further identification of Mary in terms of the parents.[29] Like
their newly departed youth, their newly departed daughter is
gone forever, and at the simultaneous completions of the clause
and the couplet there is no more to say:

> Here lyes to each her parents ruth,
> Mary, the daughter of their youth:

Line 3 begins a new independent clause, and the concluding
rhyme of the second couplet seals off another isolated, self-
sufficient assertion:

> Yet, all heauens gifts, being heauens due,
> It makes the father, lesse, to rue.

However, the word *Yet,* the first word of the second couplet,
makes a small syntactic gesture of connection between the two
couplets and thus of continuation beyond the matter-of-fact
finality of the two opening lines. That syntactic gesture corresponds exactly to the same word's ideational gesture, its signal that
some sort of modification of the preceding assertion is possible
and will follow. Moreover, the vowel sound of the first rhyme
pair, *ruth / youth,* returns in the second, *due / rue;* and the cognates *ruth* and *rue* have a sort of polyptotonic "rhyme"—just
as *ruth* and *less to rue* "rhyme" ideationally. And yet the two
couplets, one a flat hopeless statement and the other a philo-

---

29. Although immediately meaningful, use of *each her* for "each of her" is
unusual; I know no other examples of the construction; it appears to be analogous to such standard constructions as "all her" for "all of her" and "both
her" for "both of her." Compare "every / These happen'd accidents" in *Tempest* 5.1.249–50 and "some your servants" in *Sejanus* 5.59. I see no clear reason
why Jonson chose *each her* over the more available and more obviously ser-
viceable "both her." Perhaps he hoped to approximate the division of parents
effected in the use of the singular pronoun *tibi* with two appositives in *Hanc
tibi, Fronto pater, genetrix Flaccilla* in line 1 of Martial V.xxxiv, the last lines of
which are the model for the last line of "On My First Daughter."

sophical bromide, are effectively isolated from one another—two assertions on the same topic but from spheres of thought as separate as Earth and heaven.

The second couplet may be a mere bromide, but it is also full of entirely unostentatious energy, energy generated by quiet interaction between valid and invalid assertions. That interaction, I think, contributes a lot to the ultimately invaluable feel this confident, easy couplet has of philosophic insecurity and poetic ineptitude. The lines contain one valid assertion (nothing on this Earth lives forever), and two that are—in very different ways—invalid. The metaphor of gifts and debts in line 3 contains an inaudible assertion of injustice (gifts by definition are not loans; givers surrender all proprietary rights). I say the reported injustice is inaudible for two reasons: first, because the wit of the oxymoronic paradox by which heaven's earthly gifts are never more than loans had sunk into cliché and from cliché had passed into entirely undemanding commonplace centuries before the first readers of "On My First Daughter" were born and, second, because the gift-debt metaphor is vehicle for a proposition so obviously true as to be a truism. Similarly, I think, the unarguability of the truism that nobody lives forever holds us off from pausing to observe the couplet's other invalid assertion—pausing to doubt that anyone could ever have hoped to comfort or to be comforted by the thought that a dead baby would have died in sixty or seventy years anyway (there may be some conceivable comfort for the parent of a dead infant in the thought that the child has *scaped world's and flesh's rage / And, if no other misery, yet age,* but none from stoic realization that all human life is transitory).

The third couplet takes a third approach to the topic—narration of the immediate facts of the child's death:

> At sixe moneths end, shee parted hence
> With safetie of her innocence;

Once again, the couplet is closed, final, isolated. Moreover, the new couplet asks to be recognized as another exercise in appropriate commonplaces, one poetic (the euphemistic metaphor of a journey), and one theological (the child died before worldly contact could endanger her soul). And yet, without jarring a reader's sense that this is just an instance of the traditional mechanical prettification and diversion everyone is used to, this couplet eases its reader into some emotionally valuable, casual (and thus genuine) assumptions. This third couplet is not what it would be if line 5 reported that Mary died at the age of six months and line 6 began with the sort of distinction that "but" or "however" would make—the distinction *Yet* makes in line 3 between two separate frames of reference for considering the fact of death. Here consideration of the child's death and consideration of the future life of her soul cohabit in a single thought, casually joined by *with*. The fact that she died unstained by contact with earthly ambitions and temptations is relevant only in a theological frame of reference. Here (a) the fact that calls for comfort and (b) the comfortable thought that the child died freed, by baptism, of original sin and free of mortal sin as well are part and parcel of the single traditional metaphor of travel. Note also that the metaphor emerges gradually—first in the word *hence* (until which *parted* is effectively only a synonym for "died"), and, as I will explain shortly, fully in *safety*.

The primary sense of *with safety of her innocence* is (and was) "with her innocence intact," but "a safety" was apparently "a passport," a document guaranteeing safe conduct to a traveler.[30] The idea of the child setting forth with her innocence as a pass-

---

30. *OED*, which fully exemplifies *with safety of* meaning "without damage to" (1.c), approaches the additional gloss on *safety* I propose here (see headings 3 ["A means or instrument of safety"] and 4.1 [which includes "Under safety of" meaning "under the protection of"]). But *OED* overlooks "passport" or "safe conduct" as a sense of *safety*, the sense that appears to lie behind Herrick's metaphoric use of the word in the opening lines of "The Plaudite":

> If after rude and boystrous seas,
> My wearyed Pinnace here finds ease:
> If so it be I've gain'd the shore
> With safety of a faithful Ore. . . .

The noun "safetie" meaning "passport" or "safe conduct" also appears in a stanza of William Wyrley's "Glorious Life and Honorable Death of Sir John

port could have been presented in a full-blown conceit that would have advertised itself as a chosen, arbitrary, carefully closed way of thinking about the facts. As it is, *with safety of her innocence* does not transform the flat assertion that Mary died at the age of six months, but rather infuses it with an image of a young woman (someone old enough to travel alone) departing after a six-month visit—departing *for* somewhere else. As a reader progresses over the two lines, the child grows up—is conceived of as living out the life she lost—and does so in a clause that is nonetheless a statement of harsh fact rather than a fanciful, inevitably ineffectual substitute for it. The lines cause one to idly generate an adolescent or adult Mary in one's own mind; a comforting fancy becomes an incidental reality of the reader's experience of the facts. The difference between evoking that experience and openly presenting and recommending a way of thinking is the difference between rhetorical success (making a viewpoint *on* the facts inherent *in* them) and a merely admirable, merely interesting mere appeal.

There is similar, and similarly unobtrusive, persuasiveness in the syntactical continuation in a subordinate clause of the logically complete sentence that closed in line 6 with the formal close of the couplet:

Chandos" (a verse monologue—printed in 1592 as an appendage to Wyrley's *The True Use of Armorie*—in which Chandos philosophizes his life and "tragike death" in the *Mirror for Magistrates* manner); Wyrley's Chandos says that, in honor of St. George's Day, Edward III prepared

> A royall feast, proclaiming it before
>   In Fraunce, Flaunders in Henault, and Almaine,
> All knights that would vouchsafe to take the paine
>   Should safetie haue for to returne in peace
>   When as the iusts and knightly sports did cease.
>
>   (37)

"Safety" is used similarly by Richard Niccols in the final couplet of "Concordia. *In Manus,*" Epigram 15 in his "Vertues Encomium" (in part 2 of his one-volume collection called *The Furies. With Vertues Encomium. . . .* [1614]): "Concord in peace, a Musick is therefore; / In war a safetie honour'd euermore" (sig. E2).

> At sixe moneths end, shee parted hence
> With safetie of her innocence;
> Whose soule . . .

This is the first time that the conclusion of the couplet rhyme pattern has not been followed by a logically independent new clause. Like the life of the infant in the coffin, the sentence in lines 5 and 6 is finished—enclosed in its boxlike couplet. And, just as a reader's imagination has casually continued the child's life, the syntax of line 7 expands the syntax of the preceding couplet beyond limits that nonetheless remain in force. (If I did not fear seeming to interpret the syntax by wantonly and ingeniously suggesting a sort of syntactic equivalent of onomatopoeia, I would point out that the phrase "Whose soul" is to the body of the sentence apparently concluded at the end of line 6 as the departed soul is to the corpse.)

The phrase *whose soul* also continues one's simultaneously fanciful and realistic thinking about Mary. The mention of *soul* in this context signals the expected statement that Mary's soul is in heaven. However else its particulars cause it *also* to be perceived, the completed clause (*whose soul heaven's queen . . . hath placed amongst her virgin-train*) must be perceived as making that statement; and, as the pronoun *that* in *while that severed doth remain* indicates, the next clause proceeds as if it followed a simple assertion that her soul is in heaven. The *whose soul* construction, however, is very different from "her soul." The phrase at once preserves the distinction between the mortal, earthbound body and the immortal soul and also invites readers to continue conceiving physically of the Mary who departed for heaven. Bearing in mind that I am talking not about *what* one thinks but about how one thinks it, it is reasonable to say that the phrase *whose soul* asks one to think as one would if one were told that Mary *and* her soul were in heaven. That way of thinking is sustained by *she,* the pronoun at the end of line 7: *Whose soule heauens Queene, (whose name shee beares).*

Before following the subordinate clause that begins the fourth couplet (lines 7 and 8) to its verb in line 9, I want to comment on the incidental actions of the parenthetic second of the two *whose* clauses that constitute line 7. In its relation to the first half of the line, that second clause both duplicates and continues the physics of the preceding six lines. The two halves of the line, each beginning with *whose,* are urgently comparable; and, like a pair of rhyme words or the two lines paired in a couplet, are at the same time urgently different—different in that the two pronouns have different antecedents. The first *whose* refers to Mary Jonson and is followed by references to the Virgin Mary (*heaven's queen*); the second *whose* refers to the Virgin Mary and is followed by reference to the infant Mary (*she*).

That *a, b, b, a,* pattern of the persons of the line (a pattern that—because, as the parenthetic clause points out, they have the same name—can be stated as *a, á, á, a*) is internally unified. But—since the second *whose* expands ideationally from *heaven's queen,* an element in the syntactic expansion begun by the first *whose*—the same sequence participates in the poem's newfound freedom from the bounds of closed couplets. The sequence thus can contribute to a reader's vague sense of an analogous liberation of Mary from the finality of death. (Any parenthetic clause, after all, asserts and exercises a right and power to go beyond limits whose existence and validity it also acknowledges.)

Structurally, the parenthetic clause is a self-confessedly gratuitous syntactic digression; and yet, at the same time, the repetition of *whose* suggests otherwise. The substance of this clause is also digressive; and yet naming is the primary action of tombstone inscriptions and of the first couplet of this poem—and *bears,* which here means only "carries," is in accidental relation to the topic of motherhood and birth (in fact, lines 7–9 end up having presented us with two mothers and a child who bears).[31]

---

31. Compare the action of *heaven's* earlier in the line. At just the point that the syntax is escaping the limits of the form, *heaven's* echoes, and thus asserts a link to, the two previous genitive uses of the same word in line 3. The word *hence* in line 5 also participates in the echo pattern of the three *heaven's.* In Renaissance pronunciation the word "heaven," even where not spelled "heav'n," was dissyllabic or monosyllabic as rhythm—formal or informal—

Above everything else, the introduction of the parenthesis and of what it says generates a special kind of confusion—one that cannot possibly confuse the reader (anyone can follow a sentence interrupted by a brief parenthesis, and no one can ever have confused Mary the subject of this poem with Mary the queen of heaven), but a confusion of one line of thinking with another in a clause whose substance demands an easy, trivial, incidental exercise in perceiving that a word, "Mary," that says one thing also says another.

The fourth couplet is completed in another parenthesis. This one—line 8, *In comfort of her mother's tears*—is not set off in physical parentheses on the page, and this one is an immediately germane modifying phrase for the clause it interrupts, but line 8 is one more obstacle in the way of the long, structurally onomatopoeic climb toward grammatical predication in *Hath placed amongst her virgin-train.* The now-completed couplet, like all those that precede it, is very ordinary in import (this is just so much prettifying, just cute mythmaking, just sentimental hackwork); but this couplet now concerns three beings who are complexly like one another: two are mother and daughter; two are virgins named Mary; two are mothers tragically bereaved of their children. This plodding, perfunctory little poem is opening more and more paths of mental possibility.

---

dictated. Moreover, Renaissance writers and readers seem to have delighted in interchanging pronunciation within a single poem or line; for example, line 3 may well have been pronounced something like "yet all 'hens' gifts beeng heavens due." The word *hence* and the monosyllabic *heaven's* in line 7 presumably sounded nearly alike. (For a fuller discussion of such matters, see the notes on "spirit" and "spirits" in line 5 of Sonnet 86 and on "ev'n" in line 6 of Sonnet 15 in my edition of *Shakespeare's Sonnets* [New Haven, Conn., 1977, 288–89, 156].) Note also that *hence,* which says "from here" in line 5, embodies a sound that denotes the destination of the departed, heaven; *hence* thus manifests the same general sort of incidental, logically casual, purely verbal paradox that I attribute to *whose* in line 7 and *Where* in line 10 and that occurred back in line 2 when the sound of *their* made an altogether inconspicuous, wholly insignificant pair with *Here* in line 1.

> At sixe moneths end, shee parted hence
> With safetie of her innocence;
> Whose soule heauens Queene, (whose name shee beares)
> In comfort of her mothers teares,
> Hath plac'd amongst her virgin-traine:

Virgin-train is a specific allusion to "the hundred and forty and four thousand" virgins—"they which were not defiled with women"—whom St. John describes as singing "before the throne," "redeemed from among men," and "without fault before the throne of God" (Revelation 14: 1—5). Although St. John's use of the word "virgins" is akin to the narrow one to which the word is limited in modern English, Jonson's contemporaries were used to understanding it less anatomically than we do and, in context of discussions of the salvation of infants, were used to hearing "virgins" used as we would use "innocents." The virgin choir in Revelation 14 had figured for several centuries in both formal theological and informal popular discussion of infant salvation.[32] *Virgin-train,* then, is an easy, pretty, periphrasis by which the poet introduces another traditional particular of Christian comfort.

Yes, but *virgin-train* appears here in company with another easy periphrasis, *heaven's queen* for the Virgin Mary. Together they constitute a quietly persuasive court metaphor that complements and continues the process by which the particulars of a series of pious commonplaces implies and embodies the happy, thriving adolescence of which the dead infant has been deprived. These lines fulfill just the sort of parental ambition that they supersede: they present Mary as she would have been had she achieved the likeliest secular fond ambition of a London parent: lady-in-waiting to the queen.[33]

32. See pages xix—xxvii of E. V. Gordon's introduction to the Oxford edition of *Pearl* (1953), and R. Welleck, *"The Pearl:* An Interpretation of the Middle English Poem," in *Studies in English,* 4, Prague, 1933.

33. Although the possibility is of only biographical significance and no way pertinent to the experience of reading the poem, the unrealized earthly future shadowed forth in lines 5 to 9 of this poem on Jonson's dead *daughter* reflects an element of a vision Jonson had of his dead *son* in 1603. Jonson told Drummond

When, in line 9, a reader reached the syntactic equivalent of salvation in arriving at long last at the verb of the clause begun in line 7, that clause concluded in the middle of a couplet. As the mortal finality of the first three couplets was superseded by a syntax that went on to report on the afterlife, that syntax has now come to rest at a point that cannot be final because, although the necessities of the couplet form have been superseded, they have not been neglected. Like the fact that the baby is dead, the fact remains that the poem cannot end until it reaches a rhyme for *train*. The necessary next line immediately sends a reader's mind back toward the facts of the other domain:

> Hath plac'd amongst her virgin-traine:
> Where, while that seuer'd doth remaine,
> This graue partakes the fleshly birth.
> Which couer lightly, gentle earth.

That necessary line—line 10, *Where, while that severed doth re-main*—does complete the couplet, but it also opens a new, still incomplete syntactic unit. The next line completes that, but it in its turn requires a rhyme for *birth,* a rhyme that the syntactically unnecessary last line provides. The last couplet thus presents us with one more miniature, purely literary, but nonetheless real experience of our capacity to deal matter-of-factly with the coexistence of mutually exclusive systems for perceiving simultaneous finality and infinity.

The greatest achievement of which this poem makes its reader capable derives from the experience of following Jonson's sentence smoothly from *virgin-train* at the end of line 9 to *This grave partakes* in line 11.

The logical hinge on which the passage turns is the word *Where*.

The action of that word is the most difficult thing in the poem to talk about.

---

of Hawthornden about it in 1619. Drummond concludes his account of the apparition with this sentence: "He appeared to him, he said, of a manly shape, and of that growth that he thinks he shall be at the Resurrection" (H&S, 1 : 140).

Readers have no trouble with *Where* or with the logic of the lines. Once again, my evidence for saying so is the nearly universal silence of editors and commentators.[34] I suspect that line 10 is effortlessly understood as "while that severed doth remain *there*" would be. And yet, once again, the words on the page are there and are read, and the words say "amongst her virgin train: / Where . . . this grave partakes the fleshly birth." I still insist that the lines make easy, ready sense, but I also insist that the construction is meaningless—unreasonable, the assertion of a physical impossibility, an impossibility as great as being dead *and* alive or in heaven *and* on Earth.

---

34. I say "*nearly* universal" because, in the essay cited previously, Ann Lauinger has commented at some length on the syntactic relation of *Where* at the beginning of line 10 to what precedes and follows it. Faced with a discrepancy between, on the one hand, a sense of "amongst her virgin train: Where . . . / This grave partakes the fleshly birth" effortlessly derived by synesis (effortlessly derived on the basis of the probabilities of the given situation) and, on the other, the sense signaled by a syntax that places the grave in heaven, Lauinger tries to give the impression that the discrepancy doesn't exist and that her essay has demonstrated that. Unless I misunderstand entirely, there is something like a shell game going on in her sentences about the syntactic action of *Where* in line 10: "In terms of both syntax and sense, line 10 belongs with the two lines that follow it. Although the subject of line 10 (the child's soul) and its initial *where* refer back to the virgin-traine of line 9, the two halves of the couplet are separated as decisively as body and soul after death" (230). Later Lauinger says,

> The intended sense of line 10 must be something like, *While that,* i.e., the soul, *remains in heaven parted from the body.* However, the medial placement of *sever'd* makes it probable that we will interpret that word as part of the subject before realizing that it forms part of the predicate. A first rendering of the line is thus likely to be, *While that which has been severed,* i.e., the soul, *remains in heaven.* A reading so evidently undoctrinal as this, which seems to set temporal limits to the soul's enjoyment of heaven, will obviously put readers on the track of a revised interpretation. But the earlier reading lingers and lends its problematic coloring to our amended understanding of the line. (232)

The process of conscious interpretation and revision Lauinger supposes is not one I can imagine occurring—particularly in view of the silence of all the editors—professional crux finders—who annotated the poem in the years before her 1989 essay.

If my experience of talking about these lines with students and colleagues holds true, you should now have looked back at the lines to see just where and how I have misread them. You are an intelligent person and, if you read essays like this one, surely a careful reader. The issue between us here, I think, is not whether the lines, which *seem* straightforward, *are* straightforward: in things made of words seeming is being. The issue is whether or not the lines, which seem straightforward, can be demonstrated to be so according to the probabilities of semantics and syntax.[35]

The thing that makes the action of *Where* so hard to talk about here is that, when—under pressure from my analysis—one goes back to prove to oneself that the lines contain a semantically and syntactically acceptable sense, one can find a reading as straightforward in theory as the lines are in fact. "Where" often had the sense "whereas" (it still does; I have systematically used it that way throughout this essay). And that reading of *Where* not only makes sense but makes the general sense that I argue is derived suprasyntactically on the basis of contextual probabilities (on the basis of what one comes to the poem already knowing about heaven, Earth, there, and here): "amongst her virgin-train. Whereas . . . this grave. . . . "

I do not, however, believe that any reader reads, or ever read, *Where* as "whereas" in line 10 of this poem. For one thing, modern editors who gloss that use of *where* in line 99 of Jonson's "On the Famous Voyage" do not gloss the word here. For another, those of my colleagues with whom I have discussed the word *Where* in this poem do not come up with the "whereas" explanation until we have been talking, puzzling, and squabbling for some time. Most important, I doubt that readers actually read

---

35. For instance, the contexts in which one hears the current American idiom "I could care less" make it understood as it would be if it were "I could *not* care less." That, therefore, is what the expression means. However, it demonstrably—but only demonstrably—means just the opposite and demonstrably—but only demonstrably—does not make sense in the contexts where it is customarily used.

Where as "whereas" because its context is so insistently one of place. The poem is concerned throughout with here, where Mary lies, and there, where her soul has gone; and the principal overall action of line 10 is to reassert the initial focus on *here*— is to reassert the physical facts: the grave and the corpse.

Lines 5–9 have more efficiently blurred a reader's focus on the painful facts of earthly reality than any comforting words I know. Now Jonson attempts, and succeeds in taking, a daring but necessary further step toward effective comfort. Had Jonson left his readers where line 9 delivers them, the poem's achievement would have been less because, although lines 5–8 start from the facts of physical death, they leave them behind; the consolation the lines embody is therefore vulnerable to resurgent awareness that a poor little baby is dead.

To succeed fully, the poem must persist in including the ugly facts that evoked it, the inescapable facts that one would like to escape. One way to characterize this poem would be to say that it substitutes "and" (the baby is dead *and* immortal) for "but." The poem deals constantly with separation—both in its substance (the child is divided from the parents, as is her soul from her body), and in its stylistic incidentals (for instance, the unity inherent in the word *parents'* in line 1 is qualified by the *each her* construction, and the philosophical father and emotional mother are considered both separately and differently in the body of the poem). But—as the fused realities and overlapping organizational systems in lines 5–9 illustrate and as the poem's abundance of genitives witnesses—the poem just as persistently demonstrates a unity in divided things.

Reading this poem is a mentally miraculous exercise in practical paradox. That exercise culminates in line 10. Line 10 is syntactically conjunctive. *And* it reconnects consideration of metaphysical fact with consideration of physical fact. *And,* thus, it reasserts the distinction between the two. *And,* if I am right about the way our minds deal with *Where,* line 10 enables its readers momentarily to think as they would if they were capable of confusing here and there—capable of thinking of one creature as physically present in two places at once—and capable of conceiving of body and soul as physically separated *and* physically one, and capable of conceiving of Earth and heaven as absolutely distinct *and* absolutely indistinct from one another.

Line 10 evokes a sort of syntactic pre-experience of the reunion of bodies and souls on resurrection day. Line 10 lets the poem do what the grand verbal double-shuffle of "the glory of the terrestrial" and "the glory of the celestial" and of "the natural body" and "the spiritual body" in 1 Corinthians 15 only suggests can be done. This is 1 Corinthians 15:50–54 as it appeared in the Anglican burial service (note the seeming contradictions about corruption and uncorruption):

> This I say brethren, that flesh and blood cannot inherit the kingdom of God, neither doth corruption inherit uncorruption. Behold, I show you a mystery. We shall not all sleep, but we shall all be changed, and that in a moment, in the twinkling of an eye by the last trump. For the trump shall blow, and the dead shall rise incorruptible, and we shall be changed. For this corruptible must put on incorruption, and this mortal must put on immortality. When this corruptible hath put on incorruption, and this mortal hath put on immortality, then shall be brought to pass the saying that is written, Death is swallowed up in victory.[36]

What the action of the word *Where* imitates, the rest of line 10 specifically alludes to: *while that severed doth remain*. Once again, words that insist on severance also suggest union. Here that suggestion is in the word *while,* a word whose action is emblematic of the larger stylistic paradox in which it participates. *While* here means "for as long as" and thus points forward toward resurrection day. And *while* here means "at the same time as" and thus asserts the distinction between the concurrent realities of body and soul. Moreover, like the word that precedes it, *while* has la-

---

36. *The Book of Common Prayer: 1559,* ed. John E. Booty (Washington, 1976), 312. In subsequent citations, I will refer to Booty's edition as *BCP.*

tent potential as a word meaning "whereas" and indicating a distinction in logic ("whereas the soul remains severed").[37]

Like the final couplet of "On My First Son," the last two lines of this poem adapt and improve on an ostentatiously epigrammatic, syntactically isolated pair of conclusive closing lines at the end of a poem by Martial.[38] And like the final couplet of "On My First Son," the last two lines of this poem are a syntactical continuation of the lines that precede them and also feel as iso-

---

37. Note also the double action of *doth remain:* (1) "remains in heaven" ("to remain" indicating continuation in place); (2) "remains separated" ("to remain" indicating continuation of a condition).

38. The Martial poem, V.xxxiv, concludes with these lines: *mollia non rigidus caespes tegat ossa nec illi, / terra, gravis fueris: non fuit illa tibi.* The Loeb editor translates them as "And let not hard clods cover her tender bones, nor be thou heavy upon her, O earth: she was not so to thee!"

The sudden revival of interest in Martial among seventeenth-century English poets is probably the direct result of Jonson's fondness for him. Jonson's request at the end of "On My First Daughter" omits the central idea of Martial's conceit, the idea of relative weight—the idea that distinguishes Martial's variation on a timeworn conceit (as Charles R. Forker points out, fanciful appeals to the earth to lie lightly on a grave occur as far back as Euripides and Meleager [*Notes and Queries,* April 1983, 150]). Nonetheless, even given the crucial omission, "On My First Daughter" seems responsible for more than a century of imitations and echoes of the last lines of Martial V.xxxiv; the tradition culminates in Abel Evans's mock epitaph on his fellow writer, the architect of Blenheim Palace:

> Under this stone, reader, survey
> Dead Sir John Vanbrugh's house of clay:
> Lie heavy on him, earth, for he
> Laid many heavy weights on thee!

(The text is as given by Leigh Hunt in an essay called "John Vanbrugh" [reprinted in the Vanbrugh volume of the old Mermaid series, ed. A.E.H. Swaen, 1896].)

The idea of the child's weight is entirely absent from Jonson's couplet, but—although this concerns the poet rather than the poem and is therefore irrelevant to the present essay—I want to suggest that the diction of the last three lines reflects an interplay of puns and translations in Jonson's mind. Although Martial's *gravis,* "heavy," has nothing to do with the English word *grave* in line 11, and although "severe," the English for a standard metaphoric use of *gravis,* is only phonetically related to the verb "to sever" in line 10, I suspect that Jonson chose some of his words in response to those connections.

lated and emotionally summary as their models in Martial. The final couplet of "On My First Daughter" is variously comparable to the first. Where the first couplet, a syntactically independent two-line unit, was extended logically by *Yet* in line 3 and included in a four-line unit determined by phonic and polyptotonic relationships among *ruth, youth, due,* and *rue,* the last couplet, also capable of syntactic independence, is introduced as an appendage of the preceding syntax and, as the rhyme words of the second couplet repeated the vowel sound of *ruth* and *youth,* the final rhyme pair, *birth, earth,* repeats the concluding consonantal sound from the first pair. The last couplet establishes an overall 2-8-2 pattern—a sort of down-up-down pattern—for the twelve lines of "On My First Daughter": two lines on physical graveside fact; eight lines on the spiritual facts of the case; and two final terrestrial lines that, except for the implication of a spiritual realm inherent in the specificity of *fleshly,* limit themselves entirely to the material world.

> This graue partakes the fleshly birth.
> Which couer lightly, gentle earth.

The distinction between the last lines and those that immediately precede them is also established in a new heightening of a reader's sense of the ugliness of the mortal facts of burial and decay—and, in a similarly intense new intellectual refuge from physical reality, the openly fanciful cradle image of the last line. Jonson's insistence on the grimness he has sought to alleviate begins in line 10 with the word *severed,* which—though it functions here as a legalistic synonym for "separated"—carries with it connotations of suddenness and force (*OED,* 5).

Partakes is a similar case. It contains the sound "part," which echoes *parted* in line 5 and complements the idea *remain* expresses in line 10, and which, like *parted* and *severed,* is extrasyntactically pertinent to a poem that persistently concerns itself with parts and wholes. The word *partakes* also contains "takes" and thus sustains and continues the idea of rightful seizure introduced in line 3. Here *partakes* is effectively glossed by a reader's knowledge of the function of graves (set between *grave* and *fleshly birth,* any verb at all would be taken as intending to say "contains"). And that sense is an ideational neighbor of a standard sense of "to partake": "to share in." But the verb "to partake" was already permanently colored by its repeated use in the Communion service, from which "partakes of"—"share in"—came to imply the specialized sense "share in *eating.*" [39] In conjunction with *fleshly birth,* the word *partakes* infuses the line with the traditional idea of death and the grave as devourers. [40] In *fleshly birth, birth* has the now-archaic, and never common, sense "baby," "child" (for which *OED* cites Coverdale's version of Jeremiah 20:17: "That the byrth might not have come out, but remayned still in her" and this collective use from Chapman's Homer: "When you come to banquet with your wife and birth at home"). Jonson's phrase (perhaps the accidental product of his need to rhyme *earth*) can infuse the line with a vague analogy between little mortal Mary and the incarnate Christ, but its principal action is to insist upon the horrible fact of a tiny, fragile corpse hideously decomposing in the ground—to insist graphically on—and thus fully acknowledge and include—the horror that the poem tries to overcome. [41]

On the other hand, the subordinate clause with which the poem ends literalizes—and thus debases—the Christian idea of the afterlife, presents it in a way generically akin to the cheapest,

39. See, for example, these phrases from the Communion service; "partakers of his most blessed Body and Blood" (*BCP,* 263), "beseeching thee, that all we which be partakers of this Holy Communion, may be fulfilled" (264), and, in particular, "meet [that is, suitable] partakers of those holy mysteries" (258).

40. See, for example, Psalms 49:14: "Like sheep they are laid in the grave; death shall feed on them," and Proverbs 1:12: "Let us swallow them up alive as the grave. . . ." Note "swallowed" in the Pauline paradox that concludes the passage I quoted earlier from the burial service.

41. A modern reader may also hear pertinent reverberations of "the remains" in the verb *remain* at the end of line 10. Note, nonetheless, that *OED* does not record that euphemism for "corpse" before 1700.

sentimental twaddle: "She is only sleeping." However, as in the lines on Mary in heaven, Jonson does not ask us to "look at it this way"; he causes us actually and voluntarily to include the idea of a sleeping baby in our conception of the situation in which the speaker gives instructions to the earth. What Jonson does is wrap a gauzy, sentimental fancy so willfully flimsy as to be trivial in a plain one that does not involve any falsification of the essential facts of death. Graves are indeed covered with earth. And direct address to personified inanimate elements is so common, so mild, and so undemanding an appeal to the emotional energy of the pathetic fallacy that one accepts the poet's impotent imperative as a simple and traditionally expressed assertion of strong feeling about conditions beyond human control.

However, this particular instance of the stock poetic posture occurs in a context (a baby is lying in a grave; graves are obviously and traditionally bedlike)—whereas the verb "to cover" automatically calls up the cheerful analogy of a sleeping baby who will later awaken (as this one will in fact on resurrection morning). The key element in this line's success is not so much the word *cover* as the epithet *gentle;* it intensifies the personification of Earth and particularizes it. *Gentle,* which repeats some of the ideational content of *lightly* and thus gives a rhymelike feel of supralogical rightness and quasi-physical, quasi-natural complexity to the line, was a stock epithet of polite address—one that Shakespeare's plays have made familiar to all probable modern readers of Jonson's poem and one that carried with it an inherent implication of benign condescension to the person addressed. The epithet, never in any way insulting, was applied, like "good," to servants, and commonly preceded a request by a speaker in a position to command.[42] Here it personifies *earth* as

---

42. For simple examples, see *The Two Gentlemen of Verona* 2.7.42, *Romeo and Juliet* 4.3.1, and Shakespeare's several condescending uses of the epithet in *3 Henry VI,* 1.1. The epithet bespeaks its user's sense of the relative dignities of himself and the person addressed. See Volumnia's address to the triumphant Coriolanus (2.1.172), and Subtle's greeting to Mammon in *The Alchemist* 2.3.1.

a nurse or nursery maid in whose care the departing parent casually and confidently leaves the child.

Jonson's achievement in the couplet is emblematic of his achievement in the whole poem. He does not deny—or ask us to deny—any of the truth of the situation. He does not offer us alternative ways of thinking about the child. Instead, he makes the stuff of comfortable conceits inherent to the process of registering insistently bare facts. The poem is artistically daring. And it is most so in daring also to be pedestrian and to use its careful insufficiency as a means of making the poor, category-bound human mind superior to its own limitations—the limitations that language reflects and services—and sufficient to an impossible mental task that remains impossible to us even as we perform it.

PART THREE

Shakespeare's *Twelfth Night*

Twelfth Night is one of the most universally admired works in the Shakespeare canon, but its admirers have never much cared to say why. What is it in the experience *Twelfth Night* gives its audiences that causes them to value it so highly? In the three essays that follow I speculate in detail about that experience. In particular, and among other things, I suggest that, like the Gettysburg Address and "On My First Daughter," *Twelfth Night* creates a music of ideas—a music of ideas that is inconsequential in all that word's senses, a music that makes us superior to the limitations of syntax and logic (and thus effectively though temporarily superior to the human limitations of which syntax and logic are such telling evidence), and a music that is an unobserved source of the value the play has for us.

1 · *TWELFTH NIGHT* 1.1:
THE AUDIENCE AS MALVOLIO

In his account of *Twelfth Night* in *Shakespeare's Festive Comedy,* C. L. Barber suggests—though in passing—"that we enjoy the play so much simply because it is a wish-fulfillment presented so skillfully that we do not notice that our hearts are duping our heads."[1] My concerns in approaching Shakespeare's festively

---

[1]. *Shakespeare's Festive Comedy* (New York, 1965), 244. A flood of influential, valuable, culturally focused essays on *Twelfth Night* appeared in the 1980s—notably Catherine Belsey's "Disrupting Sexual Difference: Meaning and Gen-

named festive comedy are—at least superficially—very different from Barber's. And yet, in groping toward an understanding of what it is we so love about *Twelfth Night,* I have arrived at a hypothesis that is essentially only a variation on the one Barber momentarily considered. The following discussion sets out to demonstrate that the first scene of *Twelfth Night* is nonsense— demonstrable nonsense, but (since it has made, and presumably always will make, perfectly good sense to its audiences) nonsense that is *merely* demonstrable. My concern will be similar to those of the essays that precede this one—here, the miraculous discrepancy between what the variously bizarre clauses of the forty-two-line first scene of *Twelfth Night* should reasonably be expected to convey and what they do in fact convey. And again my purpose is to suggest that nonsense is often not only a valuable ingredient but the vital ingredient in the greatest literary works, to suggest that nonsense can be the physical means by which our minds approach metaphysical experience—the experience of phenomena *like* the metaphysical phenomena we know exist but cannot ordinarily know except by arbitrary and diminishing metaphor. Although the particulars I talk about are small and thus clearly different from the large ones that C. L. Barber talked about when he wrote about *Twelfth Night,* what I say here is also concerned with a holiday aspect of *Twelfth Night*—or, more particularly, with a holiday aspect of its first scene. I suggest that to experience that scene is to be given a

---

der" (in *Alternative Shakespeares,* ed. John Drakakis [London, 1985], 166–90), Phyllis Racklin's "Androgyny, Mimesis, and the Marriage of the Boy Heroine on the English Renaissance Stages" (*PMLA* 102 [1987]: 29–47), Stephen Greenblatt's "Fiction and Faction" (in his *Shakespearean Negotiations* [Berkeley, Calif., 1988]), and Jean E. Howard's "Crossdressing, the Theater, and Gender Struggle in Early Modern England" (*Shakespeare Quarterly* 39 [1988]: 418–40). Readers surprised that the following pages take no notice of those essays or of several other good ones that have followed their leads must understand that I ignore them here only because my concerns in thinking about *Twelfth Night* are essentially foreign to the concerns of those essays.

small but metaphysically glorious holiday from the limitations of the ordinary logic by which sentences determine what they will be understood to say, and that that holiday is a brief and trivial but effectively real holiday from the inherent limitation of the human mind.

Twelfth Night is in manifold ways an ideal object for an investigation of the preciousness of nonsense. Nonsense—ordinary gibberish-like nonsense—is a topic in *Twelfth Night*. Sir Andrew, for instance, recommends that kind of nonsense as the highest form of comedy (2.3.28); and rational-sounding, but only formally sustained, excursions into blatant nonsense are the stock in trade of the play's chief comedian, Feste. Moreover and more obviously, the story line of *Twelfth Night* depends on a series of invalid *and* valid conclusions to which the characters jump from variously inadequate evidence. Analogous activity by the audience has a special and potentially philosophic pertinence to a play about discrepancies between signals and what they are understood to convey, discrepancies between what is there to see and hear and what contextual probabilities say is there. I suggest, indeed, that *Twelfth Night* and its first scene, which I present as an emblem of the whole, are wonderful, and that our sense that the play and the scene are wonderful (in the metaphoric sense of the word) is directly related to the fact that both play and scene are literally wonderful—are amazing, specifically so in being capable of comprehension, in seeming coherent.

I will now look in minute detail at the first scene of *Twelfth Night*, a scene that does not invite such inspection. I do so *because* it does not need analysis to be understood.

The business of demonstrating that a scene that has always made sense cannot be demonstrated to contain the sense it so obviously conveys is difficult. In the case of this first scene of *Twelfth Night*, the task is made a bit easier by the fact that a few commentators, mostly editors faced with the need to gloss and paraphrase, have had some trouble with the first three lines: *If music be the food of love, play on, / Give me excess of it, that, surfeit-*

ing / The appetite may sicken, and so die.[2] In his 1747 edition of
Twelfth Night, the indefatigably rational William Warburton said
"There is an impropriety of expression in the present reading of
this fine passage. . . . I am persuaded, a word is accidentally dropt;
and that we should read, and point, the passage thus: 'that, surfeiting The app'tite, Love may sicken, and so die.'" Twentieth-
century scholarship, of course, will not hear of such wanton
emendation, and few listeners in any age would hear Warburton's ugly new line with pleasure. More important, the emendation may be rejected as unnecessary—obviously so because the
unemended line was clear to Warburton before he set about
making its syntax reflect the sense he apprehended from it. Warburton's emendation is a brutal variation on the justifying process
common in explanatory footnotes on verse, a process by which
reason is used to squeeze the obvious content of a sentence into
the container. For instance, one could explain that love, wanting
its food because it has lost its appetite for music, will starve to
death—or that love (an appetite), will die of a surfeit. However,
such explanations come after the fact of effective understanding;
they do not gloss lines that need glossing; they explain—or pretend to explain—why one understands the sentence.

Almost two hundred years after Warburton—in the New
Cambridge edition of *Twelfth Night* in 1930—Dover Wilson responded differently but just as rationally to the occupational
hazard of insisting that a sentence delivers the meaning signaled
by its syntax; Wilson simply capitulated to syntactical probability. "'Appetite,'" he said, "means not 'love' as is generally assumed, but 'love's appetite for music.'" Wilson was absolutely
right. The syntax does say that. He was just as absolutely wrong.
The sentence does not say that; Wilson's parenthetical "as is generally assumed" admits as much (just as Warburton's incidental

---

2. Except where I specifically say otherwise, all Shakespearean citations are
to the Revised Pelican Text, ed. Alfred Harbage et al. (Baltimore, 1969). The
editor for *Twelfth Night* in the Pelican edition was Charles T. Prouty.

"this fine passage" advertised the impropriety of his critique of the passage).

Before I leave this first sentence, I want to analyze it, despite the fact that—or, rather, because of the fact that—analysis and explication are perfectly unnecessary as aids to comprehending it.

As we read or hear Orsino's first three lines, we understand a sentence that cannot be demonstrated to mean anything—any particular thing—at all. *If music be the food of love, play on* is as clear as it sounds. So are its implications. Orsino is intent upon nourishing love, and, since the line has no context but its speaker and the loverlike extravagance of his conjunction of topics, the love in question is the love he himself feels. *Give me excess of it* feels clear too. The preceding line, I think, makes us understand *excess of* as a hyperbole for "lots of"; the literal meaning of *excess* does not come into play—the word is not its usual self—until we reach *surfeiting*. In *Give me excess of it, that, surfeiting . . .* , the word *that* is obviously *so that,* but on analysis *surfeiting* turns out to have been a problem. I say "turns out" because—since *surfeiting* occurs in a still-unfinished, and therefore promissory, syntax—a listener is not invited to care that the surfeiter is momentarily specified as the speaker (the "I" implicit in the *me* of *Give me*), and is immediately specified otherwise in the next line; *surfeiting,* it turns out, pertains not to what preceded it but to what follows it: *the appetite* is the surfeiter. That makes perfect sense, but what sense does it make of the sentence? I think one never knows—or cares. One understands, but does not know what one has understood. The lines, however, assure one generically. Metaphors are by definition clarifying devices, and the action of the food metaphor here remains a clarifying action, even though it also and simultaneously generates a confusion.

Music is to love as *food* is to the body. *Love* is the eater, *music* the *food.* If *love* is the eater, then only *love* can be the surfeiter. But we all just sat still for the assertion that the *appetite* is the surfeiter. Is *the appetite,* then, *love? Love* is indeed an *appetite.* An *appetite* for what? For the beloved, obviously. But in this conceit its food is *music*. A physical truism underlies these lines: gorging on a delicacy leads to a revulsion against that delicacy, death of desire for it. An excess of music will cure lust for music. The lines obviously say that Orsino wishes to free himself of an addiction to music. Oddly enough, that is in fact what he immediately achieves: lines 7 and 8 —*Enough, no more. / 'Tis not so sweet now as it was before*—report just such a cure. However, only a fanatic Puritan would want to cure an addiction to music. The overt topic here is music (the *it* of line 2), but music is of interest to the speaker as *the food of love*. Music nourishes love and causes it to grow. The speaker wants love to grow. The dubiety of lovers toward their condition—as toward their beloveds—was and is a psychological truism and a mainspring of love literature. It is remarkable, but usual, that a lover should record both the will to foster his passion and the will to starve it. The act of glutting one's passion is a conflation of the two ambitions, a violent compromise that feeds both urges and starves both. Here, though no probable listener will so much as pause to accept the inference that Orsino is worrying about a pathological dependence on music, the sentence sounds both true and simple because the physics implied here is, as Shakespeare says in Sonnet 129, natural to sexual desire and sexual possession. What one has in these lines, then, is a straightforward sentence demonstrably about appetite for music that is obviously understood as a sentence about sexual appetite. This synesis—this construction that asks to be understood to say what context makes probable rather than what is actually said—works because love is an appetite.

The next line, line 4, is an exclamatory interruption of the previous line of thought: *That strain again. It had a dying fall.* Even though the word *strain* appears here in context of *excess* and *surfeiting,* the reference is obviously and exclusively to a strain of music; and the line is as straightforward as it seems. The line does, however, act in a manner that in another—and ideationally insignificant—dimension has a kind of likeness to the preceding three lines. In that first sentence the significances of individual words, phrases, and clauses shift—first they signal one thing, then another. Moreover, the ideational substance of the three lines is, as I said, one thing and two things—the two being what the syntax says and what we understand. Line 4 overtly acknowledges what could be usefully called the first pair of twins in the play: *That strain again.* The repeated musical strain is and is not the one it echoes. And, in an altogether other dimension, the phrase *dying fall* in the second half of line 4 presents a casual twin for *and so die* in line 3. Similarly, and of course beyond the consciousness of the mind that apprehends the sense of the lines, the word *That,* the first word of line 4, is and is not a repetition of the *that* of *that surfeiting:* the sounds are identical; the senses (a conjunction meaning "so that" in line 2 and a demonstrative adjective in line 4), are not. (That no-way-unusual phenomenon continues through the eight further *that*s in the scene—notably in the blurred, conflicted anaphora of line 6 [where *That* is a pronoun and thus repeats and fails to repeat the adjective that began line 4], line 10 [where *That* is doubtful—a pronoun colored by the adverb indicating extent], line 15 [the adverb], and line 21 [a pronoun meaning "in which"]. The pronoun *that* also appears in lines 18, 33 [where a second *that,* this one an adverb, also occurs], and 38.)

The next sentence, lines 5–7, begins with *O*—another disjunctive exclamation—although, since Orsino continues to comment on the same musical particular he pounced on when he last interrupted himself, this one is disjunctive only in manner.

I could comment in detail on the ostentatious disjunction and the equally ostentatious coherence of this scene (as, for instance, in its conjunction of restrictiveness and expansiveness or in the action of the three exclamatory *O*s in lines 9, 20, and 33); and on the ostentatious disjunction and equally ostentatious coherence of Orsino's thinking here and later; *and* on the ostentatious disjunction and equally ostentatious coherence of the whole play. It would take a lot of time and space to do so. Fortunately, doing so is probably unnecessary.

Let it suffice to say that there is a common denominator among the various kinds of disjunction in this scene (change of tone, topic, semantic significance, logical direction, and Orsino's whim) and larger disjunctions in the play at large. For instance, the standard shifts between one scene, group of characters, and sets of concerns and the next scene, group, and set of concerns; or the less commonplace but strikingly plentiful incidental self-contradictions characters perform in *Twelfth Night;* or the sudden, incidental, and unexplained discrepancies between what we expect will occur and what does.

As examples in that last category, consider the following. In 1.2 Viola plans to get employment as a singer. In the opening lines of 2.4 Orsino apparently asks her to sing. She makes no reply, and Orsino seems to expect none. Curio breaks in to say that Feste (whom we do not expect to be on call at Orsino's house), is not in the room but is about the house somewhere. Orsino sends for him. Feste comes and sings the song. In the following scene (2.5), we expect Feste to "make a third" (2.3.160) with Andrew and Toby as audience to Malvolio's reception of the Olivia-Maria letter; instead we get the completely unexpected Fabian (who, by the way, steps in to replace Feste again in the last scene when he reads another letter—the letter from Malvolio to Olivia). At the end of the last scene most of the loose ends of the plot are tied off, some more firmly than an audience demands, but Antonio—still under arrest—is ignored; however, the other sea captain, the absent one who saved Viola and is now also under arrest, is suddenly treated as necessary to the completion of the happy ending.

Sudden shifts in character also belong in this list—things like Toby's sudden viciousness toward Andrew at their final exit (where Andrew says *I'll help you, Sir Toby, because we'll be dressed together,* and Toby says *Will you help? An ass-head and a coxcomb and a knave, a thin-faced knave, a gull?* [5.1.197–99]); and Feste's mean-spirited *I do not care for you,* spoken in not-quite-obvious jest to Viola (3.1.28); and Orsino's surprising but momentary emergence as Othello in 5.1 (*Why should I not, had I the heart to do it, / Like to th' Egyptian thief at point of death, / Kill what I love?* *(A savage jealousy / That sometime savors nobly)* . . . [111–14]). All these large disjunctions are, in their various kinds, countered by equally various conjunctive factors, and, as I will suggest shortly, so are the various kinds of disjunctions within the first speech and the first scene.

Moreover, since I have now strayed so far from the text of scene 1, I may as well point out that all the phenomena I have mentioned—simultaneous conjunction and disjunction, simultaneous coherence (in its literal sense) and incoherence (in the metaphoric sense by which "coherent" and "incoherent" refer to the logicality or illogicality of discourse), repetitions, the double identity of the first sentence—all share the same physics, and all share that physics with the operation of simple literary constructions (a sentence is one thing *and* a union of disparate parts whose disparity the mere existence of the sentence advertises) and complex ones (rhymes—in which two words are insistently the same and just as insistently different—puns, rhythm—where a pattern both repeats and does not repeat—and so on). The most obvious—and traditionally the most fascinating—embodiments of the common underlying principle shared by the phenomena I have talked about are, of course, twins.

I want now to return from that extravagant, tentative gesture of aesthetic generalization to the more solid ground of Orsino's first speech. These are lines 4–8:

> That strain again. It had a dying fall;
> O, it came o'er my ear like the sweet sound
> That breathes upon a bank of violets,
> Stealing and giving odor. Enough, no more.
> 'Tis not so sweet now as it was before.

In those lines Orsino's overt and noticeably abrupt change of whim follows upon a complementary semantic metamorphosis in *stealing and giving,* a change as complete in its dimension as the ostentatious one announced by *enough, no more,* but, if commentators' silence is any measure, a metamorphosis that goes—

and therefore should go—unnoticed. In its chronologically linear doubleness of effect, the sentence on the *sweet sound* and the *bank of violets* is comparable to the first sentence, whose principal double identity (in what is heard and what is understood) is more static, but which is also linearly double in that it sets out to recommend the nourishment of love and ends up recommending that love be starved to death. When *stealing* is heard in line 7, it participates in the process by which the musical phrase that *came o'er* the *ear* ("crept up on it" and "moved across it"), is likened to a *sweet sound stealing* (moving with unperceived motion). *Stealing,* however, is thereupon paired with *giving,* which, in a previously alien sense of "to steal," is a logical opposite of *stealing.* The incidental logic in which *stealing* and *giving* relate to one another is both irrelevant to the overt assertion (*stealing* says "moving unperceived") and relevant (a breeze both delivers odors and carries odors away).

Before going on, I want to pause for another venture into more general comment.

I am obviously suggesting that the various unnoticed vagaries and anomalies of this first scene are, though undeniably unnoticed, nonetheless efficient factors in our experience of the lines—that the enrichment provided by the manifold kinds of incoherence in this coherent whole is felt. That assertion cannot be proved, of course, but two facts of lines 5–8 and their critical history strike me as evidence for my case. First, unlike several much more questionable elements of the speech, the word *sound* has been a crux. People have wanted to change it to "south" (meaning "south wind") or "sough" (meaning "sigh"). Reasoning the obvious needlessness and injustice of emending *sound* is easy: *sound* is a simple metonomy, substituting effect (sound of a breeze) for cause (breeze); moreover, this passage is elaborately echoed in 2.3.50–53 (the "contagious breath" passage, where music, disease, and odor are reassociated in context of Toby's minidisquisition on synesthesia ["To hear by the nose, it is dulcet in contagion"]). I do, however, take the perseverance of editorial doubts about *sound that breathes* as significant. One of the curious things about opaque but efficiently clear passages in Shakespeare and elsewhere is that while they themselves often go unremarked, small rashes of unwarranted scholarly illumination break out in their vicinities.

The other fact of critical history that I want to point to here pertains to Orsino's *Enough, no more. / 'Tis not so sweet now as it was before.* That line and a half, made an identifiable unit both by logic and the rhyme in *more / before,* presents the first narratively pertinent event since Orsino's first imperatives: it is an event on a larger scale than the linguistic gymnastics I have been discussing; it presents graspable evidence for one of the two elements most often pointed to by commentators: that Orsino's mind is a very opal. I have not made a statistical count, but I think scornful characterizations of Orsino tie with adjectives praising the beauty of the verse as the commonest comments the scene has evoked. The critics seem almost to compete with one another to find contemptuous labels for Orsino and to outdo each other in scorning him (for instance, in his introduction to the 1965 Signet edition of *Twelfth Night,* Herschel Baker calls Orsino "a narcissistic fool"). I do not mean to imply that such attacks are unjust—just suspiciously shrill and urgent. I suggest that attacks on Orsino are what a psychologist might call acts of transference; vague uneasiness generated by the skittishness of the syntax becomes exaggerated discomfort with the character who speaks it. We note something wrong with Orsino, but not the "wrongness" of the sentence.

The wrongness of Orsino's next lines (lines 9–14) is extravagant, but, again, is only seen to be so in the unlikely event that it is closely examined. These lines too are effortlessly assimilable by a listener—are so, I think, both in the Folio punctuation and in the only slightly less bizarre texts that result when—as most editors do—editors substitute for the Folio's full stop after *sea* in line 11.

A very few editions have retained the Folio punctuation for line 11—among them the Signet (New York, 1965), and, awkwardly for my purposes, the text I have been following here, the

Pelican text. If line 11 is punctuated as the Folio punctuates it, lines 9–14 read as two independent assertions—roughly like this (the following mockup also retains the Folio's comma after *capacity* in line 10):

> O spirit of love, how quick and fresh art thou,
> That notwithstanding thy capacity,
> Receiveth as the sea. Nought enters there,
> ' Of what validity and pitch soe'er,
> But falls into abatement and low price
> Even in a minute.

The Folio punctuation could make *Receiveth* an error for "Receivest"; it suggests that the first of the Folio's two sentences be understood as "O spirit of love, how quick and fresh art thou that—notwithstanding thy capacity—receivest as the sea." Or—by retaining the full stop after *sea* in line 11, but ignoring the logic implied by the comma after *capacity* at the end of the previous line—one could isolate the word *notwithstanding* and leave *capacity* the receiver: "O spirit of love, how quick and fresh art thou that—notwithstanding [that is, even though thou art quick and fresh]—thy capacity receiveth as the sea." Cases could be made for the Folio punctuation and the inflectional revision it demands and for the modification by which *notwithstanding* stands logically alone as an elliptic reference to the preceding exclamation. But they are irrelevant to my concerns here. It is the effectively standard editorially punctuated reading I care about: that is the one that has satisfied—seemed right to—generations of scholars, critics, and audiences ever since Nicholas Rowe emended the punctuation in 1714. These are the lines as punctuated by Rowe and the majority of editors since:

> O spirit of love, how quick and fresh art thou,
> That, notwithstanding thy capacity
> Receiveth as the sea, nought enters there,
> Of what validity and pitch soe'er,
> But falls into abatement and low price,
> Even in a minute.

Notwithstanding the ease with which it is assimilated, the re-punctuated sentence is a chimera. Its head is an exclamation: *O spirit of love, how quick and fresh art thou.* As the words are heard, *quick* has to mean "lively"—"sprightly," in fact—and *fresh* has to mean practically the same thing: "vigorous," "youthful." The trunk of the sentence starts out to be its tail: the word *that* obviously means "who" or "which" and introduces a justification of the exclamation. However, the forward progress of the sentence is delayed by an ostentatiously logical reservation: *notwithstanding thy capacity receiveth as the sea. Notwithstanding* is a logical gesture, but its action is ultimately illogical. Up to this point, the modification meshes with the logic of the clause it interrupts: "how quick and fresh art thou, who, though you are sealike in one respect . . ." The modification has, however, altered the senses of *quick* and *fresh:* the notion of capacity recurs to the food metaphor and activates the senses "keen" and "hungry" for *quick* and *fresh.* The change in the senses of *quick* and *fresh* thus asserts an extralogical pertinence of this sentence to the preceding lines. A second later, the word *sea* invokes the senses *quick* and *fresh* have as "water" words, words indicating the quality of water—specifically, water that is not saline, is not seawater; and—since the essential equation is between *the spirit of love* and *the sea*—the simile suddenly but perfectly contradicts the now relevant aqueous sense of *how quick and fresh art thou.* The semantic meanderings of *quick* and *fresh* thus at once give a sound of rightness to the sentence *and* render it nonsensical.

During the complex ideational process by which *quick* and *fresh* transmogrify, the idea of *capacity,* which is the focus of the phrase *notwithstanding thy capacity receiveth as the sea,* temporarily becomes the focal idea of the sentence at large; and the lines continue as if the word *That,* the first word of line 10, had never been heard, as if there were no syntactical-logical link between line 9 and line 10, and as if *nought* in line 11 were—as in fact it is in the Folio punctuation—the subject of an independent clause, *as if* line 9 had ended with a full logical stop ("O spirit of love, how quick and fresh art thou!")—and line 10 had begun with "Notwithstanding."

Note that I am not suggesting that we fail to hear the word *that* or fail to acknowledge the syntactical unity between line 9 and the lines the word *that* tacks to it. I am suggesting something more complex: that the length and ideational bulk of *notwithstanding thy capacity receiveth as the sea*—a modifying gesture under cover of which, by the way, we easily adapt to the idea of a *spirit,* the sealike *spirit of love,* as a place—invite us to forget the clearly marked logical nature of the sentence's beginning and to hear its conclusion as an independent entity: "Nought enters there but falls into abatement and low price."

The improbable annotator who noticed that the lines as we are used to hearing them can be demonstrated to be incomprehensible might plausibly, but foolishly, pacify that paradox momentarily by decreeing the word *That* in line 10 to mean not "which" but "to such an extent that": "so quick and fresh that. . . ." Such an explanation would solve the undeniable, undeniably invisible syntactical problem, but would do nothing for the logic. The explanation is a benevolent lie and an inefficient one: "How quick and fresh art thou—so quick and fresh that, notwithstanding thy capacity receiveth as the sea, nought enters there . . . that does not fall in value." Why should the power of the sealike spirit of love to convert its contents to flotsam and jetsam testify to its own quickness and freshness?

No matter how one may—after the fact—contrive to include the word *That* in the logic of the sentence, I suggest that what actually happens is that listeners altogether forget the syntactic signal of the word *That*—just as they forget the quickness and freshness for which the *spirit of love* was initially celebrated. The logical force of the next word, the word *notwithstanding,* comes finally to pertain only to one of the significances that the phrase *quick and fresh* takes on as the lines progress: "keen and hungry"; and thus the logical force of *notwithstanding* vanishes almost as completely as the logical force of the word *That.*

Unless one insists that *quick* and *fresh* have meant only "keen" and "hungry," the phrase *notwithstanding thy capacity receiveth as the sea*—a standard *concessio,* a gesture of simultaneous acknowledgement and dismissal—does not ultimately dismiss the facts it admits. The two-and-a-half-line assertion beginning *nought enters there* is altogether consonant with the idea of infinite capacity, the idea the word *notwithstanding* presents to us as contrary (though negligible) evidence—evidence for doubting the validity of the assertion that *nought enters there . . . but falls into abatement and low price.* Nonetheless—although (a) *abatement* and *low price* present a contrasting complement to *quick* and *fresh,* and although (b) the fact that the *spirit of love* has become a geographically imagined place (into which anything one falls in love with may fall, thereupon falling in price as well) is worth exclamation, and although (c) the fact that *nought enters there of what validity* (weight) *and pitch* (height) *soe'er* that does not shrink in size and value is itself exclamatory in substance—lines 11–14 have no logical relation to line 9, *O spirit of love, how quick and fresh art thou,* the exclamation that ostensibly occasioned them.

If the act of comprehending these lines ultimately results in the understanding I describe, why do we tolerate them in passage and tolerate them so casually that even editors let them pass— justly let them pass—unquestioned and unjustified? I think at least part of the answer lies in this: the logic signaled by the word *notwithstanding* does indeed reach satisfactory, though momentary, completion. *Nought enters there* is potentially—and, for the instant before the syntactic metamorphoses engendered by the syntactically unnecessary modification set in motion by *of what validity and pitch soe'er,* is in fact—complete. In the course of lines 9–14 a logically meaningful assertion is briefly audible (this again is the now virtually standard Rowe punctuation):

> O spirit of love, how quick and fresh art thou,
> That, notwithstanding thy capacity
> Receiveth as the sea, nought enters there.

That temporarily extant proposition makes exactly the use of its materials that the *notwithstanding* construction calls for: "even though *x* is true, something contrary to the attendant probabilities of that fact is also true"—"even though your capacity is infinite, nothing fills it." That proposition also has shadowy and paradoxical pertinence to the traditional courtly love situation in which the frustrated lover pleads with his beloved who, although made for love, will admit no male into her vagina (her "nought").

The proposition, though proper to two distinct genres—the syntactic and the substantive—is *only* generically satisfactory. Whatever Orsino may be telling us about the *spirit of love,* and however he may imagine that spirit physically, he cannot here be telling us that the *spirit of love* is isolated. However, before a question can form in a listener's or reader's mind, the potentially complete sentence continues—thus promising to reveal a logic we will recognize as appropriate to the facts it treats. The sentence continues in a construction that, by its kind, acknowledges that an audience to the proposition it augments may feel that that proposition needs justification: *of what validity and pitch soe're.*

The addition also starts a transformation in the proposition for which it seems to be supporting bluster: the *of what . . . soe're* construction does not idiomatically present hyperbolic testimony to the speaker's conviction of the total truth of the unlikely assertion his sentence has so far made; what is called for for that purpose is some Renaissance equivalent of such a phrase as "of any kind at all." The *of what . . . soe're* construction is, however, a logical neutral zone, a buffer between phrases that assert rather than modify; the construction provides a moment in which our minds can coast upon generic assumptions and gears can shift silently. Here our minds shift into place for the *nought . . . but* construction—the "nothing that does not" construction.

If what I say is true is true indeed, then the momentarily full stop after *nought enters there* satisfies the expectations generated by the *notwithstanding* construction; and *of what validity and pitch soe're* neutralizes our probable response to the questionable proposition conveyed in the momentarily perfect, but only momentarily extant, *notwithstanding* construction. Now, at the beginning of line 13, the word *But* fulfills the new syntax generically promised by line 12, and does so at the same time that—also by generic means—it assures us that the sentence was just as aware as we were that there was something factually dubious about the propositions that nothing at all enters the sealike *spirit of love.*

What I am suggesting is that listeners or readers deal satisfactorily with so many logics on the way to what is substantively the most important verb of the sentence, the word *falls,* that the process overwhelms the large illogic of the whole—an illogic that would impinge on their consciousnesses if the sentence were not layered with so many other logics.

The verb *falls,* by the way, has strong idiomatic credentials for its rightness in a sentence about falling in love—even though its particular function in the particular sentence is to assist in a proposition to which we do not accede.

The last line and a half of Orsino's first speech is a summary emblem of most of what I have been saying about the whole: *So full of shapes is fancy / That it alone is high fantastical.* Those words can be paraphrased, as Coleridge paraphrased them, as a play on two senses of *fancy:* "So full of shapes is love [fancy], that it alone is preeminently capable of making images [of fancying]." The paraphrase, however, is necessary only to explain what it is one has understood from the sentence, a sentence urgently and self-evidently true the moment it is heard—even though one does not know precisely what in particular it asserts. The certain but ungrasped core assertion is variously supported—supported by the confirming gesture of the pregnant polyptoton in *fancy . . . fantastical;* supported by the significant feel of *full of shapes* paired with *alone;* supported by echoes of preceding locutions (the word *that,* the ideational relevance of *full* to the capacity of the sea, and the phonetic relevance of *full* to *fall* [line 4], *falls* [13] and perhaps to the pertinent, heard, but unsaid word "false" [compare Sonnet 124.6]); and supported by the pertinence of the commonest meaning of *fantastical,* a term of abuse for "a fantastic," "*un fantastico,*" an affected, capricious, show-off.

That line and a half is also emblematic of the whole in that the phrase *so full of shapes is fancy,* the second half of line 14, modifies the lines that precede it (". . . falls into abatement and low price / Even in a minute—so full of shapes is fancy") and is also the opening element of a new assertion.

Anyone familiar with the contexts and expectations the act of academic criticism brings with it might see a direction for my line of argument, a kind of conclusion that has often been—and here could be—a justification and a satisfying product for stylistic analysis. As I have described them, the sentence structures of Orsino's first speech are indeed opal-like. Their syntactic sea changes can, in short, be justly called imitative of, and correlative to, the skittish mentality of Orsino, their variously fantastic speaker. Although it may well be that the quality of our experience of lines that operate in multiple logics and drift from one logic to another in passage is indeed *a* source of the disproportionately vehement and nearly universal critical contempt for Orsino and of our strong sense of his instability, I am, as I suspect we all are, suspicious of such neat critical revelations.

Moreover, I have my eye on larger, more nebulous, less immediately satisfying, but more essential conclusions. I am concerned here not so much with these lines as clues to Orsino as I am with the process of experiencing them. To return, for instance, to the word *surfeiting* in line 2, successive signals specify three identities for the surfeiter: the speaker (the "I" implied in *Give me*), his appetite for music, and his infatuation. The three fuse in the sentence, which is thus a quasi-physical working embodiment of the traditional hyperbolic conceits in which a lover is "all love"—is his appetite, is his desires. One could call the syntactic fusion of the surfeiter's identities a metaphor for a lover's confused state of mind, but it is a metaphor that, unlike the food metaphor in line 1, does not feel like a metaphor, does not

feel like a needed, modifying, remedial act of explanatory clarification. Since the sentence sounds like simple, single-minded
exposition, it effectively makes an unsimplified and unsimplifi-
able confusion into a simple coherent fact.

A similarly insistent but similarly uneasy union of disjointed
elements occurs a few lines later, when Orsino's heart, his dear
beloved, a hart (a male deer), hounds pursuing it, and Orsino's desires chase themselves in a circle (lines 16–24). The exchange on
the topic of hunting, however, does not lend itself to traditional,
speciously comfortable critical ceremonies in which style is declared to be imitative and informative. That exchange is also a
purer instance of clear nonsense:

> CURIO: Will you go hunt, my lord?
> DUKE: What, Curio?
> CURIO: The hart.
> DUKE: Why, so I do, the noblest that I have.
> O, when mine eyes did see Olivia first,
> Methought she purged the air of pestilence.
> That instant was I turned into a hart,
> And my desires, like fell and cruel hounds,
> E'er since pursue me.
>
> (16–24)

The potential crisis comes in line 19, specifically at the word
have. Why should Orsino hunt what he has? More important,
why do we not worry? If we did worry, a little strictly legitimate
crushing would make the lines bow to us. One could quiet oneself by suggesting that Orsino's "I do [hunt]" means "I do hunt
with," explaining "hunt" in the always rare—and here unpro-
voked—sense "to exercise" (as in "I hunt my hounds regularly
from the age of six months"). Or one could convince oneself
that Orsino's response works from the conceit by which "his
true love hath his heart, and he has hers."

But no parachute to rationality will effectively make this exchange logical or—and this is vital—make it *feel il*logical as it is

heard or make it feel in need of explication. As far as I know, only one commentator has commented at all on the real but ordinarily impalpable illogic of the lines. In 1901, in his New Variorum edition, Horace Howard Furness said this: "For the sake of the threadbare pun on *hart* and *heart,* the Duke gets his metaphor confused. In [line 19], he hunts his heart, the noblest part of him; in [line 21], he is himself the hart and his desires hunt him." Most editors, however, blandly annotate the exchange on hunting in one or another variations of this confidently concise note by the New Arden editors (1975): "For the hart/heart quibble (common in Shakespeare), cf. 4.1.58. Similar allusions to the story of Actaeon's transformation by Diana (Ovid, *Metamorphoses,* III.138 ff.) as typifying hopeless passion, were common: cf. Daniel, *Delia,* Sonnet 5." In context of the present microscopic exercise, the New Arden note may seem insufficient, but in practice it is altogether sufficient. For a modern student reading the note, for a modern scholar able to write it, and for Shakespeare's contemporaries, the well-known tracks of a traditional conceit and the appropriate and appropriately commonplace mythological filigree work make a listener superior to expository logic. The action of the lines is assumed to be what our generic expectations call for, what the habitual activities of the hart/heart pun and the mythological analogy make them. We do not notice what Orsino says; we hear what he must be saying. We listen to nonsense as if it were sense.

The last two speeches of scene 1 continue to exercise our capacities for ignoring evidence and responding instead to the dictates of contextual probability. Our capacity for hearing what is silly as solemn, what is solemn as silly, what is base as noble is akin to our capacity to hear sense as nonsense, and Valentine's speech (lines 25–33) provides an example. In answer to Orsino's "How now? What news from her?", Valentine says:

> So please my lord, I might not be admitted,
> But from her handmaid do return this answer:

> The element itself, till seven years' heat,
> Shall not behold her face at ample view;
> But like a cloistress she will veilèd walk,
> And water once a day her chamber round
> With eye-offending brine: all this to season
> A brother's dead love, which she would keep fresh
> And lasting in her sad remembrance.

Valentine's description of Olivia's lifestyle is demonstrably, but *only* demonstrably, comic—is demonstrably, but not efficiently, comic. Consider the image of Olivia dutifully walking her appointed daily rounds like a nun circling a cloister or following the stations of the cross and, like a gardener with a watering can, systematically dampening her parlor every day. Also potentially comic is the grotesque suggestion of curing meat, salting down dead flesh to preserve it from decay, that inheres in *all this to season a dead brother's love, which she would keep fresh and lasting.* But the speech has never evoked laughter: we respond to its manner rather than incidentals of its matter.

Scene 1 ends with what is probably its extreme exhibition of our ability to override linguistic signals on our way to easy comprehension. This is the last speech, Orsino's response to Valentine's report on Olivia:

> O, she that hath a heart of that fine frame
> To pay this debt of love but to a brother,
> How will she love when the rich golden shaft
> Hath killed the flock of all affections else
> That live in her; when liver, brain, and heart,
> These sovereign thrones, are all supplied, and filled
> Her sweet perfections with one self king.
> Away before me to sweet beds of flowers;
> Love-thoughts lie rich when canopied with bow'rs.
>   (34–42)

In the third-from-last line of the scene, the phrase *Her sweet perfections* is syntactically free-floating. Is the phrase appositive to the three "sovereign thrones"? Does it modify a noun phrase extrapolated from the verb and thus say that the acts of supplying and filling will perfect her and, thus, are *her . . . perfections*? The word *perfections* does relate to the idea of completeness and to the idea that Olivia is exquisite, but no gloss or punctuation can worry the phrase into the grammatical logic of the sentence. Rather, *her sweet perfections* so obviously relates to the general context that it is hard to believe that *some* gloss or punctuation cannot be found to demonstrate that the sentence is as clear in grammatical fact as in effect.

I have so far dwelt principally on the syntactic illogic of scene 1 and with the way syntactic gestures (like the one made by the word *notwithstanding* in line 10) make the speech sound logically coherent when its coherence actually derives from substantively incidental patterning factors. I have mentioned a few of those factors in passing (for instance, the echo of *and so die* in *dying fall*).

The variety and number of others is astounding—not least astounding because they do not call attention to themselves. Some are simple—like *die/dying*—and local. Some are simple and reach out further—like the ideas of music and food in the first sentence, their echo in *sweet* as an atrophied taste metaphor applied to *sound* in line 5, the mere repetition of *sweet* in line 8, the ideational reprise of sweetness and loss of sweetness in the idea of seasoning something to keep it fresh in lines 31 and 32, and finally in the *sweet beds of flowers* in the last two lines of the scene. Those last lines also echo the *bank of violets* breathed upon by the *sweet sound* back in line 5. One could go on with the list indefinitely by, for example, pointing to the link the topic of disease makes between the first speech (where *sicken* occurs in line 3) and the exchange about hunting (where *purged* and *pestilence* occur in line 21)—or to the vague echo of the hunting passage in Orsino's lines about Olivia's heart and Cupid's *rich golden shaft* (36–38).

Valentine's speech (25–33), the one substantial speech in the scene that is not spoken by Orsino, is directly related to the governing topic of the whole but contrasts with the rest of the scene merely because Valentine speaks it. The news Valentine brings Orsino and the expository service he performs for us come clothed in phonetic and ideational echoes of Orsino's speeches. In line 25, *I might not be admitted* is an ideational echo of *nought enters there* in line 11. *Return* (26) echoes *turned into a hart* (22). *Behold her face at ample view* (28) echoes *when mine eyes did see Olivia first* (20). The first syllable of *cloistress* (29) echoes the essential idea of lines 1–3 (the word *cloyment* actually appears in 2.4.98, during a reprise of this scene and its language: "their love may be called appetite, / No motion of the liver but the palate, / That suffers surfeit, cloyment, and revolt; / But mine is all as hungry as the sea / And can digest as much"). *Water, brine,* and the sound of the first syllable of *season* (30–31) variously echo the *sea* simile in line 11. The word *season,* as a sound that in another context could indicate time of year, echoes *seven years' heat* earlier in Valentine's speech. And the sense of *to season* actually operative in context of line 31 (namely "to preserve, as one preserves meat by salting") echoes the food metaphor of lines 1–3 and the idea of decay in lines 9–14. *A brother's dead love* (which, because the word *dead* effectively acts twice [modifying both *brother* and *love*], is comparable in its physics to the more complex double action of *stealing* in line 7) echoes the metaphoric uses of *die* in lines 3 and 4 and the idea of falling *into abatement and low price* in line 13. The word *dead* and the word *fresh,* the two adjectives in line 32, relate complexly to the word *quick* and the word *fresh* in line 9, and the phrase *fresh / And lasting,* which runs across lines 32 and 33, relates in other complex ways to the variously similar unit *quick and fresh* in line 9 (as *validity and pitch* [in line 12] and *abatement and low price* [in line 13] did earlier).

A network of phonetic, ideational, and potential-but-unexercised ideational rhymelike links spreads out from the word *fall,* its sound, sounds that resemble it, its sense, its potential senses, their homonyms, their cognates, their synonyms, and their antonyms. The noun *fall* (which itself reaches back toward the topic abruptly discontinued after *sicken and so die*) occurs in line 4 as a musical term meaning "cadence." In line 13 the verb *falls* occurs in a standard metaphoric extension of its essential, physical sense (but in a construction where *enters there* and the syllabic flow from the preposition *into* to the not-quite-colloquially used word *abatement* momentarily activates the literal sense of *falls into:* "falls into a" points toward a noun indicating some *thing*—a ditch, *a* hole, *a* mire—that can be fallen into); *falls* is bracketed on one side by *pitch* in line 12 (where, though used metaphorically, it indicates height, but where its locally dormant musical sense is a semantic mute witness to a oneness of this part of speech with the first eight lines)—and on the other side by *low* (used metaphorically) later in line 13. In line 14, *full* in *so full of shapes is fancy* echoes the sound of *fall* (and, in a semantically irrelevant way, also echoes the idea of satiety and gluttony in lines 1–3). In line 15 *high* relates to the idea of falling, much as *pitch* and *low* did. In line 23, the hounds are *fell* and *cruel,* but the sound and a locally irrelevant potential sense of *fell* relate to *fall.* Phonetically the pattern made by the noun *fall* (4), the verb *falls* (13), *full* (14), and *fell* (23) culminates in *filled* in the last speech of the scene, where Orsino imagines the time

> when the rich golden shaft
> Hath killed the flock of all affections else
> That live in her; when liver, brain, and heart,
> These sovereign thrones, are all supplied, and filled. . . .

The casual rhyme in *killed* and *filled* presents a capsule summary of the first three lines of the play and is a rough common denominator for a scene that has worked with ideas of filling and killing from the very beginning.

The incidental topics of this scene recur as incidental or primary to all the scenes that follow it: music, gluttony, disease, hunting (in a recurring concern for finding people and in a complex alliteration of various ideas of following), dogs, payment (of debts and for services), sibling relationships (of course), the word *alone* (and its significances and its etymological roots and their significances), achieved or frustrated entrance, the sea, seeing, and onstage judgements of onstage performances. Those incidental topics are to the play as some of them—and some of the sounds that allude to them, and the sounds of some of the words incidental to discussing them—are to scene 1: like the syntactic gestures, repetitions, rhythms, and phonetic and ideational puns and rhymes that can give a speech a formal coherence that effortlessly substitutes for a logical one, the recurring topics of the play make it feel pregnant with profound significance that critics acknowledge by their respect for *Twelfth Night* but never do—and, I think, never could—deliver to us.

What is more to the point here, the action of perceiving a sentence as two things at once—what is there and what the listener perceives to be there—recurs throughout the play. Take, for example, the subscription of the Maria-Olivia letter: *She that would alter services with thee* (2.5.145). That subscription has, as far as I know, never been glossed. It needs no gloss. *Why* it needs no gloss, however, is fascinating. Considering our everyday, working assumptions about the relationship of language and understanding, it is amazing that this obviously simple assertion *is* obviously simple. Try to make another sentence in which "to alter" and "to exchange" are synonyms. Just try. *She that would alter services with thee* is made meaningful by its context, informed by a context relevant to "an altar"—an altar in a church—sustained by the relevance of both the liturgical and sexual senses of "service," and smoothed over by an implied logic that says that—since "to exchange" and "to change" are synonyms, and "to alter" and "to change" are synonyms—"to exchange" and "to alter" must also be synonyms. (For a similar but cruder example of semantic double-dealing, see Feste's use of the word *welkin* ["sky"] to mean "proper sphere of action": *Who you are and what you would are out of my welkin. I might say 'element,' but the word is overworn* [3.1.55–57]; *element* can mean "air" and can therefore replace *welkin,* but that does not make *welkin* a universally available substitute for all senses of *element.*)[3]

After scene 1, disjunctions between what is signified and what is understood from the signal become common on the stage. The audience is often conscious that a character ignores obvious signals in the words he hears. Consider, for instance, Viola's riddling *I am all the daughters of my father's house, / And all the brothers too,* which Orsino lets pass—apparently because Viola diverts his attention by suddenly swerving back to Orsino's obsession: *Sir, shall I to this lady?* (2.4.119–21). In some cases the contextual signals are so strong that members of an audience can easily join an onstage listener in taking the generically evident import of a sentence for its actual substance; the best example is *save I alone* in Viola's answer to Olivia when, as the boy bachelor Cesario, she swears she will never love any woman: *I have one heart, one bosom, and one truth, / And that no woman has; nor never none / Shall mistress be of it, save I alone* (3.1.155–57).

The relation of what I have said about an audience's—about our—superiority to the "hard" evidence of the language of

---

3. In the following passage (2.3.50–52), "contagious" in "contagious breath" may be like "alter" in 2.5.145 and "welkin" in 3.1.58; Feste has just sung "o mistress mine":

ANDREW: A mellifluous voice, as I am true knight.

TOBY: A contagious breath.

ANDREW: Very sweet and contagious, i' faith.

"Contagious"—which means rather the opposite of what context suggests Toby wants it to mean and which is not known elsewhere as a synonym for "attractive"—is a synonym for "catching," and "catching" was presumably already capable of saying "attractive" (*OED*'s first example of the adjective in that sense is from 1654, but "to catch" meaning "to charm," "to attract," "to captivate" goes back at least to Chaucer. *OED* [s.v. "to catch," IX: 37] cites *Henry VIII* 2.3.76–77: "Beauty and honor in her are so mingled / That they have caught the King"). Note that as soon as Feste enters the scene, Toby proposes singing a catch and that, in the next speech after Andrew's "Very sweet and contagious, i'faith," Toby repeats his suggestion and that the ensuing catch occupies everyone's attention for most of the balance of the scene.

Twelfth Night relates so obviously to the behavior of the characters in the story that there is little need to illustrate the parallel.
The equation in my title probably does the job by itself. I suspect that the intended implications of "The Audience as Malvolio" are now clear. Those implications are both variously just
and variously unjust. My title singles out Malvolio as the preeminent example of a character who mistakes evidence.

What is most interesting in this context is that many audiences, some students, and even some scholarly critics see Malvolio's self-delusion as a contributing factor in his acceptance of the
forged letter and its contents. The credentials of and in that letter are awfully convincing. The letter gives Malvolio plentiful
and persuasive evidence that Olivia loves him—much stronger
evidence than Viola has when she says "She loves me sure . . .
I am the man" (2.2.21–24). Viola just happens to be correct.
Sherlock Holmes himself would accept Maria's letter as a love
letter from Olivia to Malvolio. Malvolio's self-delusion is a factor in our initial acceptance of the justice of the deception, but,
when he later makes a fool of himself, he does so because he has
been made a fool *of,* tricked, not because he is a fool. Malvolio,
however, *is* a self-deluded fool, and that fact colors and confuses
our understanding of cause and effect in the letter scene. Similarly, we are inclined to think it ridiculous that Malvolio should
even imagine that Olivia might love a self-important servant. On
the other hand, although we may find Olivia ridiculous in loving a woman dressed as a boy, we accept the idea that she could
be infatuated with a genuine Cesario—with a self-important
servant. (The parallel between Malvolio and Cesario is, in fact,
carefully spelled out in 3.1.92–114; in particular, note the interaction of line 111—*Myself, my servant, and, I fear me, you*—with
the preceding lines about Cesario's and Orsino's identities as servants. Note too that Cesario is notably and persistently "surly
with servants"; see the exchange with Valentine that opens 1.4
and Cesario's manner with Maria in 1.5 and with Malvolio in
the opening lines of 2.1—where Cesario is as gratuitously
haughty as Malvolio is.)

If one wanted to draw a lesson from *Twelfth Night,* the one to draw would be the one Viola and Sebastian—and only Viola and Sebastian—seem to learn in the course of the play: do not let overpowering evidence overpower you—the lesson they could be said to respond to when they perform their minuet of supportive evidence in 5.1.233–40 (*My father had a mole upon his brow / And so had mine*)—supporting evidence for a truth self-evident to us, a truth we are impatient to hear them acknowledge. If one drew that moral, then the relationship between the characters in *Twelfth Night* and their audience, which so often listens to context rather than content, would be like that between "the picture of we three" (a picture of *two* donkeys or—sometimes—a picture of *two* fools) and its beholder.

But I do not want to draw that moral (or, for that matter, any moral). I do not want to draw that moral because that moral does not yield itself up; it must be drawn. To draw that moral one would have to be a jackass.

Audiences to *Twelfth Night* do not, and therefore should not, feel like fools looking at fools, or jackasses looking at jackasses. In fact audiences feel good. Audiences do not just laugh a lot (as they do watching *Comedy of Errors* or *Merry Wives*); all theatrical and critical evidence suggests that audiences feel actively good. I submit that, although common sense says that the reason *Twelfth Night* is a joyous and liberating play is that so many of its characters and events are joyous and free, common sense is wrong. I submit that much of our joy in *Twelfth Night* derives from triumphant mental experiences like our modest but godlike achievement in comprehending scene 1. The processes the language of scene 1 sets free are not unusual to ordinary verbal experience. Consider again an example I cited when I talked about the Jonson poems: the current American idiom "I could care less," meaning "I could *not* care less." The triumph of understanding that idiom is of the same sort as those evoked by the various comparable but more complex constructions I have talked about here. What is special about the mental triumphs that the language and the action of *Twelfth Night* enable us to perform is their number, their concentration, and their variety. If the act of comprehending "I could care less" is comparable to doing a mental somersault from the high trapeze, then our easy, graceful, matter-of-fact acceptance of the two-and-a-half-hour experience of *Twelfth Night* is comparable to doing the triple over all three rings of a three-ring circus at once and being one's own catcher.

2 · GETTING INTO THE SPIRIT OF *TWELFTH NIGHT*: THE AUDIENCE AS MALVOLIO AGAIN

In subtitling my discussion of 1.1 "The Audience as Malvolio," I relied on context to define "like Malvolio" as "prone to take signs for substance." There is, however, a chronologically primary other implication in the idea of being like Malvolio. Audiences to *Twelfth Night* are not, I think, ever really "like Malvolio" in the sense in which that label says "petty, punctilious, formal, mean-spirited, and generally out of step with the festive freedom the play celebrates, demonstrates, and generates." I do suggest, however, that as audience to *Twelfth Night,* we are regularly—if momentarily—discomfited by a recurrent need to fight back fleeting urges toward being like Malvolio—being like the character in the play whose presence makes getting into the festive spirit an issue for the characters. I think we often catch ourselves feeling distaste for festival frolic, and I for one catch myself fussing pettily about details I neither want to bother with nor want to admit to being small-minded enough even to notice.

In talking about *Twelfth Night* I have been, as I was when I talked about the Gettysburg Address and "On My First Daughter," principally concerned with manifestations of a phenomenon whereby listeners and readers casually and effortlessly perceive sense in texts that—that *therefore*—"contain" the sense they deliver but that can be demonstrated to be nonsense. Now, however, I want to consider the effects and aesthetic value of comparable phenomena in *Twelfth Night:* ones whereby for various reasons listeners and readers feel obliged to dismiss or deny inconvenient responses that the play evokes—phenomena whereby one's mind says "Nonsense" to its own responses.

This new topic, which presents a variation on simultaneous rightness in one dimension and wrongness in another, is peculiarly difficult to discuss responsibly. I will back and fill elaborately on the way to making clear what I am and what I am not saying. For instance, the rejections I referred to respond to a sense of discrepancy between our responses and those that we feel are expected of us. To speak of responses expected of us—to speak of responses that are appropriate (or, to use a term generally crucial to *Twelfth Night,* suitable)—to talk about what we are "supposed" to think—is to implicate this discussion in the issue of authorial intention, and—since the whole idea of "getting into the spirit" of a play is meaningless except in reference to an audience's sense of audience obligation—I may reasonably rehearse some truisms about literary intentionality.

To begin with, although the New Critics of the 1940s and 1950s properly taught us the folly of importing theses about "the author's intent" into texts that do not of themselves betray—or show a capacity ever to have betrayed—that intent, it would also be folly to deny that a sense of authorial intent—or, better, a sense of a work's intent—is a constant of our experience of man-made objects. We infer intent from generic and contextual signals (in fact, we are surprised when we come on a mechanism that does not show its purpose or when we find ancient earthworks and cannot guess their purposes). We are particularly quick to assume intent for objects made of words, and we are at our quickest, most confident, and most casual when we do so for the closed, deliberate verbal objects we call literary.

Among the least remarked and most remarkable things about communication in language is our capacity to fill lacunae and correct errors in what we read and hear.[4] We routinely finish one another's sentences, furnish words for which a speaker is groping, recognize malapropisms, see that a child who says "tomorrow" when he means "yesterday" does in fact mean "yesterday," see that a "not" has been omitted before a verb in a newspaper, and perform any number of similar, almost always appropriate adjustments to things we hear and read. Our experience of the first scene of *Twelfth Night* is a series of less demanding, more complicated variations on the emendation process we go through when we assume a misprint or take the word for the deed in a malapropism. We can only do such things because we assume that what we hear and read makes sense. And sense is defined in relation to realities superior to the realities of the actual sentences we emend. We know those Platonic realities from contextual probabilities.

As I said, my concern in this second discussion of *Twelfth Night* is not with the circumstances and processes of the sorts of casual, confident adjustments we perform on a malapropism or an ellipsis. What concern me here are mirror images of such mental circumstances and processes. The circumstances that concern me here are ones that lead us to emend (or try to emend, or try to make ourselves feel that we have emended) our responses. And the processes now are ones wrought upon our responses, not upon the stimuli that evoke the responses. I mean to discuss only two examples of such circumstances. One example is brief and local: the mental circumstances generated in us by Fabian's and Feste's speeches just before Malvolio's *I'll be revenged on the whole pack of you* at the end of the play. The other is the mental circumstances repeatedly generated over the whole length of the play by demands for laughter that we as audience cannot easily meet.

---

4. E. H. Gombrich discusses the phenomenon as it occurs in our perceptions of the visual arts (*Art and Illusion,* rev. ed. [New York, 1961], 211–22). Later he briefly extends his comments to speech (232).

I will begin with—and spend most of the discussion on—the larger example, a relatively simple one, but one that is nonetheless very ticklish: audience response to Toby Belch's almost perfect incapacity to delight us with his constant, always strenuous efforts to be comical.

Before I get to my thesis about Toby, I want to say that, whereas audiences to comedies customarily give some conscious attention to measuring their satisfaction or want of satisfaction with the comic activity presented them, audiences to *Twelfth Night* have onstage company in doing so. From the play's sixth line—in which Orsino says that the music he has so praised *is not so sweet now as it was before*—evaluation of performance is a recurring theme of *Twelfth Night*. And specifically comic performances are more often evaluated than any other.

Such evaluation pops up casually—as, for instance, it does repeatedly in 2.3, the scene in which, within fewer than sixty lines of dialogue, Andrew volunteers his opinion that Feste was *in very gracious fooling* the previous night (when he spoke of *Pigrogromitus, of the Vapians passing the equinoctial of Queubus*), offers the general aesthetic proposition that nonsense *is the best fooling, when all is done,* and responds to Feste's favorable comments on Toby's comic form with *Ay, he does well enough if he be disposed, and so do I too. He does it with a better grace, but I do it more natural* (21–23, 28–29, 75–77).

A bit less casual, but also incidental, is Viola's soliloquy on Feste's trade (*This fellow is wise enough to play the fool. . . . This is a practice / As full of labor as a wise man's art* [3.1.58–64]). And, from one end of the play to the other, characters evaluate Feste's jokes and decide that the jokes are worth the tips he begs in exchange for them.

Up until Olivia's entrance at line 28, 1.5 is entirely taken up with a sort of audition by Maria: she tries out her skills as a jester, and Feste—the established professional—judges her efforts (*Apt, in good faith, very apt*). Then, as Olivia enters, Feste discusses good and bad wits: *Wit, an't be thy will, put me into good fooling. Those wits that think they have thee do very oft prove fools, and*

I that am sure I lack thee may pass for a wise man. For what says Quinapalus? 'Better a witty fool than a foolish wit' (29–33).

The instance of critical evaluation of comedy that is most vital to the events of *Twelfth Night* occurs about forty lines later and in reference to a particularly successful comic effort, Feste's proof that Olivia is a fool. She says, *What think you of this fool, Malvolio? Doth he not mend?* Malvolio thereupon speaks his first lines in the play: *Yes, and shall do till the pangs of death shake him. Infirmity, that decays the wise, doth ever make the better fool* and, after responses by Feste and Olivia, *I marvel your ladyship takes delight in such a barren rascal. I saw him put down the other day with an ordinary fool that has no more brain than a stone. Look you now, he's out of his guard already. Unless you laugh and minister occasion to him, he is gagged. I protest I take these wise men that crow so at these set kind of fools no better than the fools' zanies* (68–72, 78–84).

The reason for that lengthy preamble to my discussion of Toby's comedy is my desire to suggest that our difficulties with Toby are particularly pertinent to this play and more insistent than they would be in a play that did not itself so persistently dwell on the natures of satisfying and unsatisfying comedy. *Twelfth Night* is a play that puts a special kind of moral pressure on us to sympathize with Toby's brand of heavy, hearty jocularity and *also* presses us to measure the comic quotients of a succession of comic turns.

In essence, my thesis about Toby is as follows: (1) Toby is delightful by kind; that is to say that everything about him tells us (and presumably told the first audiences who met him) that he is a comic character (as many, many years of commentary have said, Toby is like Falstaff—a lovable swaggerer, a ne'er-do-well, a bluff, hearty eccentric, who, though we might elsewhere share his fellow characters' low opinion of him, commands our affection as long as he stays up there on the stage where he does not challenge the day-to-day moral economics of our practical experience); (2) although Toby is likeable by kind—is a theatrical commodity of a kind attractive to consumers—what he does and says fails to live up to the generic expectations he evokes: he is a funny character who is not funny; (3) we feel—and some-times succumb to—an urge to pretend to ourselves that we take appropriate pleasure from Toby's antics. (If my experience of the two is reliable, to be entertained by Toby is comparable to at-tending a New Year's Eve party: no one is having a good time; some people are pretending to enjoy themselves; everybody feels that he or she is somehow wanting in geniality and that it is at least vaguely shameful to be so.)

There are a lot of troubles with that thesis, and—because the thesis is more complicated than it sounds—there are several ap-parent difficulties that are only apparent. One of the real ones is that I might be wrong about Toby. There might be—or might once have been—someone somewhere who is or was amused by Sir Toby's strenuously comic lines and antics. Whereas the rest of us merely offer a dutiful cooperative chuckle now and again in observance of the generic obligations Toby brings with him, the chuckles of a genuinely delighted audience member would be simple, fresh, and involuntary.

I may indeed be wrong, but—although I surely exaggerate when I imply that *nobody* ever found Toby funny—I have rea-son to think not only that my response to Toby is not idiosyn-cratic but that it is usual. I base that belief on my experience of audiences to *Twelfth Night*. I have spent an unlikely percentage of my professional life watching audiences at performances of Shakespeare plays and listening to them. Such study, of course, is far from scientific (for instance, I suspect that when I observe audiences I am likely to read their responses in the only available light, the light of my own). Still, for what it is worth, let me of-fer what I hope will be more a reminder for people who have seen *Twelfth Night* repeatedly than a report of controlled field re-search. Audiences confronted with Sir Toby Belch sound as if they are trying to demonstrate to one another that they are hav-ing a very good time. Whole audiences—or, rather, working majorities of the whole—have the sound and feel of the small but vocal minority in all modern audiences to Shakespearean comedy that is composed of people who have recent or particularly scarring experience of a Shakespeare course and who laugh, as if on cue, at any reference at all to cuckolds' horns.

If one grants, however, that twentieth-century audiences are not amused by Toby, can one not assume that the audiences for whom Shakespeare wrote would have found him as delightful as he seems intended to be? In saying that Toby is not funny, am I not simply providing evidence for what everybody remembers being told in high school, namely that Shakespearean comedy is no longer funny, but once was? No. Moreover, both parts of that commonplace are dubious.

As for the first part, the percentage of Shakespearean comedy that is now inefficient is much smaller than the commonplace would suggest. Consider what a lot of genuine laughter one hears from Shakespearean audiences; consider audience responses to Rosalind's interviews with Phoebe, or to the wooing scenes in *The Taming of the Shrew* and *Henry V,* or to Lavatch's marriage plans in *All's Well That Ends Well,* or—in *Twelfth Night* itself—to Feste's proof that Olivia is a fool and to the letter scene and to plenty of other scenes, exchanges, and routines as well. The behavior of modern audiences suggests that most comic material in Shakespeare is still comic in its effect as well as in its kind and probably is not very different for us from what it was for its first audiences.

As to the second—and here more pertinent—part of the popular commonplace about Shakespearean comedy, in most situations where we are likely to make the assumption, it is probably valid to assume that those scenes and jokes that now lack power to amuse us once had that power. But that assumption is not, I think, universally valid and, in particular, is invalid with respect to most of the comedy of Sir Toby Belch. There is a difference between most of Toby's comedy and the sort of failed comedy that to us seems only unavailable and only unavailable because of the passage of time. I propose to discuss that difference at some length.

Leaving aside Toby's own particular brand of failed comedy, unfunny comedy in Shakespeare is of several sorts. Some of it just doesn't suit our tastes. For instance, much of the verbal comedy of *Love's Labor's Lost* is not to the taste of twentieth-century audiences (and may not have been to the taste of many sixteenth-century audiences), but, I think, we recognize it as good of its kind. With some help from editorial glosses on unfamiliar usages, we can see what the jokes are—even if we ourselves take no pleasure beyond the little that comes from having "solved" them.

Some Shakespearean comedy appears unimpaired by time but does not seem ever to have been much good. And yet we do get its jokes. Consider the "knock me here soundly" routine performed by Petruchio and Grumio (*The Taming of the Shrew,* 1.2.5–41). The exchange seems contrived and is prolonged beyond its power to please, but one does not feel that—given one's own personal tastes—one's response is deficient or other than it would have been had one been born in sixteenth-century London. The same seems true of the verbal wit of things like the "sheep"/"ship," "lost mutton"/"laced mutton" sequence in *The Two Gentlemen of Verona* (1.1.72–100).

Some of Shakespeare's inefficient comedy, however, does indeed seem to rest absolutely on shared knowledge to which modern audiences are not party and to which scholarship cannot make them party. One good example—one that occurs in the role of Toby Belch and is atypical of it—is his reference to *Mistress Mall's picture*. It occurs in Toby's speech of inordinate admiration for Andrew's dancing skills: *Wherefore are these things hid? Wherefore have these gifts a curtain before 'em? Are they like to take dust, like Mistress Mall's picture?"* (1.3.112–14). Toby seems to allude to some sort of lost anecdote—something that was for Shakespeare's contemporaries as "the curate's egg," and "I say it's spinach and I say the Hell with it," and "Ready when you are, C.B." are for us.[5] *Mistress Mall's picture* sounds like a reference to

---

5. The phrase "for us" is cavalier. The "us" in question is people my age and of my background. In fact, lots of educated English speakers—particularly

a lost anecdote of the limp sort collected in *A Hundred Merry Tales* and similar jest books (something on this order: an unlovely lady gives a merry young man her portrait; he puts a curtain over it so he won't have to look at it; she finds out; he nimbly excuses himself by saying that he feared it might get dusty). The allusion is probably irretrievable—and, since whatever energy it once had must have depended on casual familiarity, even if the reference were someday pinned down in *Notes and Queries,* the line could probably never be brought back to life either for readers or in the theater.

Some lost Shakespearean comedy *can* be revived in performance—brought to life, not footnoted by actors pointing to parts of one another's bodies and leering insistently. For instance, immediately after his reference to Mistress Mall's picture, Toby returns specifically to Andrew's abilities as a dancer: *Why dost thou not go to church in a galliard and come home in a coranto? My very walk should be a jig. I would not so much as make water but in a sink-a-pace* (1.3.114–17). The line about making water in a *sink*-a-pace is still funny and can be made twice as funny if the actor playing Toby pronounces *sink-a-pace* as, on insufficient evidence, I suspect an Elizabethan Englishman would have pronounced it:

Americans—will not know that "the curate's egg" refers to a *Punch* cartoon that showed a particularly meek-looking young curate breakfasting with a particularly imposing bishop; the bishop, noticing that the curate is not eating, inquires whether his egg is rotten; the abjectly courteous curate replies, "Only in parts." The second reference is to another cartoon about unwillingness to eat—a cartoon from the early days of *The New Yorker:* a woman is shown trying to get a small boy to eat his vegetable; the caption reads: "It's broccoli, darling." / "I say it's spinach, and I say the Hell with it." The last of the three references is to a joke about an especially elaborate and expensive shot for a movie extravaganza being made by Cecil B. De Mille—a shot that must be got perfectly in one take because the action involves blowing up the whole set. De Mille takes special care not to miss the shot. He arranges that the scene be photographed by three separate cameras. When the scene is over and the set is rubble, De Mille calls to the first cameraman and asks how the shot went. The answer is that everything went perfectly but that the film broke. The second cameraman reports that he forgot to take the cap off his lens. Then De Mille calls to his third cameraman, who cheerily shouts back, "Ready when you are, C. B."

"sink uh piss." [6] But, as far as I can see, the sink joke is the only one in Toby's role that is at all susceptible to scholarly enlivenment. In fact, the sink joke is just about the only effectively funny line Toby has. The speech I quoted contains both the exceptions to the rule for Toby's comic efforts: it has the one line that seems diminished by the passage of time, and it has the one funny line too.

The rest of Toby's part is a trial for an actor (actors can demonstrate talent playing Toby, but I have never known one to score a triumph in the role—never heard an audience get really excited about welcoming Toby back for the curtain call)—and a trial for audiences as well—a trial in which the play contrives to make them feel obliged to prove that they are not like Malvolio but are instead jovial and carefree like Toby. The big difference between our responses to nonamusing comedy in *Twelfth Night* and nonamusing comedy elsewhere in the Shakespeare canon is that in *Twelfth Night* our experience occurs in a context where to admit, even to oneself, that one is not reveling in the revelry of Toby Belch is tacitly to imply that one is spiritually wanting in the way that Malvolio is.

Like most Shakespearean comics, Toby has a few jokes that are simply weak. For instance, just before the "Mistress Mall"/ "sink-a-pace" speech, Andrew boasts that he *can cut a caper,* and Toby responds with *And I can cut the mutton to't* (1.3.108–9). The

6. My guess is that the *a* in the last syllable of *sink-a-pace* was pronounced on the model of such modern pronunciations as those of *a* in the final syllables of "furnace," "boniface," "preface," "palace," "solace," "Horace," "Christmas," "pirate" and "determinate." As to my insufficient evidence that "sink-a-pace" was pronounced in a way confusable with "sink-'o-piss"—I have only a scathing comment on Barnabe Barnes's infamous "urine" sonnet (a sonnet in which he grossly and comically overexploits the standard conceit by which a lover wishes he were his beloved's glove [as Romeo does in *Romeo and Juliet*], or lapdog, or whatever): Barnes's sonnet (63 in his sequence *Parthenophil and Parthenope* [1593]) proclaims his wish to be a glass of wine and to journey through his beloved's digestive system and emerge as urine. In 1596, in *Have with You to Saffron Walden,* Thomas Nashe, commenting on Barnes, says "or if you would have anie rymes to the tune of stink-a-pisse, he is for you" (Q2 verso).

wit of that response is wan, but it is genuine. The plays between the metaphoric and literal meanings of "to cut" and between "a capriole" and "a pickle" cannot provoke much mirth, but the natures and capacities of their limited physics are evident and comfortable. (The caper cutting joke is of the same kind as the better-meshed multiple pun in *in a sink-a-pace.* Just as the dance terms *cut* and *caper* also pertain in the culinary context introduced by *mutton,* so the word *in* [which, in relation to the context of dance, means "after the pattern of"—as it does in the phrases "go to church in a galliard" and "come home in a coranto"—and means "into" in relation to *make water*] and the three syllables of *sink-a-pace* generate a small but measurable thrill of mastery in the mind that perceives the neatness of the purely accidental coincidence of two related assertions within one phrase. The wit of the "sink-a-pace" joke is superior to that of the caper-cutting joke not in kind but because the introduction of mutton feels forced—does not feel like a lucky accident—and because the in-a-sink-a-pace joke is three layers deep.)[7]

Toby's typical foolery, however, is very different and falls as dead as the caper-cutting joke for very different reasons. Typically, Toby is as he is when two new characters, Sir Toby Belch and Maria, enter to begin the play's third scene and Toby says his first speech: *What a plague means my niece to take the death of her brother thus? I am sure care's an enemy to life* (1.3.1−2). That speech is a bully. By that I do not mean to say that Toby is a bully (although he is one), but that the *speech* is. It tells any audience familiar with stage morality that we are to recognize Toby as lovable and admirable (comparable bullying occurs at the first entrances of Little John and Friar Tuck in dramatizations of the Robin Hood stories and at the first entrances of heroes' comical sidekicks in B-grade western movies).

7. The three layers of sense in the joke are "urinate while hopping up and down in a frantic dance," "urinate into a sink," and "urinate into a sink of urine." (The gentle play between the two senses of *in*—"while performing" / "into"—comes close to making it reasonable to call the sink-a-pace line three-and-a-half jokes deep.)

When Maria responds by scolding him (*You must come in earlier o' nights. Your cousin, my lady, takes great exception to your ill hours*), Toby's second speech not only advertises *him* as comic but advertises itself as comic too: *Why, let her except before excepted* (6). What matters about that line is not that it is not funny but that it sounds as if one ought to find it so. Because *except before excepted* echoes a legal phrase, *exceptis excipiendis*—a legal phrase unfamiliar to modern audiences—readers of modern student editions can get not only the impression that the phrase was once as familiar as, say, "habeas corpus" but the impression that the reference was once amusing. I see no reason to suspect that Toby's allusion to the never-familiar Latin for "with the aforementioned exceptions" would ever have seemed apt—which is to say, would ever have seemed witty. It has no reference. It is funny only to the extent that pure nonsequitur is funny. This nonsequitur is not in fact pure (Toby does echo, and thus allude to, Maria's phrase *takes exception*), but it might as well be. Wit requires that its impertinence be balanced by equal, but previously unobserved, pertinence, and there is no such delightfully surprising pertinence here.

And there is none in Toby's next sally. Maria continues to scold:

MARIA: Ay, but you must confine yourself within the modest
　　　 limits of order.

　TOBY: Confine? I'll confine myself no finer than I am. These
　　　 clothes are good enough to drink in, and so be these
　　　 boots too. An they be not, let them hang themselves
　　　 in their own straps.

$$(7-12)$$

Toby's answer is comic in manner. The responses of editors testify to that. Editors treat the speech as it asks to be treated. For instance, in her notes for the Riverside Shakespeare (1974), Anne Barton reports that in his use of *confine* Toby is "quibbling on the sense 'dress.'" And the editors of the New Arden edition of *Twelfth Night* (1975) give this valiantly cooperative note on *Confine? I'll confine myself no finer than I am:* "another rejection of

Maria's advice, turning to a tipsy quibble whereby 'confine' is made to mean 'dress myself up.'" Less traditionally, but just as valiantly, C. T. Prouty tried this in the Pelican Shakespeare: "*finer:* both 'tighter' and 'better'" (rev. ed., 1969).

Lest I seem to mock those glosses or imply that I might do better or other than those editors, let me insist that I presented the foregoing sampler of editorial glosses on Toby's use of *confine* only to illustrate the proposition that the "confine" speech, like many others from Toby, successfully demands that one try to find more wit in it than it delivers. In my experience, audiences in the theater make their own variation on the same sort of dutiful effort that editors make in annotations like the ones I quoted. Audiences do so for the "confine" speech, and they do so for a succession of similarly pallid, similarly demanding lines—lines like *A plague o' these pickle-herring* (1.5.115)—all the way through Toby's long, verbose tenure on the stage.

The role of Sir Toby Belch is the longest in *Twelfth Night:* by the count Marvin Spevack gives in volume 1 of his *Complete and Systematic Concordance* [Hildesheim, 1968], Toby has 364 lines (16.5 percent of the play) to 339 (13 percent) for Viola, 318 (12 percent) for Feste, 313 (12 percent) for Olivia, and 286 (11 percent) for Malvolio. I mention those figures because the relative length of Toby's part is usually a surprise to people (it certainly was to me). That sense of surprise suggests that Toby does not have the impact that the size of his role would lead one to expect.

A second reason for mentioning those figures is that the size of the role provides a probably unnecessary excuse for not prolonging my efforts to demonstrate that Toby's comedy misfires and misfires in the way I say it does. Since literary analyses designed to illustrate failure are even more tedious and even more dubious than other literary analyses, I will probably be forgiven if I simply declare that what is true of Toby's first two speeches is generally true of his others.

Before I move on from my thesis about Toby—and as a first step to introduce the larger thesis to which my comments on

Toby are auxiliary—I should dispel an assumption that has probably been invited by what I have so far said. It would be reasonable but wrong to assume that, having spent so long insisting that an audience's experience of Toby is of frustration—is an experience in which one feels that one should be delighted and is unable to be so—I must be demonstrating a flaw in *Twelfth Night*. That assumption is partially valid. I do indeed dislike the experience of Toby's sweaty efforts to be amusing—an experience that, as I watch the play, I would prefer to be spared. But that assumption is also vitally invalid. I think that *Twelfth Night*—a play that, in my opinion, is one of the most beautiful man-made things in the world—is better, is a more delightful experience, for the mildly, casually, but undeniably *dis*pleasing experiences it includes within an audience's experience of the whole.

That last proposition probably sounds bizarre—more bizarre, sillier, and more wantonly ingenious than I think it is in fact. The idea that a work of art can be better for elements in it that its audiences dislike is an idea that all but begs for dismissal by caricature ("Well, Byron's *Manfred* must be a very great work indeed: there's nothing anywhere in it that I don't find acutely unpleasant"), but consider a Shakespearean paradox remarked, I guess, by most people who have met Shakespeare plays in schoolrooms—and remarked out loud by the brashest among them. First one is told by teachers and by authoritative introductions to student texts that this or that Shakespeare play is a masterwork. Then the same teachers and introductions spend a good percentage of their time and energy on elements that seem "wrong" and on neutralizing them (by, for instance, explaining that oddities in *Macbeth* result from probable accidents in the transmission of the text or that now-troublesome elements in the histories—notably the rejection of Falstaff in the last scene of *2 Henry IV*—are misunderstood by modern audiences whose values differ sharply from some convenient, scholar-isolated values—values that can plausibly be said to make sense of corresponding troublesome elements in a given Shakespeare play but that do not seem in fact

to have been any more active in the consciousnesses of Shakespeare's contemporaries than they are in our own).[8]

The expert assistants to the plays furnish one of two kinds of
help. Either they offer the opportunity to think that our responses
to plays we love are invalid and are not "really" part of our experiences or, even more ridiculously, that the plays we love—
which is to say the plays we *have,* the plays printed and played all
these years—are not in "fact" what we love but only variously
mangled remnants of long-lost originals that had the perfection
we feel in Shakespeare's best plays but cannot rationally demon-

---

8. When I refer to "wrong" elements in the most admired of Shakespeare's
plays, I refer to things like the following. The wounded captain's narrative in
the second scene of *Macbeth* is incoherent (and was once routinely declared to
have resulted from some kind of distortion in Shakespeare's lost original). The
events of *Othello* are not credible: its plot rests on an unlikely series of lucky
lapses in probability. *Much Ado about Nothing* is similarly reliant on the improbable reticence of Margaret. As a plot device to insure that Friar Laurence's message does not reach Romeo, the quarantining of Friar John creaks horribly.
Hamlet's behavior to Ophelia in the "nunnery" scene does not make sense:
Hamlet does not know that Polonius and the King are eavesdropping. Edgar
has no reason to withhold knowledge of his identity from his desperate father,
and Rosalind has no reason to retain her disguise after she reaches safety in
Arden. As audience to "Pyramis and Thisbe," the gentlefolk in *A Midsummer
Night's Dream* are gratuitously harsh and disquietingly insensitive of the feelings of Peter Quince's troupe of amateur actors. Prospero is a hero of charity
and is also a petty, petulant, irresponsible tyrant. In 4.3 of *Julius Caesar* Brutus
tells Cassius about Portia's death and, moments later, hears the same news himself and hears it as if for the first time.

Shakespeare's plays are not the only acknowledged masterworks that are also
acknowledged to be crucially faulty. Consider the standard and, I think, just
complaints about the end of *Huckleberry Finn.* The people who care most about
that book complain loudest that it degenerates into puerile farce at the end.
The last part of the book is undeniably a letdown, but what could better fill its
place? If Huck were not engulfed at last in the limitations of boyhood (and/or
the limitations of human beings in society, no matter what their ages), the spiritual grandeur available to Huck and Jim on the river would insist on being recognized as an accidental fulfillment of a dream of freedom and potential for responsible moral action and choice—a temporary condition attainable only on
a raft. A spiritually satisfying conclusion to the journey—one that retained the
philosophic size of the trip itself—would be and would show itself to be wish-

strate them to possess. (The logic is akin in its unspoken premises to that of a girl named Maureen, who was my sister's best friend when they were both about eight years old. After she had eaten and enjoyed a paper cup full of what we all supposed to have been chocolate ice cream, Maureen read the label on the paper cup, discovered the contents to have been frozen malted milk, and said, "I wish I hadn't eaten it. I don't like malted milk.")

Be that as it may, I should get back to my purpose—my purpose in introducing the paradoxical conjunction of belief that the most admired of Shakespeare's plays are at once beautiful beyond expressing and are, if not deeply, at least casually flawed. It seems to me reasonable to suppose that, if the highest-held of all literary creations are all in some way or other marred, that fact justifies considering the possibility that aesthetically displeasing elements in aesthetically pleasing wholes may be of the essence of the pleasure we take in them.

That possibility is certainly consistent with what I have said so far in this book. After all, as my repeated disclaimers have already acknowledged, the generally unnoticeable syntactic and logical oddities I have noticed and admired in the Gettysburg Address, the Jonson epitaphs, and the first scene of *Twelfth Night* are all things that, at least in terms of the norms of syntax and the limits set by the particular premises of logical propositions, are "faults." All evidence to the contrary notwithstanding, my purpose has always been to wonder admiringly at and to marvel over the improbable logical and syntactical events I have discussed, but—because of the kinds of conclusions to which the kinds of evidence I have used usually point—the evidence has indeed been to the contrary. The phrase "the preciousness of nonsense"—a transformation of the old, mild expletive of dismissal that is this book's title—encapsulates the paradox.

I do not, of course, mean to suggest that I think my present thesis will be more palatable because it is in harmony with my

---

ful thinking, philosophic fantasy. The farcical ending is undeniably bad, *and* it lets the book as a whole be better than I can believe it could otherwise be.

earlier ones about the aesthetic value of unobserved nonsense in the Gettysburg Address, the Jonson epitaphs, and *Twelfth Night* 1.1—theses that even their sponsor cannot pretend are now self-evident truths. Nonetheless—since any reader who has come this far probably sees *some* sense in my case for nonsense—I do think it is worth emphasizing the kinship between, on the one hand, my present contention that "bad" parts of masterpieces may contribute to the special essence we recognize when we distinguish between good things and great ones and, on the other, the contention that the syntactic and logical gaps and lapses that have concerned me in the discussions that precede this one are sources of the joy we get from the works that house them. The common denominator is real but inefficient stress.

Like the logical and syntactic crises to which I have said Lincoln, Jonson, and Shakespeare make us superior—to which, in fact, they make us oblivious—the gentle but insistent pull between the responses we want to give Toby and those he evokes and comparable, comparably gentle pulls I will talk about later are real difficulties for perceiving minds, but are difficulties that those minds handle with casual, godlike ease. Like the phenomena I have considered previously, active but casual failures—if they are so gentle as not to become the focus of our attention—put minds that perceive them under stress—but under stresses with which those minds can cope without strenuous effort, stresses that are real but ultimately inefficient. They are irritants, irritants as insistent as, but no more demanding than, gnats or cobwebs. The difference between the stresses I talked about earlier and the stresses I am talking about here is that the slight but persistent irritation Toby's failure to provide the delight the play implies he is successfully providing impinges on our consciousnesses and is felt as a fault in the play—not, I think, *thought* to be a fault, but *felt*.

The distinction I make between *thought* and *felt* is between a considered judgment—a verdict—and a sense of unease—a feeling of uneasiness, an incidental annoyance. The difference is like the one between saying why people do not like a play or movie or poem that people do not like and discussing something that makes us uneasy within a work we delight in. The last parts of *Tartuffe* and *Huckleberry Finn* are examples in the latter category. And (however interesting those two notoriously unpopular plays may be to Shakespeare specialists) the last parts of *Love's Labor's Lost* and *Measure for Measure* are examples in the former. The self-consciously violent lapse from genre at the end of *Love's Labor's Lost* and the blind determination with which *Measure for Measure* pursues its generically appropriate but locally inappropriate happy ending generate an uneasiness that overwhelms everything else. In each of those two instances, the play's sudden odd behavior becomes an issue; rather than a passing mental inconvenience, the oddity demands that it be thought about and either puzzled away or moralized and said to be Shakespeare's illustration of a philosophic point or argued to be a reason to dismiss the play as an aberration.

That brings me to consideration of a further minor complication inherent in thinking about Toby's comedy—a complication that precludes the relatively comfortable conclusion that what I am arguing is that Toby's ineptitude as a comic creation spoils the parts of the play he dominates. That would be easy to understand—and to recognize as the logical but wrongheaded conclusion of a literary critic more intent on his thesis than on *Twelfth Night* as audiences experience it. In fact, Toby's scenes are, on the whole, funny. *He* is not funny, but *they* are. And it is exactly that that keeps Toby's leadenness as a theatrical commodity from dominating our experience of his scenes and thus making our disquiet more urgent than our contentment.

Do what he may to dampen them, Toby's scenes are funny. They are funny because Andrew Aguecheek is in them, and because Andrew—the one among his company in the outskirts of Olivia's household who puts least energy into showing off comic talent for the approbation of his fellow characters—is consistently funny. What Andrew works at is to seem sufficiently debonair to pass for a worldly, fashion-wise man about town, and a lot of his humor derives from his efforts to ape behavior that he supposes to be sophisticated and clever. Andrew thus tries his hand too at wit, but with only one exception that I can see, his ineptitude always seems clearly to be *his*—the amusing ineptitude of the character and not the ineptitude of his creator—not, that is, the slightly embarrassing product of an artist's failed effort to make a comic character efficiently amusing.[9]

When Andrew is present—which he is most of the time in Toby's scenes—Shakespeare works Toby even harder to amuse us than he does when Andrew is absent—and with even less success. Meanwhile, Andrew gets laughs without effort of his own and without apparent effort by the playwright (as Andrew says, he does it more natural). The result is an improbably peaceful neighborhood of responses in which mild but persistent irritation with Toby as a comic character coexists with delight in comedy upon which he is felt to be a burden.

The best example of double identity as comic failure and comic success is 2.3—the nocturnal revels scene, a scene that, because it becomes as irritating to us in terms of our experience (our experience as theatrical consumers) as it is to Malvolio in his, is also a severe test of our much-prized identities as jolly good fellows—identities that the scene makes more urgently desirable than any other in the play. Act 2, scene 3 is thus also the ideal place to examine the interactions of uncomfortably contrary responses evoked in differently pertinent dimensions of our experience.

The opening and closing of the scene are emblematic of the valuative stalemate the scene generates in other more disturbing

---

9. The exception is 2.3.155, Andrew's contribution to an exchange between Toby and Maria. Toby summarizes the probable results of Maria's letter plot against Malvolio, and Maria says, "My purpose is indeed a horse of that color." When Andrew interjects, "And your horse now would make him an ass," an audience cannot be sure whether the weakness of the wit is the character's or the play's. Note the labored play on "ass" and "as" in the "capper" with which Maria responds: "Ass I doubt not."

ways. The scene begins and ends with Toby and Andrew alone together. Toby's first speech is typically promissory of more wit than it shows and typically demanding of more merriment than it evokes: *Approach, Sir Andrew. Not to be abed after midnight is to be up betimes; and 'diluculo surgere,' thou know'st.* And, also typically, Andrew's literalistic response—apparently innocent of comic intent on the character's part—is more successful in amusing us than Toby was: *Nay, by my troth, I know not, but I know to be up late is to be up late.* Toby thereupon does some insistently comical blustering and then explains painfully how it is that to be up after midnight is to be up early and how it is that to go to bed after midnight is to go to bed early (6–8) and then (with the phrase *consist of* in *Does not our lives consist of the four elements?* [9]) sets up Andrew for another innocently literal demurrer (*Faith, so they say, but I think it rather consists of eating and drinking* [10–11]). The last moments of the scene recur to the topic of bedtime. They too demand tediously that we cherish Toby for being a lovable roisterer, and they complicate our difficulties because, in order to force ourselves into compliance with the spirit we are pressed to admire and reflect, we have to overlook our uneasiness at Toby's probable motives in urging Andrew to send for money:

> TOBY: Let's to bed, knight. Thou hadst need send for more money.
> ANDREW: If I cannot recover your niece, I am a foul way out.
> TOBY: Send for money, knight. If thou hast her not i' th'end, call me Cut.
> ANDREW: If I do not, never trust me, take it how you will.
> TOBY: Come, come; I'll go burn some sack. 'Tis too late to go to bed now. Come, knight; come knight. *Exeunt.*
>
> (2.3.168–76)

On the other hand, just by recurring to the topic of bedtime, those last lines of the scene put an aesthetically comforting frame to it and thus are mildly pleasing in one of the sets of terms in which our experience occurs—just as they are mildly discomfiting in the others. (There is also, I suspect, some aesthetic en ergy—in the opening exchange, in the closing one, and in their interaction as framers—in the urgently available, unexploited raw materials for easy wordplay on knight and nighttime—energy of a kind that I will discuss at length in the discussion that follows this one).[10]

10. Although the matter is not altogether pertinent here, I want to point out a likeness between the physics of the particular phenomena I am discussing here (for instance, successful and unsuccessful comedy coexisting and balancing each other in 3.2 and the phenomenon whereby the same elements are at once aesthetically displeasing in one system of perception and pleasing in another), and the phenomenon whereby what is substantively nonsense can be something like sensible in a system of articulation based on connections irrelevant to substantive content.

Consider, for example, the response Andrew gets when he asks whether Feste received a sixpence that Andrew sent him on the previous evening. Feste's reply—in effect, a token gift in recompense of the one he has received from Andrew—is pure nonsense; this is Andrew's question and Feste's response (the physics I am talking about is present in emblem in the antistasis in *for* [as a gift to] *thy leman* and *for* [because] *Malvolio's nose is no whipstock*):

ANDREW: I sent thee sixpence for thy leman. Hads't it?

CLOWN: I did impeticos thy gratility, for Malvolio's nose is no whipstock. My lady has a white hand, and the Myrmidons are no
bottle-ale houses.

(2.3.23–27)

All the evident energy of Feste's speech goes into establishing its incoherence—or, rather, its substantive incoherence.

The key word in establishing that incoherence is the word *for*—"because"; it announces that what follows it will explain something about what went before it. What follows is ostentatiously irrelevant to "I did impeticos thy gratility." And what follows the irrelevant assertion about Malvolio's nose is equally irrelevant to that assertion.

Phonetically, however, the *M* of *My Lady's hand* relates very clearly to *Malvolio,* and, in the next clause, the *M* of *Myrmidons* relates that clause to both of the other two. Moreover, as *nose* echoes the last syllable of *Malvolio's* and is echoed in the *no* of *no whipstock,* so the *no* of *no bottle-ale houses* echoes all three. And the *wh* sound of *whipstock* separates into the opening sounds of *white* and *hand,* the corresponding element—object of the verb—in the grammar of the substantively unrelated following clause; by beginning with an *h* sound, *houses,* the object of the verb in the third of the three nonexplanatory explanatory clauses, continues the pattern.

And *whipstock,* which, aside from their phonetic link, is so ostentatiously irrelevant to *white hand,* does, after all, refer to a *hand*le. Similarly, the second of

When the scene gets under way in earnest, it presents a good deal of mildly amusing stuff (notably Andrew's reminiscences of the previous evening's performance by Feste [18–23], the sample of nonsense fooling Feste gives Andrew in thanks for his tip [25–27; see note 10], and the truly dazzling song "O mistress mine")—surely enough to build a considerable head of unforced good will in us, the audience.

Moreover, during the ensuing caterwauling—during the howling that brings Malvolio down upon the revellers (50–79)—the audience is treated to, and is presumably soothed by (and presumably takes no conscious notice of), a particularly subtle harmony of cats. The harmony gets its start in a line of Andrew's that plays on "dog" and "cat": Toby invites Feste and Andrew to join him in singing a catch, and Andrew says, *An you love me, let's do it. I am a dog at a catch* (57). The play on "dog" and "cat" echoes and thus makes a harmony with the similar and similarly recessive wordplay that preceded Feste's attempt to prove Olivia a fool back in 1.5; Olivia gave permission to make his proof, and Feste said, *I must catechize you for it, madonna. Good my mouse of virtue, answer me* (1.5.57–58). And, merely by referring to dogs,

---

the three simultaneously related and unrelated explanatory clauses relates to *I did impeticos thy gratility,* the clause to which it and its companions are so pointedly irrelevant: the context of a coin received suggests the sense "pocket up" for the nonsense word *impeticos,* but the context also includes *thy leman,* and invites listeners to include the likeness of *impeticos* to "in petticoat" in their experience of the clause; the dim but real relevance of *my lady* to *thy leman* and of hands to the business of "impocketing" (and to groping in petticoats) all pull the assertively foreign clause about my lady's white hand into relationship with the topics from which it so sharply divides.

The same kind of simultaneous pertinence and impertinence occurs on a larger scale when, later in the same scene, topics touched upon here only because they are irrelevant to the matter about which the speaker purports to be speaking recur as meaningful incidentals of later discussion. When Malvolio arrives he compounds several separate elements of Feste's reply to Andrew in "Do ye make an alehouse of my lady's house. . . ?" (82–83), and "my lady's hand" recurs crucially—but in another sense—when Maria says, "I can write very like my lady your niece; on a forgotten matter we can hardly make distinction of our hands" (146–48).

the play on "dog" and "cat" in Andrew's line participates in a play-long alliteration-like succession of casual references to dogs—a succession that starts early in scene 1 when Orsino says, *and my desires like fell and cruel hounds, / Ere since pursue me* (1.1.23–24). Within the twenty-line passage in 2.3 between "O mistress mine" and Malvolio's entrance, the "cat" in *I am a dog at a catch* is echoed in *caterwauling* (in Maria's entrance line, *What a caterwauling do you keep here?* [66]), and *Cataian* (in Toby's otherwise irrelevant response, *My lady's a Cataian* [69]).

By even mentioning the cat-based harmonies of 2.3.50–79, I automatically exaggerate their effect on an audience. As I said, however, I do not in fact suppose that audiences pay any conscious attention at all to the cat patterns. Even the wordplay of *dog at a catch* goes past most audiences and most actors—just as it does past Feste, whose response is the limply jocular *By'r Lady, sir, and some dogs will catch well* (58).[11] I do suggest, however, that

11. It is possible that "Catch" was a common name for dogs (as "Blanch," "Sweetheart," and "True" appear to have been). If so, the complex play on "catch," "cat," and dogs in 2.3 becomes even more complex. A dog of that name figures in the eclogue beginning "And are you there, old *Pas*" in Sidney's *Arcadia* (51–56 in William Ringler's edition [Oxford, 1962]): "A prettie curre it is; his name iwis is Catch" (40).

Given the play on "catch," "cat," and dogs in 2.3, and given the scene's focus on singing, one can suspect that Sidney's poem lies somewhere in the background of Shakespeare's scene.

The eclogue, a parody of Virgil's third, is a singing contest between louts. One contestant puts up his cat against a dog wagered by his opponent.

NICO.: . . . I will lay a wager hereunto,

That profit may ensue to him that best can do.

I have (and long shall have) a white great nimble cat,

A king upon a mouse, a strong foe to a rat. . . .

PAS.: . . . I have a fitter match;

A prettie curre it is; his name iwis is Catch. . . .

This is my pawne; the price let *Dicus*' judgment show:

Such oddes I willing lay; for him and you I know.

(29–32, 39–40, 47–48)

Like the catch of Toby, Andrew, and Feste in 2.3, the singing of Sidney's the cats give the passage a felt undercurrent of artistic coherence and that they help keep us back from considering the always available, regularly shunned possibility that, if we fail to delight in Toby's noisy revels, the fault might be with *them* and not where I think we usually place it—with humorless, spiritually wizened us.

The scene begins to get hard on the theatrical consumer when Toby, who has not spoken at length since he and Andrew were joined by Feste, speaks a speech that, in its eagerness to warm things up, cools us with reiteration of an invitation to calculated merriment that becomes decreasingly inviting by virtue of the implied need to stimulate it: *But shall we make the welkin dance indeed? Shall we rouse the night owl in a catch that will draw three souls out of one weaver? Shall we do that?* (54—56).[12]

What follows is two or three minutes of loud, determined jollity, namely the action that is described—in much less time than it takes to perform—in the innocent-seeming stage direction "*Catch sung.*" I have never seen any production of *Twelfth Night*— and I have seen seventy-some *Twelfth Nights*—in which actors and director contrived to make the catch other than a trial for the audience, an audience that is required to approve and that

---

shepherds displeases its audience. In the poem's last lines, the judge refuses to declare either singer the winner:

> Enough, enough: so ill hath done the best,
> That since the having them to neither's due,
> Let cat and dog fight which shall have both you.

12. Compare the first speech of the outraged Malvolio a few lines later; formally—and, of course, only formally—it is the twin of the passage beginning "But shall we make the welkin dance": "My masters, are you mad? Or what are you? Have you no wit, manners, nor honesty, but to gabble like tinkers at this time of night? Do ye make an alehouse of my lady's house, that ye squeak out your coziers' catches without any mitigation or remorse of voice? Is there no respect of place, persons, nor time in you?" (2.3.80—85). Like Toby, Malvolio overdoes his gestures of emphatic apposition. Toby and Malvolio speak to very different purpose, but, in demanding unearned repetitions of their listeners' responses, they speak to the same effect.

wants to approve generically amusing high jinks that amount theatrically to so much sweat and raw noise.

As is by now presumably obvious, the point toward which I am moving here is that, when Malvolio the spoilsport enters to end the revelry, we the audience—firmly and forever allied with the forces of free-spirited good fellowship—feel something different from, but uncomfortably akin to, sympathy with Malvolio's point of view. The moral context of the play will not allow us even fleetingly to consider the possibility that Malvolio's attitude toward roisterers has anything to be said for it, but, however dedicated we may temporarily be to "good life" and songs of good life, I suspect that, as audience to this particular example of musical roistering, we are—in our terms—as annoyed with all the pointless racket as Malvolio is. I suggest that, in their—in our—incapacity fully to enter into the comic spirit of genuinely funny scenes (scenes that cannot be dismissed the way the efforts of inept tummlers and jolly masters of ceremonies at ships concerts can, but scenes that also sweat under a weight of elaborate, inefficient effort to amuse), audiences to *Twelfth Night* come dangerously close to seeing a likeness between themselves and the harshest of the many onstage critics of comedy in this play, Malvolio—Malvolio, *self*-exiled from the carefree festival spirit Toby advertises and the object of our scorn because he refuses to do what we want to do but cannot.

In an essay called "*Twelfth Night:* The Experience of the Audience" (*Shakespeare Survey* 34 [1981], 111–19), Ralph Berry treats matters closely related to the ones I treat here and anticipates me to my profit at several points. One of the most profitable of those is in his notice of a nearly universal critical eagerness to be disassociated from Malvolio. I will quote him on that subject later. For the moment I want to quote only his comments on 2.3:

> The revels of act 2, scene 3 will secure the sympathy of the audience, and the great confrontation between Sir Toby and Malvolio does at the same time seem like the lifeforce challenging the powers of repression and sterility: 'dost thou think, be-

cause thou art virtuous, there shall be no more cakes and ale?'
As presented, there is no chance of an audience denying this
affirmation. (Or critic, one might add. There is an all but universal convention for commentators to stand up and be counted
as in favour of cakes and ale.) (111)

I agree that there is no chance that any audience will ever
refuse a call to affirm the life force, but I do not think our endorsements are quite instinctive in the particular circumstances
Shakespeare provides, and I do not think our yea-saying is ever
quite as wholehearted as we would like it to be.

Berry's point about the critics is particularly apt. I have been
bullied by the line about cakes and ale and by its morally threat-
ening, perhaps morally threatened, clack all my professional life
(and during the last parts of my childhood when teachers trotted
out their gusto for me and insisted that mine was also in play).
Moreover, unlike Ralph Berry (who locates the onset of audience queasiness in act 3 or later), I feel bullied during the whole
confrontation between Malvolio the spoilsport and the night
revelers. And the suspiciously eager endorsements of the commentators Berry mentions suggest that I am not alone.

There is probably no need for detailed illustration that after
Malvolio's entrance the wit of the merrymakers becomes even
flatter than it was before. For a quick example, take Toby's narrow, contrived, overtly effortful response to Malvolio's *Is there
no respect of place, persons, nor time in you?: We did keep time, sir, in
our catches* (84–86). Unless—as actors never do—the actor puts
pointed stress on the word *time* (thus establishing that Toby is
pretending seriously to challenge the justice of one particular
charge among the three), the cleverness of Toby's puerile effort
at riposte falls as dead as similar sallies by cheeky children do in
real life. A few moments later, when Toby and Feste taunt Malvolio by conversing in fragments of improvised song (*But I will
never die. Sir Toby there you lie.* [98–99]), the puerility of the wit
and of the tactic itself is, I suspect, hard on audiences. We cannot do other than cheer Toby and Feste on, but they are unworthy of us—both in being insufficiently amusing and, in

Toby's case, in being contemptible enough to register snobbish contempt by saying *Art any more than a steward?* (104–5). We cheer Feste and Toby on, but it isn't easy.

I want now to turn briefly to our difficulties in coping with regrettable and regretted flashes of Malvolio-like punctiliousness about matters so petty as to be beneath the notice of anyone but a twit.

In 1.1 we are empowered to comprehend effortlessly what is demonstrably incomprehensible. In the body of the play, moments of comparably godlike ease cohabit with contrasting moments when our minds suddenly, unexpectedly scramble to get bearings they do not need—or, rather, to get bearings the spirit of the play says our minds do not need. A mind skating comfortably across a performance of *Twelfth Night* repeatedly hits pebbles. But they are not big enough to cause a spill—or to cause us to pull up short and brush them from our path. And the play skims along past them and implies by its example that such free spirits as *Twelfth Night* assures us we are must be skimming along too—superior to, oblivious of, every kind of petty inconvenience to smooth comprehension. Nonetheless, as they are in all of Shakespeare, the pebbles are there and are inconvenient. Again, the difference is that this play will not let us respect anyone who takes notice of petty detail.

Take, for a relatively large example of pebblelike bother, the sudden arrival of Fabian. Not only does he arrive from nowhere at the beginning of 2.5, he arrives to occupy a place already assigned to Feste: Maria has promised us that Toby and Andrew will be witnesses to Malvolio's entrapment in the letter plot and that the fool will *make a third* (2.3.160–61). But, since no one on the stage is at all surprised to see Fabian or surprised at Feste's absence, we, like the several editions I have checked out on the matter, let the matter pass—or pretend to. It is not worth worrying about. (And besides, if we are willing to admit to wondering about Fabian's presence in the play, there is more than a century of creative scholarship behind us providing models for speculation and teaching us how to explain away discrepancies

in detail and structure as understandable in the work of an inspired hack hurrying his plays out to meet deadlines. There are
also plentiful models for a guess that Shakespeare worked the play
out two different ways, one without Fabian and one in which he
and Toby do in fact set the device against Malvolio. One such
theory might very well be entirely valid, but it would only explain why the play is as it is; the explanation would not change
the play's behavior or our experience of it. The *need* for explanation is a permanent fact of the play.)

Twelfth Night presents us with a number of other minor in-
conveniences to our theatrical comfort. And, as I said earlier, I
think we notice them—things like the gratuitously mean *I do
care for something; but in my conscience, sir, I do not care for you. If that
be to care for nothing, sir, I would it would make you invisible* (spoken
by Feste to Viola-Cesario [3.1.27–29]), and *Will you help? An ass-
head and a coxcomb and a knave, a thin-faced knave, a gull?* (spoken
by Toby in response to Andrew's offer to help Toby as the two
of them limp out of the play [5.1.198–99]). But the behavior
of critics and commentators suggests that, having noticed them,
we quickly and conscientiously respond to their presence in
our consciousnesses in much the way the cockney in *King Lear*
is said to have responded to the live eels in her pie: *She knapped
'em o' th' coxcombs with a stick and cried, 'Down, wantons, down!'*
(2.4.118–19).

The greatest concentration of pebblelike obstacles to comfortable comprehension and easygoing conviviality occurs in the
speeches Fabian and Feste speak immediately before Malvolio
storms out of the play vowing revenge (*I'll be revenged on the whole
pack of you* [5.1.367]) and immediately after Olivia has unraveled
Maria's letter plot (*Alas, Malvolio, this is not my writing . . .* [5.1.335–
45]). Those speeches too generate circumstances that lure us toward likeness to Malvolio.

The first of them, Fabian's, is the play's best statement of its
prevailing spirit. The speech follows immediately upon Olivia's
acknowledgement that the letter plot *hath most shrewdly passed
upon* Malvolio and her promise to him that, when *the grounds and*

authors of the plot are known, Malvolio will be *both plaintiff and judge* of his own cause. Fabian says:

> Good madam, hear me speak,
> And let no quarrel, nor no brawl to come,
> Taint the condition of this present hour,
> Which I have wond'red at. In hope it shall not,
> Most freely I confess myself and Toby
> Set this device against Malvolio here,
> Upon some stubborn and uncourteous parts
> We had conceived against him. Maria writ
> The letter, at Sir Toby's great importance,
> In recompense whereof he hath married her.
> How with a sportful malice it was followed
> May rather pluck on laughter than revenge,
> If that the injuries be justly weighed
> That have on both sides passed.
>
> (5.1.345−58)

The speech is generous-spirited in manner, superficially generous-spirited in substance, and, if one thinks about it, gives persuasive, but not-quite-conclusive evidence that it is generous-spirited in essence too. Its spirit is exactly the one that best accords with our wishes for the end of this play. But the speech is also acrawl with gratuitous incidental inaccuracies.

Fabian says that he—who was not present (or even known to us) when the letter plot was hatched back in 2.3 —*and Toby set this device against Malvolio.* And he says not only that *Maria writ the letter,* but that she wrote it *at Sir Toby's great importance.* We saw no such importunity or any need for any. The discrepancies are trivial, but they are of a piece and threaten to complicate our experience of the lines by presenting themselves as evidence for generous motives behind Fabian's speech—a speech that, as I said, seems generous for other reasons, generic and situational reasons, anyway. We don't want to be thinking about Fabian. At this point in a play that, at the point when Olivia's memory of Malvolio was accidentally jogged, had already reached its destined happy ending, we do not want to worry about the inner qualities of a minor character.

And yet Fabian does take more of the blame on himself than our experience can witness, and he protects Maria by implying that the idea of the letter came from Toby, who—since his rights in Olivia's continued patronage are reinforced by consanguinity—is best able to take and survive the guilt.

On the other hand, is Fabian altogether generous? The speech, remember, responds to Olivia's promise that Malvolio will be judge in his own cause. His recommendations are calculated to save Fabian's skin as well as those of his colleagues, and the speech is openly calculating in its insinuating efforts at once to justify Malvolio's suffering and dismiss it as incidental overflow from a prank (*sportful malice* [365] is an oxymoron slippery enough to have done credit to Claudius's first speech in *Hamlet*). And so on.[13]

What concerns me most about Fabian's speech is what—faced with my prolonged commentary on it—probably at the moment most concerns you: the obvious fact that, however just they may be, my comments on Fabian's speech are entirely alien

---

13. Note too, by the way, that *Upon some stubborn and uncourteous parts / We had conceived against him* (5.1.351–52) is nonsense of the sort that I talked about when I talked about 1.1. The phrase only seems to provide meaningful modification to the assertion to which it is appended. How can one hope to take any precise sense from the idea of conceiving parts—much less imagine how parts could be conceived *against* someone else?

And, as for *imprecise* sense, which side is it to which we finally understand the lines to be charging stubbornness and discourtesy? The phrase is an idiomatic crazy quilt that magically enacts the blending and blurring of blame that Fabian goes on to ask for in the last lines of the speech. *Upon* implies—accurately implies—that it introduces a reason for setting the device against Malvolio—a reason for doing what Fabian says he and Toby did. The stubborn (that is, "inflexible") and uncourteous parts ("qualities") first seem to be Malvolio's—traits that we know to be his and ones here being said to have made Fabian and Toby want to discomfit him. The sentence thus starts out as a gesture of self-justification. *We had conceived* changes the phrase's apparent motive; the phrase seems now to have slipped again into the confessional mode in which the sentence started and to be explaining the offense against Malvolio as the product of unmotivated ill will in Toby and the now selflessly self-accusing Fabian.

to the spirit generically appropriate to an audience listening while a playwright brings his comic machine to rest. These lines—like the last lines of similar Shakespearean comedies and, indeed, of most of the rest of Shakespeare's plays—ask to be taken as performers of perfunctory final housekeeping chores. This is only a play, and, as I will suggest in section 3, at this point it is urgently so.

And yet, here am I carrying on like a sophomore in a high wind—picking at nits in a speech that in its substance asks large-mindedness from its onstage audience and in its kind asks the same from us. At this point in *Twelfth Night,* it makes no difference—or, in the play's pet idiom, it's all one—whether the details of Fabian's account do or do not square with those of the events as we have seen them unfold. And surely it is silly to go motive hunting in the lines of a character whose very existence was unknown to us until the tenth of the play's eighteen scenes and who, when we heard him carefully reminding Toby of an incident involving himself, Malvolio, and a bear-baiting (2.5.6–7), sounded from the first like a hastily adopted—or adapted—child of some dramaturgical necessity equally unknown to us. Both Fabian and his peacemaking speech ask us to take them as furniture of the play as play—as stuff in a comedy.

It is foolish to treat Fabian's speech as one would a trial transcript, but every time I hear Fabian's speech my mind both follows the route I have mapped out here and feels foolish for doing so. In short, I am mentally uncomfortable about being mentally uncomfortable with Fabian's peacemaking speech. I feel myself pulling back from its admirable spirit and perilously close to its subject, the play's chief nitpicker, Malvolio—who (being more foolish than I), is braver about admitting his disinclination to go along and taints the condition of the hour by storming ineffectually off the stage.

I am similarly troubled by similar details in the lines that come next—details effectively similar, but troublesome in another and even more petty dimension, pedantry. Feste says, *Why, 'some are born great, some achieve greatness, and some have greatness thrown upon them.' I was one, sir, in this interlude, one Sir Topas, sir; but that's all one. 'By the Lord, fool, I am not mad!' But do you remember, 'Madam, why laugh you at such a barren rascal? An you smile not, he's gagged'? And thus the whirligig of time brings in his revenges* (5.1.360–66).

What troubles me in Feste's speech is that I always have checked involuntarily when Feste says *thrown* where the two previous versions of the formula have taught us to expect *thrust* and that I am tempted to go on foolishly from there to fret over Feste's absence from the stage on both occasions when the "born great" / "achieve greatness" / "greatness thrust upon them" formula is spoken.[14] Similarly, I am self-disgusted when my mind detours into worry about Feste's substitution of *smile* in *But do you remember, 'Madam, why laugh you at such a barren rascal? An you smile not, he's gagged'?* for *laugh* in its "original," 1.5.78–82: *I*

14. *Thrown upon them* is effectively synonymous with *thrust upon them,* the phrase it "replaces," the phrase from 3.4.41 that quoted *thrust upon 'em* (2.5.134) in the fraudulent Maria/Olivia letter to Malvolio. The phrases are also nearly identical phonetically. But *thrown upon them* is *not* identical with *thrust upon them,* and the imperfection of Feste's quotation of a phrase we have heard twice before calls momentary attention to itself—attention that one presumably does not want to give. There is no reason to expect Shakespeare to quote himself faithfully; characters misquote all the way through the canon. More important, it does not matter whether Feste's phrasing is identical to the phrasing it echoes. It is all one.

It is all one, too, that the line we hear as a misquotation is quoted by a character who was present on neither of the occasions when we heard it (2.5 —in the letter scene—and 3.4 —in the scene where Maria demonstrates Malvolio's madness to Olivia). Why does that not matter? First, because Feste could have read Malvolio's letter offstage or heard accounts of Malvolio's behavior. Second, and more important, because this is only a play—and a farce at that; to speculate on the source of a clown's knowledge (or, for that matter, on his use of his offstage time) is silly—particularly silly since, although an audience can be expected to notice and shrug off the substitution of *thrown* for *thrust,* no member of an audience can be imagined to remember that Feste is offstage in the scenes where Malvolio says the words Feste echoes to him here. And yet my mind has—obviously has—in fact gone down the several paths to folly that I now label as such.

marvel your ladyship takes delight in such a barren rascal. . . . Unless
you laugh and minister occasion to him, he is gagged.

Perhaps my experience is unusual. Perhaps not. One way or
the other, it is certain that each of the troublesome details that I
want to brush aside and cannot quite brush aside has a lot of
company here. The concentration of incidental discrepancies in
the two speeches that precede Malvolio's enraged promise to be
revenged is greater than any I can remember in any passage of
comparable size anywhere in the Shakespearean canon. And it is
certain too that my trivial discontent with my reactions to the
trivial discrepancies I have just been discussing occurs in the company of a lot of larger invitations to police one's responses.

The largest of those occurs when our desire to join in the fun
of the happy ending requires that we try to brush aside nagging,
always minor inclinations to agree that Malvolio has indeed been
most notoriously abused.

I said earlier that I would quote Ralph Berry on the topic of
critical eagerness to be disassociated from Malvolio. Berry takes
the eagerness of critics to assure us and perhaps themselves of
their allegiance to festival views as a symptom of an unspoken
truth about the play. So do I. (Note that critics never bother
to register the difference between Iago's behavior and behavior
they themselves would recommend, that we never feel the need
to label the behavior of Don John, Iachimo, and Richard III as
wicked, and that *Twelfth Night* does not impel commentators on
it to put themselves on public record as being of the opinion that
Andrew is silly.)

This is Berry on the shrillness of critics insisting that they are
comfortable with Malvolio's punishment (Berry has just said that
Malvolio's "final speech, leading to the appalling 'I'll be reveng'd
on the whole pack of you', is the climax of everything that happens in *Twelfth Night*"):

> The experience must be confronted, and neither denied nor in-
> dulged. 'Malvolio: a tragedy' is a sentimentalization of this play.
> But equally, one is struck by the large number of critics who, on

this issue, seem bent on represssing instincts which, outside the theatre of *Twelfth Night,* they would surely admit. I cite a few instances, though my point could easily be illustrated at far greater length. To Joseph Summers, 'Malvolio is, of course, justly punished.' Barbara K. Lewalski concurs in the natural justice of the affair: 'Since he so richly deserves his exposure, and so actively cooperates in bringing it upon himself, there seems little warrant for the critical tears sometimes shed over his harsh treatment and none at all for a semi-tragic rendering of his plight in the "dark house".' For C. L. Barber, Malvolio is 'a kind of foreign body to be expelled by laughter, in Shakespeare's last free-and-easy festive comedy'. Most certainly he is to be expelled, if *Twelfth Night* is a 'free and easy festive comedy'; but supposing the intruder belongs in the play, what then?

How can one explain this critical imperviousness to the ending? One comes to view the critics here as a representative sampling of the human mind. They *want,* as we all do, a comedy; they do not want a disturbance to the agreeable mood created in *Twelfth Night;* it is easiest to find a response based on 'Serve Malvolio right: he asked for it. . . .' [The critics] seek a formula that helps to suppress the disquiet one inevitably feels. In this they faithfully embody certain tendencies within the mind, and thus— as Shakespeare well knew—of his audience.[15]

Like this one, Berry's essay suggests that Shakespeare built "into his design a threat to its own mood" (118). He concludes by saying that "the ultimate effect of *Twelfth Night* is to make the audience ashamed of itself" (119). I agree. But, unless I misunderstand him, Berry thinks the audience is ashamed to have associated itself with Malvolio's tormentors and thus to have been accomplices in petty but real brutality. I suggest, rather, what the critical testimonials to cakes and ale and to the justice of Malvolio's punishment suggest: that, though we may have crowed persuasively, we are ashamed to have secretly been insufficiently fes-

15. Pp. 117–18. Berry gives the sources of the passages he quotes as follows: Joseph Summers, "The Masks of *Twelfth Night," University of Kansas City Review,* 22 (1955): 25–32; Barbara K. Lewalski, "Thematic Patterns in *Twelfth Night," Shakespeare Studies,* 1 (1965), 171; C. L. Barber, *Shakespeare's Festive Comedy* (Princeton, N.J., 1959), 257.

tive—ashamed that we have been unable to play zany to Sir Toby as well as we would like and as well as we would like to be thought to have done—ashamed of having been insufficient to the play's demands on us—ashamed of having failed to fit in.

Throughout his career, Shakespeare experiments with—and gets energy from—setting audiences to watch—or, rather, try to watch—a play other than the one he shows them. For example, he does that in varying ways and to varying effects in *Love's Labor's Lost, Romeo and Juliet, 2 Henry IV, Henry V, All's Well That Ends Well, Troilus and Cressida, King Lear, Antony and Cleopatra, The Winter's Tale,* and *The Tempest. Twelfth Night,* I think, is not only Shakespeare's supreme achievement but his most complex experiment with the interaction of the play we see and the one we try to see.

Some of the plays in my list of examples make us—which is to say *let* us—face up to our plights. Those plays relieve much of the uneasiness they evoke by commenting more or less self-consciously on their deviations from a behavior pattern they have invited us to rely upon. *Love's Labor's Lost* and *Troilus and Cressida* certainly do that. And, less crudely, *2 Henry IV* and *Henry V* do too. Some of the listed plays do not—notably *Romeo and Juliet, King Lear, The Tempest,* and—and above all—*Twelfth Night.*

Some of the plays in my list—*All's Well, Henry V,* and *Antony and Cleopatra,* for instance—leave us in doubt about where they want us to stand. *Twelfth Night,* on the other hand, does not leave us in any doubt about what responses it expects of us; we know where *Twelfth Night* wants us to stand. What *Twelfth Night* does is leave us in doubt as to whether or not we have succeeded well enough in standing there.

I have been insisting on the likenesses between us the audience and Malvolio. We are also like Andrew Aguecheek. Andrew—the most persistent participant in the play's themelike series of variations on the idea of following—is constantly a step or two behind his companions—often physically, always mentally. He puts most of his energy into attempting to demonstrate that he is, and has the qualifications to be, one of what he takes to be a sophisticated company. Andrew never quite succeeds in fitting in, but he never quite fails either. He seems to have doubts about his success, but, until Toby speaks his last line, no one directly tells him.

Andrew keeps insisting on his concurrence in his companions' thinking. A good percentage of Andrew's role consists of variations on "me too." Andrew's most famous "me too" line is *I was adored once too* (2.3.166). Like Andrew, audiences to *Twelfth Night* try to fit in. And, like him, they are not told outright whether their efforts are or are not fooling anybody. We want the play to find us adorable in its terms, but the play will not tell us whether we pass its muster.

3 · THE LAST FEW MINUTES OF *TWELFTH NIGHT*

At the end of *Twelfth Night* everything comes together with the neat, easy convenience available to neat, easy fictions. And nothing does. That paradox is played out in every dimension of the last few minutes of *Twelfth Night,* and I will spend the bulk of this last section describing the paradox's multiple manifestations.

Before I begin listing and describing, however, I want to do two preliminary things.

The first is to say that the paradox I focus on here manifests the physics that is the common denominator in every literary phenomenon in which the human mind takes pleasure. What our minds most like is to be in situations where they simultaneously perceive *is* as *is not* and *is not* as *is*. The paradoxically co-existent contrary actions I will talk about here all share the same physics, and all share those physics with the operation of simple literary constructions (a sentence is one thing *and* a union of disparate parts whose disparity the mere existence of the sentence advertises) and complex ones (rhymes—in which two words are insistently the same and just as insistently different—puns, rhythm—where a pattern both repeats and does not repeat—and so on). The most obvious—and traditionally the most fascinating—embodiments of the common underlying principle shared by the phenomena I will talk about are, of course, twins— which, as Orsino says, present *a natural perspective that is and is not* (5.1.209).

As a second preliminary, I want to remind you that what interests me about *Twelfth Night* is the question of what is so good about it and to say that this essay is groping toward an answer to that question.

Now I will come back to enlarge on my opening assertion that everything comes together in the last few minutes of *Twelfth Night* and that nothing does. I will begin by looking at conclusiveness and inconclusiveness in their most obvious manifestations.

The happy marriages that make the play come out as nature and the nature of fiction demand are fairy-tale easy. Toby marries Maria in a subordinate clause (5.1.354). Olivia has loved Cesario, has contracted a marriage with Sebastian, is content, and blandly welcomes Viola as an in-law: *A sister, you are she* (5.1.317). Orsino—previously governed by his love for the now truly unavailable Olivia—cheers up immediately, claims his *share in this most happy wrack* and proposes marriage to Viola: *Boy, thou hast said to me a thousand times / Thou never shouldst love woman like to me. . . . Give me thy hand, / And, let me see thee in thy woman's weeds* (258–60, 263–64). Everything is coming out exactly as it should.[16] As *Twelfth Night* draws comfortably toward its close,

16. The two Shakespeare plays most obviously similar to this one are blessed with similar good fortune. In *Much Ado about Nothing,* Claudio mourns for the girl he thinks he has killed but he willingly settles for her mysteriously—and temporarily—extant cousin. And, in *As You Like It,* Phoebe responds ruefully to the revelation of Rosalind's sex—"If sight and shape be true, / Why then, my love adieu" (5.4.114–15)—but is quickly and gracefully resigned to marry Silvius (143–44); moreover, that play introduces a new character in its last fifty lines: "the second son of old Sir Rowland" who ties off further loose ends by unexpectedly arriving with the unexpected news that, on his way into the Forest of Arden to murder his brother, the usurping duke, "meeting with an old religious man, / After some question with him, was converted / Both from his enterprise and from the world, / His crown bequeathing to his banished brother" (5.4.146, 154–57).

only a critic with the naïveté of a verisimilitude-crazed high school student or a theater reviewer for *The New Yorker* could fault the play for its good fortune in drawing so conveniently to its bias. Everything is coming out exactly as it should. And I for one am delighted.

On the other hand, Malvolio—appropriately enough— refuses to do what is appropriate to the spirit of the scene; he refuses to be included and storms out of the happy ending, promising future discord: *I'll be revenged on the whole pack of you* (5.1.367).[17] What matters from the point of view of the play as play—what matters to the play's self-interested efforts to reach the comfortable conclusion it seems so doggedly determined to achieve—is that the reintroduction of narratively necessary concern for the outcome of the Malvolio story occurs after all the other major necessities of the plot line have been scrupulously attended to. In Albany's words at the end of *King Lear* (where Shakespeare experiments again—more daringly and more dangerously—with premature signals of dramatic conclusion and lets his play behave as if it had forgotten all about its central character), the plight of Malvolio is reintroduced as a *great thing of us forgot* (*King Lear* 5.3.237). In fact, Olivia has simply forgotten all about Malvolio: *A most extracting frenzy of mine own,* she says, *From my remembrance clearly banished his* (5.1.273–74).

The issue of Malvolio recurs at exactly the point where it feels most inappropriate and where the fact that it does not fit in—

---

17. Compare *As You Like It.* In 5.4.172–73, Duke Senior's couplet could conclude the play: "Play, music, and you brides and bridegrooms all, / With measure heaped in joy, to th'measures fall." Instead, Jaques holds up the festivities with a prolonged refusal to participate in them. When Jaques does at last make his exit, the duke has to provide a new couplet to do again the job his previous couplet had been thwarted in: "Proceed, proceed. We'll begin these rites, / As we do trust they'll end, in true delights." Something comparable happens in the last three speeches of *Much Ado,* where a messenger with news of Don John's capture requires Benedick to conclude the play a second time— now with a cheerful reminder of the day-to-day life that goes on after wedding dances are over: "Think not on him till to-morrow. I'll devise thee brave punishments for him. Strike up, pipers!"

the fact of its unsuitability—is most urgent in an audience's experience. Earlier I quoted Orsino's lines to Viola, *Give me thy hand, / And let me see thee in thy woman's weeds* (5.1.264–65). If it were not for the Malvolio plot—or if the Malvolio plot had been disposed of earlier (this long last scene did, after all, begin as another "letter scene" [*Now as thou lov'st me, let me see his letter*]; and its first topic was the letter Feste is carrying from Malvolio to Olivia)—what Orsino says in lines 264–65 could have led directly into a slightly modified version of the couplet with which, in lines 376–77, he concludes the action:

> Give me thy hand,
> And let me see thee in thy woman's weeds,
> And when in other habits you are seen,
> Then be my mistress, and my fancy's queen.

Instead, Viola's response to Orsino fixes on the incidental practicalities of recostuming herself and, as an improbable result, causes the play to meander back to Malvolio by an altogether improbable route. Viola cannot put on her woman's weeds because she left them with the captain who brought her on shore in scene 2; he is in jail; Malvolio put him there.

Let me back up for a minute.

In pointing out the ease with which Shakespeare pairs his characters off at the end of *Twelfth Night,* my purpose was not to say that those pairings have the comic-opera symmetry by which W. S. Gilbert suddenly mates Sir Joseph Porter with Hebe at the end of *Pinafore* and marries Captain Corcoran to the plump and pleasing person who was his nurse when he was a baby. After all, given the farcical situation in *Twelfth Night,* the marriages of Olivia and Sebastian and of Viola and Orsino are dramatically inevitable and have, as Sebastian points out, nonfarcical, natural justice; moreover, the possible marriage of Toby and Maria was mentioned way back in scene 5 (*If Sir Toby would leave drinking, thou wert as witty a piece of Eve's flesh as any in Illyria* [1.5.24–26]), and Toby himself has introduced the idea—albeit in his hyperbolic *I could marry this wench for this device* (2.5.168). What mattered to me was that Shakespeare went to such apparent lengths to make Orsino's instant recognition of his generic obligation to love Viola seem like an authorial convenience and to announce the marriage of Toby and Maria in such a way as to make it sound like a casual act of authorial housekeeping (*Maria writ / The letter, at Sir Toby's great importance, / In recompense whereof he hath married her* [1.5.352–54]). In the last minutes of *Twelfth Night*, Shakespeare tempts his audience to condemn the play as an improbable fiction and demands that his audience consciously remember what no audience to a farce is likely to forget: that this is just a play.

He goes to the same trouble to present the *in*conveniences of the plot in a way that invites similar awareness of crude authorial stitching. The transition from the happy realignment of the four participants in the Orsino/Olivia/twins plot to the all-but-forgotten Malvolio plot is pointedly artificial—is wantonly and openly arbitrary about announcing an otherwise unsuspected, otherwise irrelevant fact by which the otherwise trivial topic of Viola's clothes leads into a reminder of Malvolio. This is 5.1.264–70:

> DUKE: Give me thy hand
>   And let me see thee in thy woman's weeds.
>
> VIOLA: The captain that did bring me first on shore
>   Hath my maid's garments. He upon some action
>   Is now in durance, at Malvolio's suit,
>   A gentleman, and follower of my lady's.
>
> OLIVIA: He shall enlarge him. Fetch Malvolio hither.

As a reminder of the lost loose end that Malvolio has become, Viola's account of the whereabouts of her wardrobe unravels the play just at the moment when it had begun to feel complete. But that sense of completeness was illusory: we need to see Malvolio's letter delivered and to see Malvolio himself delivered from prison. Thus, the undeniably disruptive wardrobe speech undeniably furthers the scene's efforts to tie off all the play's plot strands.

There is a similar contrariety in the fact that the plot device by which concern for Malvolio is gracefully reintroduced is so ruthlessly convenient that its very grace is awkward.

And, for yet another manifestation of contrariety in yet another dimension, consider the fact that—when this play takes sudden urgent interest in the captain that did bring Viola first on shore, a captain who has long faded from our memories—it does so while another sea captain—Antonio, who, in the phrase of the second officer, was arrested *at the suit / Of Count Orsino* (3.4.307–8)—is on the stage and, in so far as the silence of the text is evidence, still under arrest. The play really does forget all about him. After the speech in which he responds to the fact that *an apple cleft in twain is not more twin* (215) than Cesario and Sebastian, he neither speaks again, nor is spoken to, nor is spoken about.

All this is pretty dull and obvious. I have subjected you to it because I want to talk about similar and similarly simple rhyme-like contrarieties that differ principally from those I have so far dwelt upon in that they do not appear to invite conscious notice—even the conscious notice of professional noticers annotating texts.

It may give you some comfort if I tell you what I am driving at. I am driving toward the proposition that from moment to moment, second to second, this last scene of *Twelfth Night* and, for that matter, the whole play cause our minds perpetually to pull in contrary directions simultaneously—to perceive conclusion as inconclusive or to perceive like things as self-evidently unrelated to one another.

By way of transition from effects that call attention to themselves (at least to the degree that they cause ripples in our consciousnesses) to effects that seem to me to invite no attention whatever, consider the double effect that derives from twin facts of lines 360–66—Feste's raging speech of triumph over Malvolio. That speech unexpectedly informs us that Feste has held a particular grudge against Malvolio since scene 5 and implies that Feste has been purposefully exercising it during his subsequent participation in the group effort to discomfit Malvolio. But the vehicle for that surprising revelation is a speech that is a medley of reprises of earlier scenes—notably 1.5, which this whole last scene repeatedly and variously echoes: *Why, 'some are born great, some achieve greatness, and some have greatness thrown upon them.' I was one, sir, in this interlude, one Sir Topas, sir; but that's all one. 'By the Lord, fool, I am not mad!' But do you remember, 'Madam, why laugh you at such a barren rascal? An you smile not, he's gagged'? And thus the whirligig of time brings in his revenges* (5.1.360–66).

The relation of Feste's speech to the speech that precedes it evokes a similar effect in another dimension—one to which I will soon give a lot of attention. Olivia, in pity of Malvolio, calls him *poor fool*—"pitiable innocent": *Alas, poor fool, how have they baffled thee.* Feste then breaks in with a speech that reprises speeches in which Malvolio had baffled Feste by calling him an ineffective professional clown—a poor fool.

Let me start with the smallest of all the small experiences of paradox I mean to discuss: the experience of understanding 5.1.274, the second of a pair of lines I have already quoted: *A most extracting frenzy of mine own / From my remembrance clearly banished his.* The relationship of one's understanding of the word *remembrance* in that line and one's understanding of the word *his* is remarkable—and not least so for inviting no remark at all. *Remembrance* in the phrase *my remembrance* refers to a faculty of the mind—here, the file of active accounts in Olivia's memory bank. When one follows the signal presented by *his,* one understands it to say "my memory of him," but one gets that clear understanding through the intercession of the implied phrase "his remembrance." The parallel between *my remembrance* and *his* is easy, ostentatious, and syntactically commonplace. But, in "his remembrance," the absent/present word "remembrance" refers not to remembering but to something remembered. Compare the unworkable hypothetical phrase "from my thoughts drove out his"—a phrase that, in isolation at least, can only be understood if one talks oneself into accepting "his" as a synonym for "thoughts of him"—accepting "of" meaning "about" as a synonym for "of" indicating possession. But the *my remembrance / his* pair does not occur in isolation. It occurs after *A most extracting frenzy of mine own,* a phrase that, in *my own,* presented a more distant but more easily meaningful antecedent for *his* than *my remembrance* did: "his extracting frenzy," a reference for *his* that the *my remembrance / his* pair successfully screens us off from but that makes easy sense in reference to the raging lunatic Olivia supposes Malvolio to be.

The phenomenon I have just discussed is not unusual. Things like it go equally unnoticed every day in ordinary discourse (and are almost indispensable to the day-to-day operation of faulty logic). I would not fuss about the sleight-of-mind trick one probably performs as one hears Olivia's sentence or about the syntactically less inviting substantively straightforward reading one presumably ignores, if one did not hear Olivia's sentence in context of a veritable gymkhana of strikingly various but altogether comparable perceptions of relationship.

Consider the relationship of the phrase *Malvolio's suit*—the key phrase of the wardrobe speech—to the fact that the speech *is* a wardrobe speech—a speech about clothes. Note too that Viola goes on in her next line to identify Malvolio as *a follower of my Lady's,* and that everyone in *Twelfth Night* is some kind of follower, some kind of pursuer. *Twelfth Night* has been largely concerned with servants, with zanylike followers (like Andrew), and with suitors—lovers endeavoring to gain favor. Moreover, hunting—particularly hunting with dogs—has been a recurrent incidental of the play ever since its third speech, in which Orsino said that the sight of Olivia turned him into a hart whose desires pursue him like hounds (1.1.19–24). And all the way through the play clothing has been an incidental topic too (*These clothes are good enough to drink in* [1.3.10] and *I know your favor well, / Though now you have no sea-cap on your head* [3.4.310–11]); and Olivia's veil and Malvolio's yellow stockings are momentarily central concerns. Of course, the generically inevitable comedy topic—the

topic of what is suitable, the topic of how things ought to be—
is even more persistent in this comedy than it is in most others.

I want now to consider the effect on our experience of the
play and the value to it of several puns on *suit* that the urgently
pertinent, urgently impertinent speech about Viola's clothes and
the captain *now in durance at Malvolio's suit* does not contain. What
that speech does contain are the raw materials for one or another
pun on *suit*. Most of the untapped potential for suit play is obvious when one thinks about it (as one must as one reads this essay and as one is not invited to do as one hears or reads the speech
under normal conditions): *garments, at Malvolio's suit,* and *follower*
occur in concert with one another and with Orsino's new identity as suitor for Viola's hand. Moreover, in the words *in durance,
at Malvolio's suit* (5.1.268), the wardrobe speech also presents and
resists exploiting one of Shakespeare's pet puns, one no longer
readily available to us, that on *durance:* "forced confinement"
(usually in prison) / "a kind of stout durable cloth" (*OED,* 3).[18]

As some of the material I have already quoted demonstrates,
Viola's wardrobe speech is not unusual in *Twelfth Night.* Almost
from the beginning, the play has repeatedly presented and re-
sisted opportunities to pun on *suit*.

Consider, for instance, the opening moments of 3.4. Olivia has
been musing about her progress and prospects as a suitor for Cesario's love (*I have sent after him. . . . youth is bought more oft than
begged or borrowed*); then she speaks the following lines to Maria:
*Where is Malvolio? He is sad and civil, / And suits well for a servant
with my fortunes?* A moment later, Malvolio—newly a suitor and

18. Shakespeare puns brazenly on "durance" in *The Comedy of Errors* 4.3.
23–24, where one of the Dromios describes the officer who arrested one of
the Antipholuses as the man who "takes pity on decayed men and gives them
suits of durance," and in *1 Henry IV* 1.2.40, where Falstaff says that the buff
jerkin traditionally worn by arresting officers is "a sweet robe of durance." Restraint similar to the restraint Shakespeare shows by not cashing in the "durance"
pun occurs in another dimension of *Twelfth Night:* the play does nothing to call
conscious attention to the parallel between the captain *in durance at Malvolio's
suit* and Malvolio's own imprisonment "in a dark room and bound" (3.4.127).

newly suited in unsuitable clothes—enters and we get our first sight of him cross-gartered and in yellow stockings.

Later in the same scene, when Antonio mistakes the disguised Viola for Sebastian and rescues her, we hear this exchange between Antonio and the arresting officers (I have already quoted some of the phrases):

> 2. OFFICER: Antonio, I arrest thee at the suit
> Of Count Orsino.
>
> ANTONIO: You do mistake me, sir.
>
> 1. OFFICER: No, sir, no jot. I know your favor well,
> Though now you have no sea-cap on your head.
> (3.4.307–9)

The first time Shakespeare puts his audience's mind into a verbal situation pregnant with potential for puns on "suit" is in act 1, scene 2 and involves the very captain who intrudes so abruptly into the wardrobe speech in 5.1. I will use italics in the following exchange to force the unobserved potential for overt wordplay into view—thus totally distorting the usual and otherwise inevitably sweat-free effect of the lines. Viola tells the captain that she wishes she could serve Olivia:

> VIOLA: O that I served that lady,
> And might not be delivered to the world,
> Till I had made mine own occasion mellow,
> What my estate is.
>
> CAPTAIN: That were hard to compass,
> Because she will admit no kind of *suit,*
> No, not the Duke's.
>
> VIOLA: There is a fair behavior in thee, captain,
> And though that nature with a beauteous wall
> Doth oft close in pollution, yet of thee
> I will believe thou hast a mind that *suits*
> With this thy fair and outward character.

> I prithee (and I'll pay thee bounteously)
> Conceal me what I am, and be my aid
> For *such disguise* as haply shall *become*
> The form of my intent. I'll serve this duke.
>   (1.2.41–55)

When I talk about puns the play does not make, I am not just trying to be cute. Common sense says that to fuss about puns that don't occur is to waste time. I suggest, however, that such invisible constellations as the ones that form in words and ideas that relate to ideas expressible in the word *suit* may be the prime source of *Twelfth Night*'s greatness.

The play keeps establishing thrilling environments for the minds that perceive it.

As one sees and hears this play one's mind is surrounded by potential for perceiving connections among disparate elements and differences between things that are also "all one." That potential is surely there in the likenesses and differences among characters and among situations. A similar potential in interactions among words and the ideas they convey is manifest in so many different patterns of relationship that, at almost any given moment in *Twelfth Night,* one's mind stands a split second from a flush of mental triumph—a flush comparable to the ones one feels just before one solves a problem, or just before the shininess of a pebble in the American River near Sutter's Mill attracts one's attention, or just before one realizes that one's conversational circumstances are ones in which there is a pun to be made. The flush fades immediately because achievement brings with it awareness of its limitations. All one has done is square the circle or find a cure for cancer or find gold or make a pun. The aura of potential triumph is always brighter than the triumph can be.

For my purposes here, I have gone at least as far with that line of thinking as I need to. I would, however, suggest incidentally that, somewhere along that line of thought, lie one kind of justification for old-fashioned close readings and one kind of answer to the question why great works of literature are recognized to be so before they are analyzed and—usually—revealed to say or do things they have not previously been heard to say or seen to do.

I should now get back to the value of unmade puns.

Several pages ago, I said, "We need to see Malvolio's letter delivered and to see Malvolio himself delivered from prison." There was a play on words there. That sentence is clever—not *very* clever—but clever, overtly clever. My sentence simultaneously denied the differences between two senses of "to deliver" and called attention to those differences. It also advertised the perfect triviality of its Polonian achievement. It demanded a murmur of mental applause for accomplishing something—not for the something accomplished. There is, down deep, good reason for the popular contempt in which punning is held.

By way of contrast to my simultaneously insipid and explosive exploitation of the potential inherent in the word *deliver,* consider the splendor of what Shakespeare makes of the same potential in the last scene of *Twelfth Night.*

Shakespeare makes nothing of it whatsoever.

When she hears that the captain is in durance at Malvolio's suit, Olivia says, *He shall enlarge him* (1.5.270). A few moments later, Feste reports on Malvolio's condition in the first of two speeches that play on the verb "to deliver"—play on it in senses different from one another as well as from the sense in which "deliver him" might have said what *enlarge him* did five lines before—but so casually that I doubt that any audience ever registers the fact. Feste says that Malvolio

> holds Belzebub at the stave's end as well as a man in
> his case may do. Has here writ a letter to you; I
> should have given't you to-day morning. But as a
> madman's epistles are no gospels, so it skills not much
> when they are delivered.

OLIVIA: Open't and read it.

CLOWN: Look then to be well edified, when the fool delivers
the madman.
> [*Reads in a loud voice*] 'By the Lord, madam'—
> (5.1.276–84)

The necessary last link in the chain—the return to the substance of Olivia's *He shall enlarge him*—occurs twenty lines later, in line 305, where as far as I can tell it goes unobserved to be so: *See him delivered, Fabian; bring him hither.*

In the interval between the phrase *when the fool delivers the madman* and the phrase *See him delivered,* the play presents two other, effectively silent circuses of verbal wit. The first gets its impetus from the coincidence of the words *madman* and *madam* in *when the fool delivers the madman. By the Lord, madam*—although the two words are already reaching for one another several lines earlier in the speech that begins *Truly, madam* and ends *but as a madman's epistles are no gospels, so it skills not much when they are delivered* (276–80). Note *Truly* in *Truly, madam;* its sense both is and is not echoed in the word that triggers the overt word play in the speech—the play on *gospels* meaning Matthew, Mark, Luke, and John and "gospel" used figuratively to mean "undeniably true." Similarly, the surface wit of *when the fool delivers the madman*—the wit inherent in the simultaneously valid and invalid distinction between fools and madmen—is echoed in its physics by the available but unexploited phonetic wit in the indistinction the first syllables of "*mad*man" and "*mad*am" might—but do not—imply.

The following sequence follows upon *By the Lord, madam:*

OLIVIA: How now? Art thou mad?

CLOWN: No, madam, I do but read madness. An your ladyship will have it as it ought to be, you must allow vox.

OLIVIA: Prithee read i' thy right wits.

CLOWN: So I do, madonna; but to read his right wits is to read thus. Therefore perpend, my princess, and give ear.

(285–90)

Almost thirty lines later, at Malvolio's entrance, we hear *madman* and *madam* again—and in an exchange where *How now? Art thou mad?* is echoed in *How now, Malvolio?:*

DUKE: Is this the madman?

OLIVIA: Ay, my lord, this same.
How now, Malvolio?

MALVOLIO: Madam, you have done me wrong,
Notorious wrong.

(317–19)

As the second of those two little exchanges reaches back toward
the first, so both of them reach back to a much more complex,
elaborately sustained, but equally unostentatious display of valu-
ably wasted opportunities to make comic capital of the ortho-
graphically identical, phonetically different opening sounds of
madman, madam, and *madonna.* The display occurs in three neigh-
boring passages in 1.5. The first is Feste's famous and splendid
proof that Olivia is a fool. Although the word "mad" does not
occur until line 102 (in "madman" in the third round of play on
sounds, words, and ideas that can refer to fools, madness, and
Olivia), the interplay of variations on "mad" in Feste's proof so
urgently echo Feste's thesis that the passage flirts with, but never
succumbs to, an available temptation to pun macaronically on
the first three letters of *madonna* and say that *madonna* is Italian
for "madwoman." [19] Note the ostentatiously twinlike relationship between *Good madonna* and *Good fool* in *Good madonna, why
mournst thou? / Good fool for my brother's death* and the complexly
easy symmetry and asymmetry of the nearly identical next two
lines—lines that differ only in the simultaneously distinct and
indistinct concepts expressed in *think* and *know,* the ideationally rhyming concepts *hell* and *heaven,* and the substitution of

19. Geoffrey Hartman's wonderfully rich and suggestive "Shakespeare's
Poetical Character in *Twelfth Night*" (*Shakespeare and the Question of Theory,* ed.
Patricia Parker and Geoffrey Hartman [New York and London, 1985], 37–53)
touches momentarily but deftly on the interplay of *madam* and *madman;* Hartman says that "'madam' ('mad-dame') and 'madman' collapse distinctions of
character" (45–46). Hartman also insists throughout the essay by means of casual iterations of his own that his readers observe the iterations in *Twelfth Night*
of various senses of *all one* and of various senses of *hand.*

fool in the second line for *madonna* in the first. These are lines 47–67 of 1.5:

CLOWN: The lady bade take away the fool; therefore, I say again, take her away.

OLIVIA: Sir, I bade them take away you.

CLOWN: Misprision in the highest degree. Lady, *cucullus non facit monachum*. That's as much to say as, I wear not motley in my brain. Good madonna, give me leave to prove you a fool.

OLIVIA: Can you do it?

CLOWN: Dexteriously, good madonna.

OLIVIA: Make your proof.

CLOWN: I must catechize you for it, madonna. Good my mouse of virtue, answer me.

OLIVIA: Well, sir, for want of other idleness, I'll bide your proof.

CLOWN: Good madonna, why mourn'st thou?

OLIVIA: Good fool, for my brother's death.

CLOWN: I think his soul is in hell, madonna.

OLIVIA: I know his soul is in heaven, fool.

CLOWN: The more fool, madonna, to mourn for your brother's soul, being in heaven. Take away the fool, gentlemen.

Forty lines later conceptual interplay among foolishness, madness, and appellations for Olivia begins again, this time in a single speech of Feste's—a speech that concerns kinship (and, in *here he comes* at Toby's entrance, generates gratuitous confusion about kinship) and abruptly brings the words *madonna* and *fool* into the company of the idea of weak-mindedness expressed in the phrase *weak pia mater*. In that phrase lies substantively dormant—absolutely dormant—substantively unavailable potential (1) for echoing the previously central idea of motherhood, (2) for repeating a sense as contextually foreign to *madonna*[20] (which here

---

20. This is John Florio's gloss for "madonna": *Mistris mine. Madame. Also taken for our Lady* (*Queen Anna's New World of Words or Dictionarie of the* Italian *and* English *Tongues* . . . [London, 1611]).

means "mistress mine" and nothing else) as the surface Latin sense—"holy mother"—is to *pia mater,* when as it is here it is used as an anatomical term, and (3) for presenting—as, remember, it most distinctly does not—the shadowy approximation of the term "madwoman" (an approximation inherent in the conjunction of the word *mater* and the idea of mental disorder): *Thou hast spoke for us, madonna, as if thy eldest son should be a fool; whose skull Jove cram with brains, for—here he comes—one of thy kin has a most weak pia mater* (1.5.107–10).

A few minutes later Toby concludes his uninformative report on the gentleman at Olivia's gate; he says, *Let him be the devil an he will, I care not. Give me faith, say I. Well it's all one* (5.1.122–23), and leaves the stage. Thereupon, Olivia and the fool perform the third of the scene's three variations on *m, a,* and *d* in combination:

OLIVIA: What's a drunken man like, fool?

CLOWN: Like a drowned man, a fool, and a madman. One draught above heat makes him a fool, the second mads him, and a third drowns him.

OLIVIA: Go thou and seek the crowner, and let him sit o' my coz; for he's in the third degree of drink—he's drowned. Go look after him.

CLOWN: He is but mad yet, madonna, and the fool shall look to the madman.   [*Exit.*]

(1.5.124–32)

Malvolio enters and speaks the scene's next word: *Madam.*

This is already a long discussion, and I want to get to the last of the last few minutes of *Twelfth Night.* I will content myself with noticing only three more examples of unrealized but elaborately sustained opportunities for punning in the last scene, and I will do little more than mention those.

I have already pointed to an instance of intercourse between *poor fool* meaning "pitiable innocent" and *poor fool* meaning "inept comic entertainer." Here it will suffice to say that the play's continuing, all-but-obsessive eagerness to offer onstage evaluations of Feste's skills (*I had rather than forty shillings I had such a leg, and so sweet a breath to sing, as the fool has* [2.3.18−20]; *This fellow is wise enough to play the fool* [3.1.58]; *The knave counterfeits well; a good knave* [4.2.19])—keeps company with Feste's repeated and regularly successful efforts to make himself richer.

Intervening between the twin flurries of *mad-madam* activity—and in part overlapping them as they themselves overlap the variations on *deliver* and *suit*—is a dizzyingly fruitful field for punning—one that Shakespeare fruitfully forbids his speakers to harvest. The exchanges about the two letters (lines 277−304, about the letter written to Olivia by Malvolio; lines 318−44, about the letter *not* written to Malvolio by Olivia)—have a unifying common denominator in the altogether unexploited opportunities they offer for an outlandish variety of plays on writing, reading, right, and wrong. The verbal festival begins in line 286 when Feste talks about reading madness and introduces the idea of rightness, how "it ought to be":

> I do but read madness. An your ladyship will have it
> as it ought to be, you must allow vox.
>
> OLIVIA: Prithee read i' thy right wits.
>
> CLOWN: So I do, madonna; but to read his right wits is to read
> thus. Therefore perpend, my princess, and give ear.
>
> OLIVIA: [*to Fabian*] Read it you, sirrah.
>
> FABIAN: (*reads*) 'By the Lord, madam, you wrong me. . . .'
>
> (5.1.286−92)

The exercise reaches its entirely unnoticeable perfection in lines 318−19 of the second sequence when Malvolio says *Madam, you have done me wrong, / Notorious wrong.* The first syllable of *Notorious* is of course—and of course does not ask to be observed to be—a synonym for "epistle."

> MALVOLIO: Madam, you have done me wrong.
>   Notorious wrong.
>   OLIVIA: Have I, Malvolio? No.
> MALVOLIO: Lady, you have. Pray you peruse that letter.

You must not now deny it is your hand.
Write from it if you can, in hand or phrase. . . .
                                        (5.1.318–22)

In the lines just quoted the pattern in writing and rightness overlapped with a concurrent pattern made in different meanings of the word *hand*.

Shakespeare appears to have been partial to play-long, alliteration-like repetitions of words capable of reference to body parts. The whole of *Hamlet* is studded with references to ears—including, for example, the mildewed ear of grain that, like Claudius, blasts its wholesome brother (3.4.65–66). In *King Lear*, feet—some French and secret. In *Love's Labor's Lost*, buttocks. In *Troilus and Cressida*, arms. In *Twelfth Night*, hands. I will resist laboring the topic of hands, handwriting, commands, and such in *Twelfth Night* except to say that—whereas in *As You Like It* Shakespeare wastes the inherent energy of *hand* in an openly chuckle-hungry pun on *hand* meaning "the extremity of the arm" and *hand* meaning "handwriting" (Rosalind denies that Phoebe could have written the letter Silvius delivers: *I saw her hand. She has a leathern hand, / A freestone-colored hand. I verily did think / That her old gloves were on. . . . This is a man's invention and his hand* [4.3.25–27, 30])—in *Twelfth Night* he does not.[21]

A great while ago, I argued the rarely debated proposition that Shakespeare is a better writer than I am. Shakespeare is also sometimes a better writer than Shakespeare is in *As You Like It*. The various hands in *Twelfth Night* reach out to one another (as they do across the lines that separate Orsino's first blurry, amorphous marriage proposal to Viola [5.1.264–65] and his second [311–16]—and as the ensuing discussion of Olivia's and Maria's twin handwriting does to *Give me thy hand* and *Here is my hand*

---

21. *As You Like It* also sports a heavyhanded pun on "suit." Jaques says, "O that I were a fool! / I am ambitious for a motley coat." The duke promises him one, and Jaques's response is "It is my only suit" (2.7.42–44).

in the marriage proposals)—but in *Twelfth Night,* unlike *As You Like It,* they never clasp.

As to Feste's final song, it is an emblem of the last scene and, like the scene, an emblem of *Twelfth Night* at large.

For instance, the whole song circles longingly around seductive potential for a pun on son (a boy child) and sun (which ever art when rain is not)—a pun that would complement 3.1.37–38: *Foolery, sir, does walk about the orb like the sun; it shines every where.*

Feste stands all alone on the stage at the end of a play that is complete—is all one—and is not, alone on the stage at the end of a play that over its whole length has played with the ingredients and potential of the word *alone*—notably with those ingredients in the phrase *all one* and *that* phrase's potential to say "does not matter" (that is, to say what *What You Will,* the play's subtitle, says) and/or to say "the same," and/or to say "whole," "complete."

This is the song's first stanza:

> When that I was and a little tiny boy,
>> With hey, ho, the wind and the rain,
> A foolish thing was but a toy,
>> For the rain it raineth every day.

When that I was and a little tiny boy: that is an ordinary "when" clause—except that its fifth syllable, *and,* does not perform, cannot perform, its usual conjunctive function in this sentence; in fact, in this syntax it is incapable of any substantive function whatever. That, however, doesn't bother us: this is a song; and we are used to nonsense syllables in songs—syllables present for merely rhythmic purpose.

With hey, ho, the wind and the rain: this line follows—but does not follow from—the line that precedes it. For an instant, *With* gestures toward the kind of connection that the preposition "with" makes for the Whittier-blessed "little man," the "barefoot boy with cheek of tan." But the wind and the rain are not personal attributes. That does not, of course, matter to us. This is a song. We are used to the substantively irrelevant "with" that introduces refrain lines. I would mention, however, that here, as in all similar songs, the substantively impertinent prepositional gesture of relationship *is* a gesture of relationship—connects, makes one thing of, two lines that have no more-than-local connection at all except the one asserted by *With*—which *does* function as an asserter of connection, albeit nonlogically. *With* finally asserts no connection between the substance of one line and the substance of the next. *With* comes ultimately to assert simple connection between the lines *as* lines—as, and only to the extent that, a rope makes a cow part of a barn and makes a barn part of a cow.

A foolish thing was but a toy, on the other hand, *does* connect logically with line 1—the line from which it is *dis*connected by line 2, a line introduced by a gesture of substantively irrelevant connection. Line 3 presents the independent clause inherently promised by the "when" clause. The interrupted substantive unity of lines 1 and 3 corresponds to the interrupted formal unity they have by virtue of the *a, b, a, b* rhyme scheme.

Line 2 was a nonsense line. Line 3 is not. Its syntax meshes logically with that of line 1, and its substantive particulars pertain to childhood. Moreover, the irrelevance of the nonsense line (like the irrelevance of the other refrain lines—the second and fourth lines of each of the first four quatrains) vouches for the substantive coherence of the substantively purposeful pair it interrupts.

But what does *A foolish thing was but a toy* mean? Not much. *Foolish thing* and *toy* are synonyms: twins. The line says "a foolish thing was only a foolish thing." If it were not for the word *but*—which suggests that we will subsequently hear that a foolish thing subsequently came to count for more than it once did and more than the logic of synonyms says it justly should—line 3 would be nonsense too—though nonsense of a different kind than the nonsense of the refrain line (it would be nonsense of the sort exemplified in *That that is is* [4.2.14] or *There's never a villain dwelling in all Denmark / But he's an arrant knave* [*Hamlet* 1.5.123–24]).

For the rain it raineth every day is another substantively irrelevant nonsense line—obviously so and for reasons similar to the ones that evoked generic recognition in line 2. This second nonsense line also presents itself as a substantive continuation of the preceding line. This time the connection is urgently logical: the line begins with *For*—"because"—and momentarily promises to explain or justify the assertion made in line 3. When, as of its third syllable, line 4 turns out to be impertinent to line 3, it simultaneously shows itself pertinent to line 2, which was also about weather; the earlier, similarly irrelevant line now has a twin established in terms irrelevant to the pair it interrupted.

And, by the end of the line, the second "*b*" rhyme establishes the twinship of lines 2 and 4 in another dimension. The rhyme, however, is not perfect: the vowel sounds of *rain* and *day* are identical, but *day* lacks a final *n*. But the rhyme sounds of lines 2 and 4 are *also more* than perfect. *Day* does not rhyme perfectly with *rain*, but it *does* rhyme perfectly with *hey*, the first stressed syllable of line 2; and *rain*, though imperfectly matched by *day*, *is* perfectly matched by—is repeated by—the first stressed syllable of line 4: *rain*.

Although the legitimate union of the outlaw lines is indisputably established, *For the rain it raineth every day* still gestures toward explanation—and does not explain the *second* line—a syntactic fragment incapable of explanation in any event—any better than it did the third. Furthermore—at exactly the moment when the rhyme word, *day*, is in the act of imperfectly augmenting the otherwise-established independent identity that lines 2 and 4 (the weather lines) have from lines 1 and 3—the phrase *every day* suddenly but gently establishes *kinship* between the nonsense lines and lines 1 and 3, the pair of lines focused in the concepts of time and mutability.

This is the second stanza of the song:

> But when I came to man's estate,
>   With hey, ho, the wind and the rain,
> 'Gainst knaves and thieves men shut their gate,
>   For the rain it raineth every day.

By the time we have heard the second stanza—and heard the tune two times through—we understand the rules. We understand that, although the second and fourth lines of these quatrains have substantive and syntactic coherence, their action is effectively formal. They are of a commonplace but complex kind. Like similar lines in similar songs, the second and the fourth lines of these quatrains correspond in kind to the nonsignifying ideational interplay of *mad* and *madam,* or *read, write, wrong, right,* and *notorious.* The refrain lines are agents of nonsubstantive—that is, noncommunicating—coherence. They work to the same kind of effect to which a tune the song is sung to works—the effect to which any tune any verses are sung to works. The refrain lines work as rhythms, rhymes, and alliterations work. The refrain lines bind the stanzas to one another. At the same time, they are agents of incoherence. They are substantively and logically unrelated to the autobiography-like narrative that is beginning to emerge in the substantively efficient lines. The *With* is filler. And "because it rains every day" cannot be conceived of as witness to the truth of the assertions spread over the first and third lines.

Quatrain 3 is insistently one with quatrain 2—more so than quatrain 2 was with quatrain 1. Both 2 and 3 begin with *But when I came.* Moreover, the pattern of chronological narrative is becoming more certain. Quatrain 3, however, while progressing through the steps of a predictable young manhood, *colors* the essence of what it echoes.

> But when I came, alas, to wive,
>   With hey, ho, the wind and the rain,
> By swaggering could I never thrive,
>   For the rain it raineth every day.

In 1954, in his *The First Night of "Twelfth Night"* (p. 168), Leslie Hotson suggested that *thing* in *A foolish thing* in line 3 of quatrain 1 had—or played on—the bawdy sense that, like *fool* and *toy, thing* has as a slang term for "penis." Hotson was, quite properly, hooted down. There is nothing in the substantive context of quatrain 1 to activate any of the bawdy potential of *thing* (or *fool* or *toy*). *But* when the first line of quatrain 3 comes to *wive,* its last syllable, it retroactively generates a sexual context for the diction of quatrain 1—and for the modification quatrain 2 imposed on the state of original innocence presented there. The incidental sexual context persists in the rest of quatrain 3 and in quatrain 4. Quatrain 3 is overtly playful. *But when I came, alas, to wive* plays casually on "a lass"—a girl. And—to state the matter simply and obscenely—*But when I came alas to wive . . . By swaggering could I never thrive* says that, for the groom, marriage is a put-up-or-shut-up situation.

Quatrain 4 insists further on the likeness of the successive quatrains to their siblings. It too begins *But when I came.* This third "come to" construction, however, is subtly different from the two it echoes. Unlike *to* in *came to man's estate* and *came . . . to wive,* the *to* in *came unto my beds* actually introduces a physical destination—a place to move toward.

> But when I came unto my beds,
>> With hey, ho, the wind and the rain,
>> With tosspots still had drunken heads,
>>> For the rain it raineth every day.

The first line of this quatrain is not only subtly different from the first lines of quatrains 2 and 3; it is crudely different as well. Except as it comes vaguely to have imitated the double vision of a teetering drunk, *But when I came unto my beds* does not make sense: *beds* is plural; one can lie down in only one bed. Still, line 2 is reassuringly identical with the three previous second lines. Indeed, each time they recur, the pairs of second and fourth lines—pairs whose prime identifying quality is their impertinence—become, in another organizational dimension, increasingly pertinent—pertinent to the song *as* song. At the same time—and at the same time that a sort of autobiography-like quatrain-to-quatrain continuity is developing—the substantively coherent pairs of lines in the middle three quatrains are ostentatiously discontinuous with, and impertinent to, one another. Each begins with a signal of logical discontinuity—the conjunction *But*—and quatrains 3 and 4 make sudden topical leaps. On the other hand, the context has become more and more supportive; the narrative has become more and more clearly coherent. Now, in quatrain 4, the syntax of lines 1 and 3—the syntax that successfully carries the continuation of the autobiography-like narrative—collapses. Now, in quatrain 4, where the first line has behaved like a nonsense line, the third line usurps the formulaic opening gesture of each of the previous second lines. And—though this use of *with* is not the substantively irrelevant one *with* has as a hook to hold refrain lines—the *with* of *With tosspots still had drunken heads* does introduce a nonsense line—a line where one head is plural and where the logical relationship *with* establishes between line 1 and line 3 is similarly drunken.

Paradoxically enough, however, the second nonsense line of quatrain 4 *is* regular and is thus reassuring: *For the rain it raineth every day.* But it is not so obviously isolated from the narrative lines as it has been in its previous appearances. Now both pairs of lines have a topical common denominator: liquids. And—in context of the issue of adequate and inadequate masculine sexual performance and of the idea of swaggering—the contrast between wind and rain has begun to feel pertinent to the content of the substantive lines—as has the daily reliability of rain.

The song started out talking about its singer's distant past. Quatrains 2, 3, and 4 presented a series of events from his less distant past. The song seems to be moving toward the present. Quatrain 4, however, while confirming that impression, seems to blur together many days or weeks or years. It also concerns evening and night—and thus points toward a conclusion, toward an assertion of how things are now (or how they soon will be or how they must at last inevitably be for all mortals). Instead, the first line of the last quatrain of this song that started from the speaker's distant past and moved forward chronologically now leaps to the ultimate human past—to creation—and, in its last line, talks about the indefinite *future*.

> A great while ago the world begun,
>   Hey, ho, the wind and the rain;
> But that's all one, our play is done,
>   And we'll strive to please you every day.[22]

The present—*now*—is effectively missing. It gets lost.

The same sort of thing happened at the end of the play's dramatized action. Both in general (as, for instance, in Feste's mocking reminder of the past and Malvolio's threat for the future), and in the substance and grammatical structures of the speech with which Orsino concludes the fiction, the end of *Twelfth Night* behaves as if there were no present, only a past and a future—and lets our minds behave in something like the way they would if human minds were capable of the impossible task of imagining time without a present moment.[23] This is that concluding speech (note, incidentally, the incidental clash of dimensions we casually weather when, four lines from his final exit [from the

---

22. For the first four stanzas of the final song, I have quoted the Pelican text as usual. In this last stanza, however, I follow the folio's version of the second line of the last stanza (even though the variation between it and its counterparts in earlier stanzas is very probably accidental).

23. As Geoffrey Hartman has observed, present time momentarily evaporated back in act I. In the essay I mentioned earlier he comments acutely on what Olivia says when she accedes to the request that she remove her veil and let "Cesario" see her face: *Look you, sir, such a one I was this present.* Hartman says this: "I was, not I am; by pretending she is a painting, just unveiled, the original I is no longer there, or only as this picture which points to a present in the way names or texts point to a meaning. . . . There is no 'present'" (51).

stage], Orsino says *We will not part from hence* [will not part from Olivia's house]):

> Pursue him and entreat him to a peace,
> He hath not told us of the captain yet.
> When that is known, and golden time convents,
> A solemn combination shall be made
> Of our dear souls. Meantime, sweet sister,
> We will not part from hence. Cesario, come—
> For so you shall be while you are a man,
> But when in other habits you are seen,
> Orsino's mistress and his fancy's queen.
>
> (5.1.369–77)

All in all, the last quatrain of Feste's song multiplies the play's typical characteristics.

The line that follows the once ostentatiously predictable pattern of likeness—line 2—here loses its ceremonial initial *With* (at least *With* is absent in the First Folio text of the last quatrain; the Second Folio printer seems to have assumed that the initial *With* was lost by accident and to have replaced it; most subsequent editors have followed his lead; but, whatever the cause, the missing *With* in quatrain 5 is one more casual manifestation of simultaneous likeness and difference in *Twelfth Night*).

Line 3 of the last quatrain suddenly dismisses all of history (*But that's all one*), and just as suddenly announces that the play is done—is complete—is "all one." But, typically of the physics of *Twelfth Night,* the assertion of finality that is made in *But that's all one, our play is done*—that is made in a line made extrafinal by the word *one,* an extra, midline "*a*" rhyme that augments the end rhymes in *begun* and *done* (words that rhyme ideationally as well as phonetically)—is an assertion of finality that occurs before the quatrain can end. It has to have a fourth line. The fourth line begins with *And,* which here is at once songlike metrical filler and a real signal of continuation. The promise of future performances of future plays is as impertinent to the song as the song was to the apparently concluded play it continued. But the last line does end with *every day,* does come to complete the otherwise lost likeness between this quatrain and its predecessors.

As of the moment we hear *But that's all one, our play is done,* the singer of this song is—as, of course, he also always has been—the actor who has been playing Feste and not Feste "himself" (Feste is only a character in a play).

But this character in a play is himself an actor. Feste played Sir Topas the curate and, already costumed as Sir Topas, prefaced that performance by offering Sir Toby—whose name is not Sir Topas—an absolutely perfect and perfectly unexceptional pair of pairs of twins: two identical, nonidentical *that*s and two identical, nonidentical *is*s: *"That that is is"*. One clause later, however, when one or the other in the second pair of *that*s (there is no way to tell which and no need to) and one or the other in the second pair of *is*s (there is no way to tell which and no need to) turned out to be references to the word *that* and the word *is* instead of instances of their use, the pairs of twins became so extraordinary as to discourage any further attempt at understanding what was by then obviously mere nonsense: *"That that is is"; so, I, being Master Parson, am Master Parson; for what is "that" but that, and "is" but is* (4.2.14–16). On the other hand, in one logic or another, each of these three clauses makes sense. And—granting its merely verbal equation of two senses of *being*—so did the logic of the whole.

In the fiction performed by the actors, the speaker of that fool-like parody of jackleg scholasticism was, by the way, either Feste pretending ontological discourse on his assumed identity as Sir Topas—the role he is about to play—or Feste pretending already to be playing that role and imitating Sir Topas engaged in ontological discourse. There is no way to tell which and no need to.

Now, in *But that's all one, our play is done*—the next-to-last line of the play—the actor who has played Feste echoes lines he spoke a few minutes earlier when Feste recalled his own theatrical performance as Sir Topas: *I was one, sir, in this interlude, one Sir Topas, sir; but that's all one* (5.1.361–63). At the moment when the words *I was one, sir, in this interlude* were heard, the theatrical term *interlude* referred to the whole extended practical joke; *one in,* of course, meant "party to," "a participant in" (as variations on that locution do earlier in the play in Olivia's *to make one in so skipping a dialogue* [1.5.190–91] and Andrew's *I'll make one too* [2.5.191]). The next phrase makes *interlude* refer specifically to the onstage masquerade in which Feste played the role of Sir Topas and makes the word less a metaphor: *I was one in this interlude, one Sir Topas.* But Feste was not one in *that* interlude. He, who carried on both sides in conversation between himself and himself playing Sir Topas, was two.

And the actor is two here too. He is what Feste is: a professional entertainer. And he is here performing for *his* audience as—as Feste—he has performed both for that audience and for onstage audiences. Moreover, in the traditional *plaudite* gesture of *And we'll strive to please you every day,* he asks by implication what various characters and Feste himself have asked all the way through the play—whether Feste's efforts to please are successful (*Doth not this fool mend?*), and whether other kinds of performance are adequate (as I noted earlier, judgment of performances is an incidental of Orsino's first speech, the first speech of the play: *Enough, no more, / Tis not so sweet now as it was before*). And the actor asks the question at the end of a song that has idly echoed other persistent details of the fiction from which *But that's all one, our play is done* does and does not break free—details like play on *little thing* (3.4.282–83: *A little thing would make me tell them how much I lack of a man*); gates (1.4.14–15 [my italics]: "Therefore, good youth, address thy *gait* unto her; / Be not denied *access,* stand at her *doors*"; 1.5.99–268, passim; 3.1.80: "I will answer you with *gait* and *entrance*"); swaggering, drunkenness, and Feste's efforts to thrive financially. Consider quatrain 2 in particular. That quatrain establishes the aesthetic ground rules of the song and thus augments the independence of its identity. But the quatrain echoes early parts of the story. In act 1, scene 2 Viola—wishing "not to be delivered to the world" till she had made her *own occasion mellow* what her estate was (42, 43)— suddenly came to man's estate by means of masculine usurped attire; and—in 1.5—men shut Olivia's gates to her.

More urgently, this actor—who now seems to have ceased to play Feste once the action stopped—has stood all alone and sung a song in which the singer/autobiographer got married—and, like the well-sorted/oddly-sorted lovers in *Twelfth Night,* got married inconclusively.

I should not, however, myself be inconclusive. Although I have said as much as I have to say about the last song, the last scene, and *Twelfth Night* itself, I should say something summary. I go on record, therefore, as saying that *Twelfth Night* is about twins—deeply, totally, perfectly, about twins. I will, moreover, therefore risk further generalization on what it is that is so good about *Twelfth Night: Twelfth Night* is good because it is so witty.

Twelfth Night is a witty play.

It may well strike you as it does Horatio in *Hamlet* that *there needs no ghost . . . come . . . to tell us this.* However, the term "witty play" ordinarily means a "play with lots of witty lines in it"—a play that is a vehicle for wit, that contains wit. That is not what I mean. *Twelfth Night* surely contains wit, but *it* is also witty. The container, the play itself, is witty. When one calls a line or a phrase witty, what one is saying is that the line or phrase enables its auditor simultaneously to perceive simultaneous rightness and wrongness, that the elements conjoined in the witty assertion belong together and also—in some other pertinent set of terms—do not. In saying that *Twelfth Night* is a witty play, I am saying that in all its dimensions and in every scale—every scale from the relationship of its at once separable and inseparable plot lines to the catechism and mouse game in *I must catechize you for it, madonna. Good my mouse of virtue, answer me* or the complex phonics of *Therefore perpend, my princess, and give ear*—*Twelfth Night* consists of relationships that are at once just and unjust and of disjunctions among parts of entities that are *and remain* all one.

Index

Parenthetical words after act, scene, and line numbers for Shakespearean plays identify the cited passages quickly. The tag phrase is not always the first phrase of the cited passage but often a more distinctive phrase likely to recall the passage to the reader's mind. Particular words and phrases in the first scene of *Twelfth Night* discussed in the section of Part Three called "*Twelfth Night* 1.1.: The Audience as Malvolio" (pp. 121–49) are not indexed because the heading makes references easy to find.